Embracing Wisdom

That the exercise of our intellectual powers in the service of the Gospel can prove life-transforming is a principle that informs the writings of Thomas Aquinas and, at the same time, marks the horizon of his thought. Yet the contemporary interpretation of Aquinas' thought, with a few notable exceptions, continues to suffer from the modern divorce between systematic theology and spirituality. Even among those studies that link Aquinas' systematic and spiritual purposes, few have asked *how* Aquinas sets about composing his text in such a way that it orders spiritual operations of memory, affect, imagination, understanding, judgment, and decision to each other and to the purpose of Christian spiritual development.

Embracing Wisdom proposes a theological interpretation of the *Summa theologiae* as a spiritual pedagogy ordered to the growth in wisdom, and thus in holiness, of preachers and confessors in the late thirteenth century. It proceeds along two unequal trajectories. The first begins by examining the social and cultural transformations of the late twelfth and early thirteenth centuries, and the spiritual crisis they occasioned for the Church, a crisis which called for the creation of a new kind of pastoral agent to take responsibility for the preaching of the Gospel. The analysis that follows develops a picture of the socio-cultural role of the theologian and preacher and brings to light the rhetorical means Aquinas deploys to promote the formation of wise preachers who can mediate the Gospel by means of new cultural forms.

The successive chapters that form the second trajectory present the pedagogical structure and spiritual dynamic of the *Summa theologiae* in light of these rhetorical principles, showing how it climaxes in the Christology of the *Tertia pars*. This Christology is shown to promote communion with and conforming of the whole person to Wisdom Incarnate, transforming the student into an agent of Divine Wisdom in the world.

I0888902

Embracing Wisdom

The *Summa theologiae* as Spiritual Pedagogy

GILLES MONGEAU

PONTIFICAL INSTITUTE OF MEDIAEVAL STUDIES

Acknowledgement

The publication of this work has been assisted by a grant-in-aid from the Jesuits in English Canada.

Library and Archives Canada Cataloguing in Publication

Mongeau, Gilles M. (Gilles Michel-Joseph), 1964–, author

Embracing wisdom : the Summa theologiae as spiritual pedagogy / Gilles Mongeau.

Includes bibliographical references and index.
Issued in print and electronic formats.
ISBN 978-0-88844-422-6 (paperback). – ISBN 978-1-77110-366-4 (pdf)

1. Thomas, Aquinas, Saint, 1225?–1274. Summa theologica. 2. Spiritual life – Catholic Church – History of doctrines – Middle Ages, 600–1500. 3. Christian life – History – Middle Ages, 600–1500. 4. Theology, Doctrinal – History – Middle Ages, 600–1500. 5. Philosophy, Medieval. I. Pontifical Institute of Mediaeval Studies, issuing body II. Title.

BX1749.T6M65 2015 230'.2 C2015-905507-5 C2015-905508-3

© 2015
Pontifical Institute of Mediaeval Studies
59 Queen's Park Crescent East
Toronto, Ontario, Canada M5S 2C4

www.pims.ca

MANUFACTURED IN CANADA

Contents

Preface

When I began my philosophical studies, the question of the convergences or harmony between imagination and intellect, feeling and reason, faith and culture had already been a scholarly concern of mine for some years. I had thought to explore this question by bringing together the theological anthropologies of Bernard Lonergan and Hans Urs von Balthasar, but very early on, the writings of Jean-Pierre Torrell, OP convinced me that it would be much better to do for myself what Lonergan and von Balthasar had done, namely to apprentice myself to a great figure of the tradition. Given my training in Lonergan studies, my previous work in medieval political thought, and Torrell's insistence that Thomas Aquinas is best read as a spiritual theologian, the Angelic Doctor became the obvious choice.

Initially, I thought that I might find some interesting answers to my question in the traditional doctrine of the spiritual senses, the notion that by the grace of baptism the human senses (both exterior and interior) are "elevated" to experience divine mysteries. Certainly, Aquinas has interesting things to say about various elements of this doctrine. Two important encounters changed the direction of my thought. First, I sat in on a class given by Thomas Hibbs on the *Summa contra gentiles* and encountered for the first time his notion that this work has a narrative and dramatic dimension as well as a dialectical one. The following year, a research stay in Fribourg, Switzerland to work with Fr. Torrell convinced me that a similar question needed to be asked of the *Summa theologiae*. As I learned to read this text as a work of spiritual theology, I realized how profoundly Torrell himself had been formed by reading it over and over again for so many years. What was going on in the text itself that it could have this formative power? Might the *Summa* not only propose a spiritual theology in its content, but also foster a spiritual transformation by its literary structure and dynamic?

I found the initial answer to these questions in the research of Mary Carruthers and her retrieval of the medieval uses of classical rhetoric. Her insight that Aquinas was deeply formed in rhetorical techniques of memory and invention, and that medieval books are mediators of experience (rather than mere repositories of arguments), helped me to ask the further question: could we read the *Summa* with an eye to its rhetorical intention, that is, as a work that seeks to mediate an experience through deploying rhetorical means?

The detailed reading that followed convinced me that such an interpretation was not only possible, but very fruitful, shedding a great deal of light on precisely the convergences in Aquinas' thought between imagination and intellect, feeling and reason, faith and culture. I have been able to test the results of this research in the classroom for a number of years, and have found that this approach to Aquinas' corpus is very helpful to students: it gives them a way into the text and opens them up to being formed by the text. They discover that they can allow Aquinas to lead them through difficult epistemological and metaphysical hurdles as they arise in the text, with Scripture, imagination, and memory as supports and guides.

Thomas Aquinas was a master pedagogue, and his contemporaries appreciated this in him. In the triptych that adorns the cover of this book, Aquinas holds the Scriptures open to Ecclesiastes 12:9–10: "Besides being wise, the Teacher taught the people what he himself knew, having weighed, studied and redacted many sayings. The Teacher took pains to write in an attractive style and by it to convey truths plainly." I hope this book can help you, the reader, discover this dimension of Aquinas' theology, so that you might understand something of what his contemporaries knew, and perhaps receive through this discovery some measure of the Wisdom he sought to convey.

Anyone who has been immersed in the writing and rewriting of a book knows firsthand that the myth of the isolated thinker is just that, a myth. Scholarship today is only possible within a community of friends and colleagues to whom the scholar is indebted for professional and spiritual support. This book is no exception.

In general, I want to acknowledge all of those scholars, remote and proximate, on whose achievements this work rests. Not only do present-day theologians stand on the shoulders of giants, they are often kept aright by the shoulders of their peers. I can perhaps ask you, the reader, to remember that each footnote in this book is an act of gratitude as much as an act of scholarly responsibility.

It is important to name a few scholars whose direct encouragement nurtured this book into existence: Jeremy Wilkins; Robert Sweetman; Gordon Rixon, SJ; Reid Locklin; David Burrell, CSC; Thomas Noble and members of the University of Notre Dame's Medieval Institute, where I spent a very enjoyable semester working on this manuscript; many colleagues and friends at the Toronto School of Theology and the University of Toronto, particularly the late Margaret O'Gara, and *praeses emeritus* of the Pontifical Institute of Medieval Studies, James McConica, CSB, for his generous advice at a crucial moment in the production of this text.

I have been privileged and delighted to work at Regis College since 2003, among faculty committed to the link between serious intellectual formation and spiritual development. The many convergences in scholarship and teaching among us have greatly enriched this book, as have the puzzled frowns and enthusiastic smiles of my students.

Friends and peers play a central role in the writing of any long book. From my earliest studies, I have been blessed in belonging to a community that has met regularly for friendship, conversation, food, scholarly critique, and the continual restoration of sanity. The seeds that were planted then continue to bear fruit: thank you Michael and Isilda Attridge, Gregory Beath, Allen and Gwen Anne Jorgenson, Maicco and Trish Michielin, Patrick and Beth Patterson, Mary Tanter, the late George Schner, SJ, Paul Walker, and Phil and Helena Ziegler; thank you also to David and Leslie Demson, Kathy Baroody, Richard Greene, Matthew Levering, and Marianne Marusic.

Saint Ignatius of Loyola called those who would follow the way of the Jesuit Constitutions "companions in the Lord." Many of my Jesuit companions have contributed to this endeavor through their generous friendship and encouragement, a few in more immediate ways: Len Altilia, Peter Bisson, Robin Koning, Erik Oland, Joseph Schner, and Winston Rye.

Finally, I must acknowledge the debts of *pietas*. If I am a theologian today, it is due to the example and mentorship of three men, each a pastor and theologian, who first modeled for me the unity of the intellectual and spiritual life: Jean-Marc Laporte, SJ, Robert Foliot, SJ, and Robert Doran, SJ. To them this book is dedicated *ad maiorem Dei gloriam*.

CHAPTER ONE

A Wisdom that Makes One Holy

When the poet Dante, on his journey through the heavens in the *Paradiso*, reaches the heaven of the Sun, he and Beatrice are encircled by a ring of lights, "wreathing round us to form a flashing crown, sweeter in song than radiant to the sight." The shining souls of the denizens of the Sun revolve around Dante and Beatrice three times, then come to a stop; one of them comes forward to greet Dante:

> You want to know with what plants and blossoms
> this garland is in flower, encircling with delight
> the lovely lady who strengthens you for Heaven.
>
> I was a lamb among the holy flock
> led by Dominic along the road
> where sheep are fattened if they do not stray.
>
> He that is nearest to me on the right
> was both my brother and my teacher –
> he, Albert of Cologne, I, Thomas of Aquino.[1]

As Robert Hollander points out in his commentary on this tenth canto of the *Paradiso*,[2] the sun is a symbol of illumination which wisdom brings to the soul, and the souls that dwell in the heaven of the sun are those whom the Spirit of Wisdom has made shine most brightly. These souls are transformed into light by sharing in God's very self, whose essence it is the goal of wisdom to know.

1 Dante Alighieri, *Paradiso* 10.91–99, ed. and trans. Robert and Jean Hollander (New York, 2007), 263.

2 See Robert Hollander's notes: ibid., 266 (notes to lines 1–6) and 270 (notes to lines 40–42).

Along with Albert the Great, Thomas names Solomon, Dionysius the Areopagite, Bede, Richard of Saint-Victor, Gratian, and Peter Lombard as being among his companions. In the eleventh canto, Aquinas sings the praise of Francis of Assisi; in the twelfth, Bonaventure appears and praises Dominic. Dante is reproducing a common practice – honored in some places to this day – of having a member of the Dominicans preach the sermon on St. Francis' feast day, and vice versa. Dante writes that divine providence "ordained in her behalf two princes / one on this side, one on that, to serve as guides. / One was all seraphic in his ardor / the other, by his wisdom, was on earth / resplendent with cherubic light."[3] In the eleventh canto Thomas praises Francis' love and presents it to his fellow Dominicans and those reading Dante's poem as an ideal shared by Dominic but lost to them. Dante shows Thomas very much in love with God, even as he celebrates the wisdom that has brought him into union with God.

In the twelfth canto, Bonaventure appears to praise Dominic as a great lover of truth and holy doctrine: "Not for this world, for which men toil today, / ... but for love of the true manna, / he soon became a teacher so renowned / that he began to travel through the vineyard – which quickly withers if the keeper is corrupt."[4] Bonaventure reiterates the complementarity and interpenetration of Franciscan mystical love and the Dominican contemplation of wisdom and introduces twelve more souls, many of whom are renowned preachers and theologians.

The wisdom that Dante celebrates in the heaven of the sun is a knowledge that leads to love, a holy teaching that transforms the one who contemplates and participates in it. It was perfectly obvious to him that Thomas was among the wise, and that the wisdom in which he shared led to holiness and ultimately to union with God. That the intellectual life can make one holy and that Thomas counts among the wise is no longer so obvious to us.

Hans Urs von Balthasar points out that "In the whole history of Catholic theology there is hardly anything that is less noticed, yet more deserving of notice, than the fact that, since the great period of scholasticism, there have been few theologians who were saints."[5] He continues: "If we consider the history

3 Ibid., 11.35–39, 287.

4 Ibid., 12.82–87, 315.

5 Hans Urs von Balthasar, *Word and Redemption*, trans. A.V. Littledale (Montreal, 1965), 49.

of theology up to the time of the great scholastics, we are struck by the fact that the great saints, those who not only achieved an exemplary purity of life, but who also had received from God a definite mission in the Church, were, mostly, great theologians."[6] Their enduring influence is due to the fact that "the faithful saw in their lives an immediate expression of their teaching and a testimony to its value, and so were made confident in the rightness of teaching and acting."[7] These individuals "were complete personalities: what they taught they lived with such directness, so naively, we might say, that the subsequent separation of theology and spirituality was quite unknown to them."[8]

It is this awareness of the separation of theology and spirituality that first motivated me to begin the research that has led to this book. As von Balthasar states, "Theology and spirituality have become, as it were, each a world of its own, with hardly any point of contact,"[9] and this remains true despite the revitalization of both "worlds" after the Second Vatican Council. This is just as true in Thomist studies as in other areas of theology. Since the publication of the encyclical *Aeterni Patris* in 1879, interest in Saint Thomas Aquinas has gone from enthusiastic revival to almost complete disregard. The rise of neo-scholasticism, neo-Thomism, and transcendental Thomism notwithstanding, the interpretation of Thomas' thought has continued to suffer from a divorce of that which, for Aquinas, was inseparable, namely the enterprise of theology and the spiritual life of the theologian. The works of Jean-Pierre Torrell and others emphasize the unity of these two elements in Aquinas' work, restoring a balance within scholarly discourse. Thomas' theology, proposes Torrell, is a medium which transmits a spirituality, that is, an activity within which the theologian exercises in a specific way the virtues of faith, hope, and love and presents to others this concrete configuration of the theological virtues as an ideal of holiness and wisdom.[10]

6 Ibid.

7 Ibid.

8 Ibid., 51.

9 Ibid., 63.

10 Jean-Pierre Torrell, *Saint Thomas d'Aquin, Maître Spirituel* (Fribourg, Suisse, 1996), which has appeared in English as Jean-Pierre Torrell, *Saint Thomas Aquinas: Spiritual Master*, trans. Robert Royal (Washington, DC, 2005). In addition to Torrell many monographs and collections of essays have focused on the sapiential and transformative character of the theology of Thomas Aquinas, including: Mark Jordan, *Ordering Wisdom: The Hierarchy of Philosophical Discourses in Aquinas* (Notre Dame, IN, 1986); Matthew Levering, *Scripture and Metaphysics* (Malden, MA, 2004); Michael Dauphinais

Skopos: *Beginnings, Aims, Ends*

Before I explore this notion of philosophy (and theology) as a way of life, I would like to situate this work within the wider contemporary scholarship on wisdom, rhetoric, pedagogy, and spirituality in the medieval world. To keep things manageable, I will "triangulate" this work in relation to three authors who represent significant trends in scholarship: Mark Jordan in *Ordering Wisdom*; Peter Candler in *Theology, Rhetoric and Manuduction*; and Fáinche Ryan in *Formation in Holiness*. I will also attend to a short essay published in 1974 by Guy-H. Allard.

Jordan's work represents a real breakthrough in scholarship on Aquinas, and the present study has much in common with *Ordering Wisdom*. In the first part, Jordan shows Aquinas' awareness and use of the tools of rhetoric, and situates Aquinas' use of rhetoric in relation to the disciplines of the trivium and to philosophy, particularly ethics. His analysis of the emergence of the *quaestio* from the practices of forensic rhetoric in the study of canon law emphasizes that the *quaestio* fostered dialogue in which one could appropriate the judgments of others, particularly authorities, and uncover harmonies within apparent dissonances. Jordan also usefully identifies some of the basic tools Aquinas employs from both the trivium and the other arts.

Modern notions of philosophy, writes Jordan, make enormous and destructive claims. Aquinas, by contrast, grasps philosophy as incomplete and orders it pedagogically to theology, thereby setting limits to philosophic discourse through the creation of a hierarchy of discourses which are also different types of knowing. I will focus in a complementary fashion on the theological and spiritual discourses to which all this is ordered. I will also be more concerned to insert Aquinas' praxis in its social, cultural, and religious context.

I appropriate much of what Jordan does in the first part of his study, but I also distance myself from some of his concerns. His broader purpose is to show that Aquinas orders discourses to each other and to a persuasive end according to the modes of knowing, and so the second part of his work traces the progression of speculative discourse, the most spiritual form of knowing, from the physical through the psychological to the metaphysical. While noting

---

and Matthew Levering, *Knowing the Love of Christ: An Introduction to the Theology of Thomas Aquinas* (Notre Dame, IN, 2002); *The Theology of Thomas Aquinas* (Notre Dame, IN, 2005), ed. Rik van Nieuwenhove and Joseph Wawrykow; Thomas Hibbs, *Dialectic and Narrative in Aquinas: An Interpretation of the "Summa Contra Gentiles"* (Notre Dame, IN, 1995).

the use that Aquinas makes of the trivium for constructing persuasive philosophical discourse, Jordan's focus is on the importance of dialectic. This study, by contrast, points to the anchoring of Aquinas' text in the symbolic, the aesthetic-dramatic, and the affective elements of meaning, as well as the way in which the rhetorical form of the text mediates religious meaning. I rely here on the paradox noted by Eugene Rogers (and discussed later in this chapter), that the more theoretical Aquinas' theology is, the more Scriptural and Christocentric it becomes: Divine Wisdom has a concrete shape and narrative to which the student or theologian must be conformed.[11]

I am in substantial agreement with Guy-H. Allard in "Le *Contra Gentiles* et le modèle rhétorique," which Jordan criticizes. Whereas Jordan notices the roots of the *quaestio* in forensic rhetoric, I pursue, with Allard in his analysis of the *Summa contra Gentiles*, the rhetorical development of the whole of the *Summa theologiae* as deliberative rhetoric which seeks to "provoke concrete action and treats discourse according to the roles it can play in the city … ."[12] Allard's approach takes into account the construction of a moral and political identity as part of the quest for *beatitudo*. Although his research has been surpassed by the work of Michel Corbin, Thomas Hibbs, and René-Antoine Gauthier, Allard's perspective complements Jordan's pedagogical analysis. My approach will be more historical. I explore the historical circumstances that prompted Aquinas to construct a Christian identity and the choices that such an identity entails.

In contrast to both Jordan and Allard, I move beyond morality and politics to include spirituality. Aquinas' pedagogy is a spiritual one that does not exclude moral and political theories but sublates them within the larger horizon of divine charity encountered in Christ by the power of the Holy Spirit. Such a conception places this study in conversation with Peter Candler and Fáinche Ryan.

In *Theology, Rhetoric and Manuduction* Candler presents the process of knowing as participative and developmental, thus requiring a guide. He seeks to resurrect this pre-modern perspective against the representational and immediate panoptic knowing promoted by modernity. This older view is not solely concerned with the nature and number of objects to be known, but rather moves through a field of knowing. Candler's interpretation captures well the

11 Eugene Rogers, *Thomas Aquinas and Karl Barth: Sacred Doctrine and the Natural Knowledge of God* (Notre Dame, IN, 1995).

12 Guy-H. Allard, "Le *Contra Gentiles* et le modèle rhétorique," *Laval théologique et philosophique* 30 (1974): 237–250, at 240 (my translation).

pedagogical perspective by which I understand the *Summa theologiae* and connects with Jordan's progression through modes of discourse.[13]

Candler is interested in classic texts as pedagogical and manuductive, and focuses on rhetoric as defined by Augustine as the tool or grammar of manuduction. Candler's book is a helpful introduction to key notions, which I appropriate in many instances. To the extent that he discusses knowing as liturgical and Eucharistic, I part ways with him, not because of any fundamental disagreement but on account of differing interests. For me, *lectio divina* as a primary locus for encountering Scripture in community is a given, as well as a basic assumption for understanding the pedagogy of the *Summa*. Aquinas writes for young Dominicans who have been reading Scripture prayerfully and are continuing to do so, but his concern in the *Summa theologiae* is precisely to lead them to something more than their liturgically developed knowledge of Scripture, i.e., to the *ordo disciplinae* of the wise. In this way, Aquinas seeks to re-form and transform the *ducti* and *skopi* of knowing.

Candler seeks to understand what occurred to separate the reading of Scripture from the living tradition of the Church and reads Augustine and Aquinas from within this problematic. Again, while I endorse much of what he writes, my own concern is how this prior performance served to make theology a living mediation between religious living and the cultural matrix of thirteenth-century Europe. The crisis that interests me is the pastoral and spiritual crisis caused by the growth of the city in light of nascent urban commerce and the need for a new kind of pastoral agent to take responsibility for the Gospel. Thus, where Candler seeks to restore continuities, I will highlight the discontinuity between monastic and scholastic theologizing, even as I affirm the continuities he uncovers. Thus, while Candler's discussion of the process of manuduction in the *Summa* as a form of performative theosis is excellent in its context, from my perspective it remains too abstract and does not take into account the properly Dominican *telos* of preaching and hearing confessions.

In the fifth chapter of his book Candler highlights the radical difference between modern reading habits and those required to participate in the *Summa theologiae*'s path of knowing. I refer the reader to the excellent presentation of the manuduction of desire and the presentation of the *ductus* of the *Summa* in light of Aquinas' cognitional theory[14]; the discussion of rhetoric as communal

13 Peter M. Candler, *Theology, Rhetoric, Manuduction, or Reading Scripture Together on the Path to God* (Grand Rapids, MI, 2006).

14 Ibid., 90–107.

and as a process of *traditio* is also helpful, and corresponds with the work of Allard. But I will take seriously the ordering of memory and desire according to first principles as a significant additional practice within the Church's pedagogy, one that is particularly relevant to pastoral leadership. It is not that Candler ignores the *ordo disciplinae*, but his interests preclude him from asking how this is significantly different from other *ordines*. Over and over again, with Mark Jordan, the importance of the focus on the *ordo disciplinae* must be emphasized to show the unique pedagogy of the *Summa* within the larger pedagogy of religious life, the liturgy, and the Church as a community of memory.

Fáinche Ryan, in her study of the *Prima pars* of the *Summa theologiae*, proposes precisely this kind of focus on theology as a process of sanctification. According to Ryan, theology is an activity available to all the baptized in the Church, who practice it primarily in listening to sacred Scripture and responding to it in the Church. As she writes in her conclusion, "Prayer is the bond between the theology of the professional theologian and the theology of the factory worker and the house maker."[15] While I take seriously her perspective that Thomas' goal in the *Summa* is to lead people toward sanctification, I want to introduce a twofold distinction. First, the *Summa* explores the structures and processes of sanctification in all persons *in order to* teach the one who has the care of souls how to help them. Second, the *Summa* is *itself* a process of sanctification specifically ordered to those involved in the care of souls to make them better equipped for the mission of preaching and hearing confessions. Thus, Aquinas' concern is not formation in holiness in general and at a certain level of abstraction, but rather it is a process of formation in holiness of one who must find the right consoling word in preaching and hearing confessions.

Ryan's interest is in the graced processes that make the various kinds of knowing God in this life possible. She is particularly interested in the kind of activity beyond catechesis that forms us in the image and likeness of God. While not disagreeing entirely with her perspective on Thomas, I am not certain that in writing the *Summa* Thomas had in mind a textbook for everyday Christians. While the text can be and has been used successfully in this way in the twentieth century, it is anachronistic to assign this purpose to the historical production of the text without careful qualification. Thus, I will take seriously those studies that distinguish the genuinely salvific knowing of the *vetula* and the activity of the master of the sacred page or the knowing required of the

15 Fáinche Ryan, *Formation in Holiness: Thomas Aquinas on Sacra Doctrina* (Leuven–Dudley, MA, 2007), 184.

preacher, which is tied to leadership, like the knowing granted by grace to Moses and Paul.

In the end, Ryan reads the *Summa* not to discover the historical purpose of the text but to explore the possibilities it presents for an explanation of, and program for, the Christian spiritual life, which is legitimate. By contrast, however, I will explore how the text itself is a pedagogy designed for the training of pastoral agents whose concern was to promote the spiritual and religious development of the faithful in the thirteenth century. It is this concrete exercise of philosophy and theology as a way of life that Aquinas seeks to promote in the *Summa theologiae*.

Philosophy (and Theology) as a Way of Life

Pierre Hadot used his inaugural lecture as professor of Hellenistic and Roman Thought at the College de France in February 1983 to set out the state of his research into classical Western philosophy. He was convinced from his study of ancient texts that the only way to interpret these writings correctly is to read them within the larger context of the philosophical life as it was understood in the period. He drew a sharp distinction between philosophy as a way of life and philosophical discourse. Too often, modern interpreters of the Stoics, Epicureans, Platonists, and Aristotelians have treated the texts of these schools as abstract and a-historical formulations stripped of their context. They have neglected to attend to the rise of *philosophia* as a cultural phenomenon in ancient Greece. Hadot proposed a different method:

> As a history of ancient *philosophia*, our history of Hellenistic and Roman thought is less focused on studying the doctrinal diversities and particularities of these different schools than it is on attempting to describe the very essence of the phenomenon of *philosophia* and finding the traits shared by the "philosopher" or by "philosophizing" in antiquity. We must try to recognize in some way the strangeness of this phenomenon, in order then to try to understand the strangeness of its permanence throughout the whole history of Western thought … . Philosophy is found everywhere – in speeches, novels, poetry, science, art. However, we must not be deceived. These general ideas, these commonplaces that may adorn a literary work, and true "philosophizing" are separated by an abyss.[16]

16 Pierre Hadot, *Philosophy as a Way of Life*, trans. Martin Chase (Oxford, 1995), 56.

To be a philosopher in ancient Greece (and later in the Roman Empire) was to make a radical break with daily life and take on a whole new set of practices. Although the philosopher might continue to take part in the life of the *polis*, he did so in such a way as to preserve in himself, and to promote in others, a particular ideal of wisdom. Each philosophical school in antiquity "represents a form of life defined by an ideal of wisdom."[17] As a consequence, each school "has its corresponding fundamental inner attitude – for example, tension for the Stoics or relaxation for the Epicureans – and its own manner of speaking … . But above all every school practices exercises designed to ensure spiritual progress toward the ideal state of wisdom … ."[18] These include sets of meditative practices, exercises in self-presence and in the use of the imagination, and a kind of meditative reading to memorize and assimilate the teachings of the particular school. Hadot, grounding his insights upon the work of Paul Rabbow, whose *Seelenführung: Methodik der Exercitien in der Antike* situated the Ignatian Spiritual Exercises within this ancient tradition,[19] calls all of these practices of philosophy as a way of life *spiritual exercises*:

> The expression is a bit disconcerting for the contemporary reader. In the first place, it is no longer quite fashionable these days to use the word "spiritual." It is nevertheless necessary to use this term, I believe, because none of the other adjectives we could use – "psychic," "moral," "ethical," "intellectual," "of thought," "of the soul" – covers all the aspects of the reality we want to describe. Since, in these exercises, it is thought which, as it were, takes itself as its own subject matter, and seeks to modify itself, it would be possible for us to speak in terms of "thought exercises." Yet the word "thought" does not indicate clearly enough that imagination and sensibility play a very important role in these exercises … . [These] exercises in fact correspond to a transformation of our vision of the world, and to a metamorphosis of our personality. The word "spiritual" is quite apt to make us understand that these exercises are the result, not merely of thought, but of the individual's entire psychism. Above all, the word "spiritual" reveals the true dimensions of these exercises. By means of them, the individual raises himself up to the life of the objective Spirit; that is to say, he re-places himself within the perspective of the Whole.[20]

17 Ibid., 59.

18 Ibid.

19 Paul Rabbow, *Seelenführung: Methodik der Exercitien in der Antike* (Munich, 1954).

20 Hadot, *Philosophy as a Way of Life*, 81–82.

The written work, in this context, "is a reflection of pedagogical, psychagogic, and methodological preoccupation."[21]

Thomas Aquinas, Wisdom, and Sacra doctrina

The wisdom that Dante ascribes to Thomas Aquinas is precisely what Thomas, writing in the first question of the *Summa theologiae*, calls *sacra doctrina*. Recent scholarship in both medieval history and theology has focused on deepening our understanding of what Thomas means by this phrase *sacra doctrina*, and Bruce Marshall has summarized well the current state of research in an essay that serves as my starting point.[22]

Sacra doctrina is for Thomas saving truth: "We need *sacra doctrina* because our salvation depends on it. The goal of life for which God has made us – the enjoyment of God himself, seen face to face – is wholly beyond our powers to attain," and "unless we can rely on God to tell us what we can never find out on our own, there will be no salvation for us."[23] This knowledge is given us in Jesus Christ, the Word Incarnate, which means that the core of *sacra doctrina* is the knowledge of the truth about God – Father, Son and Spirit – and of the truth of the Incarnation: "the knowledge of Jesus Christ is, indeed, the consummation of the whole enterprise of theology."[24]

This enterprise is primarily speculative, though it includes knowledge of the practical consequences of saving truth in Christian living. We must be attentive to our understanding of the term "speculative," because modern English usage captures only a part of its meaning for Aquinas. Luckily, we can rely on an excellent study by Servais Pinckaers to guide us. He first points out that ancient and medieval *mentalités* "had an objectivist, ontological, analytical and universalizing perspective,"[25] compared with our contemporary perspective, which is subjective, psychological, synthetic, and concrete. The Latin term *speculor* "insists ... on the effort undertaken to *see* in the act of looking; it means to look attentively, to be on the lookout for, to espy a thing not yet seen or not yet seen clearly."[26] The act of "speculating" here means getting underneath the

21 Ibid., 104.

22 Bruce D. Marshall, "*Quod scit una uetula*: Aquinas on the Nature of Theology," in *The Theology of Thomas Aquinas*, ed. van Nieuwenhove and Wawrykow, 1–10.

23 Ibid., 3–4.

24 Ibid., 5.

25 Servais Pinckaers, "Recherche de la signification véritable du terme 'spéculatif,'" *Nouvelle Revue Théologique* 81 (1959): 673–695, at 674.

26 Ibid., 681.

surface, spying out, as it were, the real. "The speculative person, in this sense, is the one who has discovered a spiritual reality that is truer than the seeming of sensible realities, who has been seized by this spiritual reality. One can define the speculative person as a lover of the spiritual truth."[27] To love spiritual truth in this way means to make an effort to perceive it. Thus, while speculative knowledge in this sense is akin to the knowledge gained in contemplation (as we understand this term) the two are differentiated as "acquired" to "infused" knowledge. Both are based upon faith, both are genuine encounters with truth in God, but the process of knowing is different.[28] Nevertheless, says Pinckaers, in Thomas' general usage "this distinction is not made explicit and for him the terms *speculativus* et *contemplativus* are practically equivalent."[29] In this light, says Torrell, we must think of the *scientia* of *sacra doctrina* as a "contemplative" knowing – though with all the caveats that will properly distinguish it from the infused knowledge of mystical contemplation – which is *in via* and whose finality is "contemplatio primae veritatis in patria."[30]

Hadot's recovery of the enterprise of philosophy as a way of life, overcoming the modern misunderstanding of philosophy as primarily an academic pursuit that involves the study and interpretation of texts, also applies to Aquinas' notion of *sacra doctrina* as it is expounded in the *Summa theologiae*. Hadot, as we have seen, borrows the expression "spiritual exercises" to describe the goal of Plato's dialogues, Aristotle's *scientia*, or the Stoics' meditations.[31] He insists on this expression in preference to others precisely because it captures the way in which these philosophical writings make intellectual demands of the one who engages them. The purpose of these meditations is not, however, solely the knowledge acquired through them but rather a larger personal transformation. Aquinas himself proposes just such an understanding when he links together study, meditation, wisdom, and spiritual exercises in the *Summa theologiae*'s discussion of the relation between contemplation and the various states of religious life.[32]

This raises an important point. If *sacra doctrina* is that teaching which is necessary for salvation, it cannot be equated with theology *stricto sensu*. Theologians are not the only ones saved. The distinction Aquinas makes between *sacra doc-*

27 Ibid., 684.

28 Ibid., 693.

29 Ibid.

30 Jean-Pierre Torrell, "Le savoir théologique chez saint Thomas," *Revue Thomiste* 96 (1996): 355–396, at 369.

31 Hadot, *Philosophy as a Way of Life*.

32 Thomas Aquinas, *Summa theologiae* 2–2.185–189.

trina and *revelatio* is helpful. We should not be misled by our current understanding of the term "revelation" into thinking that there are two bodies of knowledge, on the one hand *sacra doctrina* and on the other hand divine revelation in our sense, such that the distinction becomes one between theology and Scripture, or theology and the Church's teaching, or some similar dichotomy. Henri Donneaud points out that for Aquinas, the phrase *revelationem divinam* preserves a more "verbal" meaning, namely God's act of revealing. Thus, "*revelatio* points directly to the divine act ... the act itself of revealing, of unveiling, of causing to know ... *Scriptura* or *doctrina*, on the other hand, signify the result of this revelation on the side of human beings."[33] We can say, then, that *sacra doctrina* is human participation, in all its forms, in God's act of revealing.[34] *Doctrina* is, as Mina Ofilada writes "a mediation in need of a constant process of mediating carried out by persons with a vocation, the teachers."[35] This view is precisely the one put forward by Thomas himself in the commentary on the *Posterior Analytics*, in which he notes that *doctrina* and *disciplina* pertain to the process of learning. *Doctrina* is the action of the one who makes us know, and *disciplina* the reception of knowledge from another.[36] He continues that doctrine and discipline can be taken to refer to the acquiring of any knowledge, not merely scientific knowledge. All this leads Torrell to affirm that "The term *sacra doctrina* has a very broad signification ... . In the *objective* sense ('that which' is taught) it applies first and foremost to Christian truth as a body of doctrine, with a wide application that ranges from Scripture to theology. In the *active* sense (the act of teaching) *doctrina* signifies all those activities by means of which Christian truth reaches us: God's teaching which makes itself known by means of the revealing act, the process of tradition, the preaching of the Church (including catechesis), and, naturally, theological education."[37]

This is why Thomas can give such an epistemic advantage to the *vetula*, the old woman of the well-known medieval commonplace: "She does not simply possess some cognitive items additional to those which human reason can arrive

33 Henri Donneaud, "Insaisissable *Sacra Doctrina*?" *Revue Thomiste* 98 (1998): 179–224.

34 Claude Geffré makes essentially the same point in the notes to the French translation of the *Summa*; see Thomas Aquinas, *Somme théologique*, ed. Albert Raulin (1984–1986; repr. Paris, 1999–2004), 1: 154.

35 Mina M. Ofilada, "The Role of the Teacher as a Condescending Mediator as Viewed from Aquinas's Notion of *Sacra Doctrina* and Its Bearing on the Nature of the Theological Enterprise," *Angelicum* 77 (2000): 373–396, at 393.

36 Thomas Aquinas, *Expositio Libri Posteriorum* 1.1.177–78.

37 Torrell, *Saint Thomas d'Aquin, Maître Spirituel*, 2.

at on its own. She knows the final aim of human life, and she knows the way to reach it … . [This] enables the old woman to do what even the most accomplished philosopher, absent Christian faith, cannot: orient her life, including the life of her mind, modest though it may be, to her final end. Her advantage is therefore great, and genuinely epistemic."[38]

This is why it is so important that *sacra doctrina* be a *scientia,* "a system of thought at once deductive and empirical," that "aims to explain states of affairs which we observe or otherwise accept … by tracing them back with syllogistic necessity to principles which provide a causal account of these states of affairs."[39] But surely not everyone will understand the faith scientifically in the way Aristotle intended? James A. Weisheipl offers us a first clue towards a solution. To call *sacra doctrina* a science is to indicate "the rationality, the reasonableness, the coherence of revelation. The alternative is to call faith irrational, absurd, and incoherent."[40] But as we have just seen, there is more at stake. Aquinas *does* want all Christians to know from first causes, as much as possible. He believes that *sacra doctrina* in the wide sense delineated above is *scientia.*

Eugene Rogers gives us the definitive orientation on *sacra doctrina* as *scientia*. "A science is the more Aristotelian," he writes, "the more it proceeds from first principles. Unitary first principles take propositional and real forms. For sacred doctrine, these first principles are respectively Scripture and Christ."[41] In the *Summa*, "scientific character now proceeds from first principles not on account of the [discursive] linkages they boast with a higher science, but on account of the [principial] light they shed, even if it lies beyond us."[42] As Thomas shows in question 1 itself, it is not only propositions that can shed such principial light on other propositions, but also things: "in short, one thing can explain another. One thing can even explain another without explaining it to us."[43] A distinct science emerges from a distinct revelation, "be it ever so worldly; or to put it in uncontroversial terms, when we have a distinct form."[44]

38 Marshall, "*Quod scit una vetula*," 6–7.

39 Ibid., 7.

40 James A. Weisheipl, "The Meaning of *Sacra Doctrina* in *Summa Theologiae* I, q.1," *The Thomist* 38 (1974): 49–80.

41 Rogers, *Thomas Aquinas and Karl Barth*, 18.

42 Ibid., 27.

43 Ibid., 23.

44 Ibid., 27.

> A science is the more Aristotelian, therefore, the more it accounts for or discovers that integrity, that mutual fittingness, that quality of belonging to each other, of human beings and the world. It is in unitary first principles that the integrity resides. A science accounts for its integrity by tightening the logical and descriptive links that, in human minds and language, join mind to thing, the psychological aspect of first principles to the real … . It is part of the development of forms in the world to manifest themselves and, in the presence of knowers, to render themselves better known.[45]

Scientia understood in this way unites a number of aspects: "as a habit of the soul, *scientia* conforms the mind to reality. As an academic discipline, *scientia* formalizes deductions from axioms. And, since the form that is knowledge and the form that drives things are one and the same form, we can even say that, as a structure of reality, *scientia* informs the development of things."[46] Rogers distinguishes four inter-related aspects of *scientia* that are "pulled apart" by the logic of Scripture: "The demand of the human being for intelligibility, the natural desire to know, is answered provisionally, in this life, by a *praecognitio finis* and finally, in the next, by the *scientia Dei et beatorum*; the effective structure of the soul that results from revelation is the infused habit of formed faith; the academic discipline or logic-informed study that embodies that intelligibility in propositions is sacred doctrine, a science in virtue not of noting but of believing its first principles; and the intelligible structure of reality to which the science's intelligibility corresponds remains altogether unknown to us in this life even as faith unites us to it by a self-revelation of God – climaxing in the Word become flesh – to which we now enjoy only textual access."[47] We can agree with most of Rogers' analysis of Thomas' position on *sacra doctrina* as *scientia*, but given the understanding of *sacra doctrina* we have already proposed, we must nuance the third aspect he distinguishes by changing the phrase "academic discipline or logic-informed study" to take account of the other ministrations of God's word, such as preaching, catechesis, and hearing confessions, which Thomas includes within *sacra doctrina*: thus, "the disciplined study and teaching that embodies that intelligibility in propositions … " is more reflective of Thomas' position.

45 Ibid., 30.
46 Ibid., 34.
47 Ibid., 39.

It is Christ who, as the fullness of God's revelation, "stands tacitly as the new light or form that gives rise to this new *scientia*,"[48] and thus "he is quietly named whenever Thomas uses tell-tale 'form' words: *via* and *ratio* and *iter* and exemplar."[49] Thus the various activities that make up *sacra doctrina* in the Church are participations in Christ, spiritual activities by which persons are conformed to the image and likeness of Christ. To say that *sacra doctrina* is *scientia*, then, is to propose a spiritual enterprise, a conforming of the mind to the Word who structures reality. The intelligible order which *sacra doctrina* seeks to embody in propositions and to communicate as a participation in the teaching activity of God in the Church, then, is the order which all things have in Christ, the Word who in God is the primary analogate of all truth and who as Incarnate is the "demonstration par excellence" by which God reveals all truth.[50]

From scientia *to* sapientia

To state that *sacra doctrina* is a *scientia* is, then, to propose it as a spiritual enterprise, as a conforming of the mind to the real. In article 4 of question 1, Thomas shows just what kind of a spiritual enterprise is involved. The article asks *utrum sacra doctrina sit scientia practica* like political science or ethics, where the mind is ordered for right action. This was, in fact, the position taken by most of Thomas' contemporaries, particularly those immediately concerned with pastoral formation. It is the attitude that leads to the writing of confessor's manuals and collections of homilies without moving into the realm of theory or speculation. Thomas takes a different tack, answering that while it is indeed practical, "it is more speculative than practical: it is occupied more with divine things than with human acts; though it thinks upon these latter as well, insofar as by them we are ordered to the perfect knowledge of God, in which consists eternal beatitude."[51]

Sacra doctrina is not only *scientia*, then, it is also true *sapientia*, wisdom: "This teaching is the supreme wisdom among all human wisdoms, not merely in any

48 Ibid., 57.

49 Ibid.

50 Ibid., 61–65.

51 "Magis tamen est speculativa, quam practica: quia principalius agit de rebus divinis, quam de actibus humanis: de quibus agit, secundum quod per eos ordinatur homo ad perfectam Dei cognitionem, in qua eterna beatitudo consistit." Thomas Aquinas, *Summa theologiae* 1.1.4 corp.

one order, but absolutely."[52] This is because it is the highest science, by which the wise person orders all things. It is unlike the wisdom which is a special gift of the Holy Spirit, since it is acquired by disciplined study. Nevertheless, because it is rooted in God's own truth revealed in Christ, it is the highest wisdom: "It is the most characteristic mark of *sacra doctrina* to make determinations about God as the highest cause: not only so far as God is knowable from creatures ... but also so far as God is known only to God's self, and is made known to others by revelation."[53] Claude Geffré notes in his commentary here that "S. Thomas distingue nettement ici la connaissance théologique, qui est un savoir acquis par l'étude, et la connaissance mystique, qui est un don du Saint-Esprit. Mais puisque la théologie s'enracine dans la foi, on ne peut dissocier dans l'acte théologique lui-même la part de construction rationnelle et la part d'expérience savoureuse de la Réalité même de Dieu. C'est la fausse dichotomie entre le registre de l'intelligence et celui de l'affectivité qui a entraîné ultérieurement le fossé grandissant entre 'théologie' et 'spiritualité.'"[54] Thus, to call *sacra doctrina* a wisdom is not only to identify it as an acquired intellectual virtue which orders the mind of the wise person but also to appeal to a whole way of life which, classically, assisted the disciplined study by which wisdom was acquired: one might think here of Aquinas' own delightful *opusculum* to a young Dominican who had asked him how to study fruitfully.[55]

Ductus: *The Itinerary of This Book*

This book is a work of theological interpretation. As such, it consists of two parts: the first explores the historical and methodological context for reading the *Summa theologiae* as *sacra doctrina*; the second explores the text in light of this

52 "Haec doctrina maxime sapientia est inter omnes sapientias humanas, non quidem in aliquo genere tantum, sed simpliciter." Thomas Aquinas, *Summa theologiae* 1.1.6 corp.

53 "Sacra autem doctrina propriissime determinat de Deo, secundum quod est altissima causa: quia non solum quantum ad illud, quod est per creatura cognoscibile ... sed etiam quantum ad id, quod notum est sibi soli de seipso, et aliis per revelationem communicatum." Thomas Aquinas, *Summa theologiae* 1.1.6 corp.

54 Claude Geffré makes this comment in a note to the same passage; see Thomas Aquinas, *Somme théologique*, ed. Raulin, 1: 159.

55 The authenticity of this text has been disputed. Nevertheless, it provides a good example of medieval and classical attitudes concerning the asceticism required to succeed in the life of study; Thomas Aquinas, *How to Study: Being the Letter of St. Thomas to Brother John (De modo studendi)*, 7th ed., trans. Victor White (London, 1960).

context, bringing to the fore the rhetorical *ductus* that unites Aquinas' systematic and spiritual concerns. The two parts are not related as premises to conclusion, but rather as interpretive horizon and activity of interpretation within that horizon. I hope that my readers, having become aware of and open to the rhetorical dynamics present in the text, might allow the spiritual pedagogy of the *Summa theologiae* to work in them as it did in Thomas' students, leading them to Wisdom's embrace.

The first part of the book proceeds in three steps. The first step, which takes up the whole of chapter two, makes explicit the intellectual framework within which the interpretation of the text will proceed. If the *Summa theologiae* is to be understood as holding together systematic and spiritual elements under the rubric of wisdom that orients a way of life, we must settle some basic questions of historiography. Specifically, I propose a critical realist framework that defines a notion of culture and explores the functions of meaning in human living. I then discuss the disciplines of the *trivium* as methods for the responsible control of meaning, highlighting the particular role played by rhetoric.

Chapter three articulates the second step, which consists of an exploration of the socio-cultural and pastoral context within which Aquinas wrote the *Summa theologiae*. After exploring the monastic appropriation of rhetoric as the basic context for Aquinas' religious and theological method, I will show the key social and cultural shifts that lead to the world of thirteenth-century European Christianity and explore the changes in spiritual practice connected with them. This proceeds into a presentation of the three key pastoral reform movements that converge in Thomas Aquinas' *œuvres*.

After I have recovered the historical elements of Thomas' theological and spiritual program, I will turn, in chapter four, to the third and final step of the hermeneutical part of this book. The convergence presented in the third chapter will be confirmed by a careful reading of Thomas' "public" theology, culled from his correspondence, his public tracts defending the mendicant movement, and various public academic exercises, namely the disputations and his inaugural lecture. We see in these works a Thomas fully engaged in the socio-cultural and pastoral movements of his day, taking a public role as a teacher of wisdom. From them we can develop a picture of the role of the theologian and preacher as Aquinas understood it. The chapter then proceeds to an articulation of the various textual means by which Aquinas implements this program in the *Summa theologiae*, understood – as Aquinas says it must be understood – as a document intended for the formation of beginners in *sacra doctrina*. Without negating or denying the philosophical tools Aquinas deploys in the *Summa*, this chapter will focus on the literary and rhetorical tools which engage and transform the student's memory, imagination, and experience within a systematic enterprise.

The itinerary of the first part of the book, then, can be understood as a set of narrowing concentric circles, or more dynamically as an inward spiral that moves from the theological framework for understanding Aquinas' historical context, through an exploration of that context as a means of understanding his theological project in its proper particularity, to an articulation of principles of reading that bring to light the performative or aesthetic-dramatic operators embedded in the text of the *Summa*. The second part – the exegetical commentary – also proceeds in three steps. The first step establishes, by means of a careful exegesis of the key prologues of the *Summa theologiae*, the concrete pedagogical structure and dynamics of the work. This is the work of chapter five. At the end of this chapter, I will make the case that the *Summa* is related to medieval texts of spiritual formation, and that its systematic theological achievement is also a pedagogy of spiritual development. Chapter six explores this *ductus* in greater depth, showing how it climaxes in the Christological questions that open the *Tertia pars*; this constitutes step two. Chapters seven, eight, and nine, finally, explore – and this is the third and final step – the Christology of the *Summa* as promoting communion with Wisdom Incarnate, so that the students who are the intended audience of the text might be transformed into agents of Divine Wisdom in the world, that is, might become authentic participants in *sacra doctrina*. There is, once again, a spiraling itinerary, this time one that zeroes in on the Christology of the *Summa* as key to its theological and spiritual structure and dynamic.

In the concluding chapter, Aquinas will emerge as an inheritor of the great traditions of spiritual pedagogy of the ancient and medieval worlds, one who sought to hand on to subsequent generations a new way of practicing the theological craft in a new pastoral and cultural world, and who can be a model for us of the unity of the intellectual enterprise and the spiritual life. Christian living in the twenty-first century will require more and more that we recover this unity, captured in the understanding of *sacra doctrina* as both mind-forming *scientia* and life-transforming *sapientia*. Like Dante, we can learn much of holiness and wisdom from hearing afresh the spiritual theology of Thomas Aquinas.

CHAPTER TWO

Meaning and Culture

The turn to the sapiential and spiritual elements of Saint Thomas' theology – particularly the possibility that a text like the *Summa theologiae* represents a pedagogy that is in some significant way in continuity with ancient notions of philosophy as a way of life ordered to the transformation of the person – implies that any serious attempt to understand his theology involves understanding the historical particularity of those he is addressing. What evidence is available to us to help us understand who his students were? What was the historical and cultural context that set the horizon of their understanding? What can we know, historically, of the pastoral and theological demands Aquinas was trying to meet with his pedagogy? Finally, can we learn from his writings what kind of pastoral agent he understood to be the *telos* of the formation process his theology governs?

Aquinas begins the *Summa contra Gentiles* with a consideration of the office of the wise: those who are called wise, he writes, "order things rightly and govern them well." This is because, he continues (citing Aristotle in the *Metaphysics*), "it belongs to the wise man to order." The rest of the first chapter of the *Summa contra Gentiles* considers *theoria* about God as the highest and most proper form of wisdom, as the source of all order. This continues into the second chapter, which proposes wisdom as the first principle of human beatitude, understood as a communion with God such that God's own self-knowledge becomes the immediate principle of our knowing God. Such considerations can give the impression that wisdom is only *theoria*, that is, that the pursuit of wisdom is concerned only with eternal and timeless – and necessary – truths, and that the truths of practical reason, by means of which one governs oneself and others well, are not wisdom proper, but in some way derived or secondary. A first glance at a work like the *Summa contra Gentiles* might tend to confirm this hypothesis, since matters of practical reason seem to be addressed from a more contemplative and theoretical stance.

But is this hypothesis true? Is wisdom for Thomas Aquinas primarily a matter of timeless and necessary truths? Or is Aquinas working with another and richer understanding of wisdom?

We can catch an initial glimpse of a richer possibility if we notice Aquinas' acquaintance with the wisdom literature of the Hebrew Scriptures. Aside from his extensive commentary on Job, which he understands to be a disputation on God's providence, that is, on God's government (practical ordering to the good) over all creatures, Aquinas cites the wisdom literature sixty-three times in his various works.[1] Aquinas knew the wisdom literature, and in fact opens the *Summa contra Gentiles* with a citation from the Book of Proverbs linking the meditation of truth to the practice of piety, the practical virtue that disposes one to show respect for and act upon my responsibilities to others (especially parents and elders), to God and to the state.

The wisdom tradition in Hebrew literature exhibited some consistent features that will aid our consideration of the notion of "wisdom" according to Aquinas. The biblical scholar John J. Collins writes: "Wisdom is not a matter of knowing a stock of universal truths. It is a matter of knowing the right response on a specific occasion."[2] The wisdom traditions in Israel, though they arose in different contexts, were ordered to practical and religious instruction; sages were concerned with both the handing on and the questioning of traditional wisdom, along with promoting the personal development required to respond well to the various situations of life. Norman Gottwald adds that sages sought to communicate "how to accommodate one's life to the fundamental orderliness of the world, or what to do when the anticipated order fails."[3] Wisdom, continues Gottwald, "aims for a practical and comprehensive ethics and behavioural style adequate to the situations in which its followers live, labor, and interact with one another and with others who are less attentive to wisdom."[4] It thus encompasses a wide range of truths, from scientific and philosophic observation of the natural environment and historical events, to considerations of social relations and political order, to family affairs and questions of manners, to daily work, to matters of religious belief and practice. It is a

1 This does not take into account the commentary on the Psalms, and the numerous citations from the Psalms throughout his work; in his day, the Psalms were considered to be part of the wisdom corpus.

2 John J. Collins, *Introduction to the Hebrew Bible* (Minneapolis, 2004), 494.

3 Norman K. Gottwald, *The Hebrew Bible: A Socio-Literary Introduction* (Philadelphia, 1987), 564.

4 Ibid., 566.

question of discovering the "value and meaning for life" of these various forms of knowledge.[5]

This practical yet comprehensive dimension of the biblical wisdom tradition helps to orient and deepen our understanding of what Aquinas means by wisdom. In the opening questions of the *Summa theologiae*, Aquinas asks whether *sacra doctrina* is contemplative or practical. His answer is that *sacra doctrina* is both contemplative and practical, though it is mainly contemplative. Practical knowledge is that knowledge whereby one orders one's life and activity in the world, whereby one makes of one's life something meaningful and valuable. Aquinas seems to be saying that finding and crafting value and meaning in one's life flows from a contemplative grasp of *theoria*, which promotes grounding one's life in the real order of things. This is confirmed by the prologue to his commentary on the *Sentences* of Peter Lombard. Through the wisdom of God, he writes, "the hidden things of God are made manifest and the works of creatures are produced, and not only produced but restored and perfected."[6] One and the same Wisdom in God is both contemplative and practical: it is manifestation of divine truth and producer of creatures; it is the restorer of creatures and that by which they are practically ordered to their fulfillment.

According to Thomas, wisdom is a participation in both God's knowing and God's practical governing of the cosmos. And like the biblical sage, the Christian teacher both hands on and reorders the received tradition, so that students can discover and craft meaning and value in their lives. Wisdom is thus concerned with that realm we have come to call culture, the empirical set of meanings and values that "carries meaning and value ... immediately and spontaneously to the pulsing flow of human living."[7]

What is Culture?

Contemporary cultural studies and cultural anthropology make use of many theoretical and methodological frameworks: there are materialist, functionalist, structuralist, deconstructionist and phenomenological approaches to cul-

5 Ibid., 566.

6 Thomas Aquinas, "Prologue," *Commentary on the Sentences*, trans. Joseph Kenny <http://dhspriory.org/thomas/ Sentences.htm#01>.

7 Thomas McPartland, *Lonergan and Historiography: The Epistemological Philosophy of History* (Columbia, MO, 2010), 85.

ture. Theorists such as Karl Marx, Clifford Geertz, Claude Lévi-Strauss, and Émile Durkheim among others anchor these approaches in more basic philosophical assumptions. What these approaches have in common, however, is a commitment to the empirical study of culture and cultures. According to Bernard Lonergan, "[The] contemporary notion of culture is empirical. A culture is a set of meanings and values informing a common way of life, and there are as many cultures as there are distinct sets of such meanings and values."[8] These sets of meanings and values are not free floating; they are grounded and conditioned to some degree by political, economic, technological orders that distribute the goods of human living to members of a society, and they in turn sanction and orient human living within these orders. "Not on bread alone doth man live. Over and above mere living and operating, men have to find a meaning and value in their living and operating. It is the function of culture to discover, express, validate, criticize, correct, develop, improve such meaning and value."[9]

How have Christians through the centuries ordered their life and activities in the world? Can we propose a general process by which Christian believers have found meaning and value through their human living and operating, of which Aquinas' theology could be understood to be a particular example? In order to make this case, we must first examine modern developments in the understanding of culture itself more closely.

In her book *Theories of Culture*, Kathryn Tanner provides a magisterial analysis of this development. We should distinguish, she writes, between a "high culture" notion of culture, and a human-centred one. The "high culture" notion of culture emerges in the seventeenth century as part of the reappropriation of the Greek and Roman ideal of the cultured person. "[The] notion of high culture – referring to a process of individual education and refinement, and, by extension, to the products of such processes (works of art and literature) – runs contrary to the anthropological sense of culture ... . [Contrary] to an anthropological notion of culture, high culture is an evaluative and exclusivist concept: not all persons are cultured and those who are are better than those who are not." Such an understanding of culture does not allow for a plural meaning of the term: "there is a high culture to be shared in varying degrees by cultured persons but no high cultures."[10]

8 Bernard Lonergan, *Method in Theology* (Toronto, 1990), 301.

9 Ibid., 32.

10 Kathryn Tanner, *Theories of Culture: A New Agenda for Theology* (Minneapolis, 1997), 5.

This notion of "high culture" in an evaluative or normative sense evolves from a personal to a social application during the Enlightenment. In France, a sense of culture as a particular set of universally applicable social practices that overcome local differences in *mores* – so as to facilitate the creation of a single French civilization – is promoted by those elites trying to forge a unitary French state from the various feudal and regional groupings competing with the monarchy for power. This notion of culture is embraced particularly by the rising bourgeoisie to define itself against the "vulgar and backward" aristocratic and rural populations. Under the influence of the rationalism of the *encyclopedistes*, this high notion of culture becomes an intellectual category that allows French thinkers to create a scheme of universal classification within which they can fit all peoples and nations according to the degree to which they meet the standards of French civilization.

In Germany, by contrast, *Kultur* identifies the unique spiritual, artistic, and intellectual achievements of the nation (*Volk*). It is the expression of the unique genius of the people, and contains in itself its own measure of perfection. The development of this culture is the result of the working of the inner "logic" of a people's "nature." Culture is, in this sense, "genetic." The contribution of human invention to *Kultur* lies in fully exploiting what nature has given. Cultures are thus to be evaluated on whether they have fully followed or lived up to the natural logic of their development. For German thinkers seeking to resist the onslaught of French manners and social practices adopted by many of their neighbors as an ideal to be emulated, German *Kultur* represents the bursting forth of national genius in all its vitality, while French *civilization* represents the last gasps of a nation in its senescence.

In England in the eighteenth and nineteenth centuries, culture became a means of resisting the corrosive pressures of industrialization. A rural and reflective ideal of culture governed the establishment of national institutions, particularly schools and universities. In the eyes of proponents of this ideal of culture, modern society had broken down the mechanisms whereby people controlled their impulses and desires. The resultant anarchic play of impulse and desire meant that social order was no longer maintainable. By exposing people to the best of human achievements, which were the same for all humanity, by means of a series of national institutions that held them to the highest standards of excellence, the English people would have the ability to control their impulses and desires and thereby restore social order.

The rise of British cultural evolution, which combined the aforementioned understanding of culture with French notions of universalism and rationality, produced an evaluative scale of development with British institutional forms at the apex and was the next significant step in the transformation of the notion of culture. This typically English conception was increasingly challenged by exposure to the particularist German account of *Kultur* as the organic set of achievements of a people. As this German notion gained ascendancy, the interest in empirical study of particular cultures as unique wholes fostered an increase in field work. This field work in turn dismantled the evaluative scale – with British institutions at the top – piece by piece.

The modern anthropological notion of culture emerged from this development with certain key characteristics. Culture is understood to be a uniquely human phenomenon, distinct from, and in contrast to, nature. The ancient distinction between *physis* and *nomos* is recovered and transposed, but now *physis* (nature) is conceived as animality and biology, while *nomos* (convention/law) is conceived as reason. Further, cultures are distinguished from one another precisely according to their key differences. Such differences are assumed to correspond to identifiable social groupings: a culture exists precisely as the attribute of a social group, the differences of which mark it off from other societies. Cultural values are understood to be the product of the social consensus that creates and preserves them and are prior to the persons who belong to particular social groups, thereby shaping the character of group members. Cultures, finally, are contingent human constructs, as can be seen from the great variety of cultures in existence. As Tanner notes, "One point of an anthropological idea of culture is to promote a non-evaluative alternative to ethnocentrism. Evaluation may come later but it is not built into the category of analysis that enables others to be described … . The contextual preoccupation of anthropological accounts of culture also disengages, at least for a time, the anthropologist's own culture-specific standards of truth, beauty, and goodness."[11]

More recently, this anthropological notion of culture has been criticized from various post-modern perspectives. It is seen to be insufficiently historical, ignoring the process of production of common meaning over time. The notion that a culture is an organic whole is challenged by the fact that no participant in a culture ever knows it as a whole but rather calls upon particular resources of meaning to meet particular circumstances. This in turn leads critics to challenge the notion that there is a social consensus that creates and preserves a cultural system. Neither can a culture be interpreted as a direct determinant of social order, nor can social order be a direct determinant of cultural values.

11 Ibid., 36–37.

What does occur is that particular historical agents with differing levels of cultural skill and with creative freedom make different use of cultural forms to meet particular situations both personal and social. According to this understanding, culture is subject to change both from external influence and internal forces. Once change and difference are admitted as realities within a culture, it is no longer possible to view it as a "sharply bounded, self-contained unit."[12]

Postmodern criticisms do not discard the elements of an anthropological notion of culture but radically historicize them. Precisely "because they are the products of historical processes, none of these features of culture can be simply presumed. Homogeneity, consistency, order, are no longer unempirical, a priori presumptions; sometimes they occur, sometimes they do not ... . Historical struggles precede any clearly defined meaning or organization of cultural elements; and these definitions are never so firm as to stop their flow." Cultures are still considered as wholes, but "contradictory and internally fissured wholes. Even successful struggles of cultural consolidation are likely to contain internal inconsistencies ... . Whether or not culture is a common focus of *agreement*, culture binds people together as a common focus for *engagement*."[13] Such a historically-minded revision, Tanner proposes, means that "culture refers to the whole social practice of meaningful action, and more specifically to the meaning dimension of such action – the beliefs, values, and orienting symbols that suffuse a whole way of life."[14] This is what Lonergan intends when he writes that the function of culture, understood empirically, is to discover, express, validate, criticize, correct, develop, and improve the meanings and values by means of which people find direction in and give direction to their living and operating.[15]

12 Ibid., 53.
13 Ibid., 56–17.
14 Ibid., 70.
15 Thus, Lonergan's reception of an empirical notion of culture does not exclude the question of normativity; he locates normativity not in the achievements of this or that particular historical culture but rather in the ongoing personal and communal self-transcendence that authentically responds to God's love poured out in human hearts. While a discussion of this in response to such critics as John Finnis in his 1992 Etienne Gilson Lecture, *Historical Consciousness and Theological Foundations*, most recently published in *Religion and Public Reasons: Collected Essays* 5, ed. John Finnis (Oxford, 2011), 139–162, would take me too far afield, the reader is referred particularly to McPartland's *Lonergan and Historiography*. A position on the normativity of practical reason

By understanding culture in light of postmodern developments Tanner highlights the role played by concrete forms of life within a culture, but Robert Doran, developing the work of Eric Voegelin within a Lonerganian framework, suggests that these forms of life are projects of discernment whereby persons search for, discover, and implement a direction for themselves within the movement of life. Following Voegelin's historical study of world cultures, Doran posits the emergence of a human-centred principle of meaning in various places around the world. It is an act of resistance against cosmos-centred forms of culture. The human-centred principle can be stated as follows: order in the soul is the measure of order in the city, and the measure of the soul's order is God.[16] In terms of the history of Western culture, the human-centred principle emerges with the origins of philosophy in classical Greece. "Its origin lies in an act of resistance directed not simply against a corrupt state of affairs in the philosopher's social environment," for example, Socrates' resistance to the Athenian oligarchy, "but ultimately against the destruction that the process of decline threatens to perpetrate on the philosopher's own integrity ... ." The philosophic community offers its insights into the common good and human integrity "in a publicly available and evocative manner, through both direct and indirect communication, that is ... through linguistic but also symbolic, artistic, intersubjective, and incarnate carriers of meaning."[17] The divine is in this context a world-transcendent measure of authenticity. This emergence of human-centred meaning is, as we have just seen, an act of resistance to a cosmos-centred principle, and thus establishes, as a matter of historical development, a dialectical relationship between them, such that within a concrete culture there is a dialectical tension between them. This dialectic of culture, however, is not meant to be resolved in favor of one pole or the other:

> In the dialectic of culture, an exclusively [cosmos-centred] set of constitutive meanings informs a culture that is not only dominated by myth and magic, but also powerless against the oppressive forces of contemporary imperialistic or totalitarian ambition; and when [human-centred] consti-

---

very similar to Lonergan's but within an explicitly Thomist framework, can be found in Martin Rhonheimer, *Natural Law and Practical Reason: A Thomist View of Moral Autonomy*, trans. Gerald Malsbary, Moral Philosophy and Moral Theology 1 (New York, 2000).

16 Ibid., 485.

17 Ibid. For a definition and discussion of the various carriers of meaning, see Lonergan, *Method in Theology*.

tutive meaning informs the way of life of the community at the expense of [cosmos-centred] attunement to the rhythms and processes of the body and of non-human nature, the very intentionality of the [human-centred] breakthrough to a world-transcendent measure of human integrity is canceled by human pride; humanity usurps the prerogatives of divinity, and the governing constitutive meaning of the culture becomes mechanomorphic.[18]

The discovery and implementation of a direction for oneself in the movement of life and the consequent selection and mediation of cultural values within a culture can thus be understood as a project of negotiating, as best one can, the integrity of this dialectic of culture. It is not a question of either/or, but of whatever concrete balance of both/and meets the needs of the present situation simultaneously in the culture and in the life of a cultural agent. The ability of cultural agents to do this more or less authentically is what generates the internal fissures and contradictions of the whole, which is a concrete culture, and creates the movements of progress and decline that engage the members of a culture in the struggle over that culture.

Kathryn Tanner's understanding of Christian identity as a task to be achieved can be situated within Robert Doran's more explicit identification of the dialectical nature of culture. The unity and historical continuity of Christian identity resides in this task, which tends to "revolve around a similar set of claims and ritual actions ... claims and ritual actions that because of their lack of definition amount in practice to a similar set of questions to be answered in the effort to be true to God. Who and what Jesus was, the difference he made in human life, the practices and beliefs that came into the world with him, are understood to be of crucial significance for how one is to live." The lack of definition to which she alludes is not a relativism but rather the very condition of possibility of appropriating and interpreting the claims and practices of Christianity. "Even without agreement in results, unity among Christian practices is therefore sustained by a continuity of fellowship, by a willingness, displayed across differences of time and space, to admonish, learn from, and be corrected by all persons similarly concerned about the true meaning of Christian discipleship ... . Christianity has its identity as a task; it has its identity in the task of looking for one."[19]

18 Ibid., 146.
19 Tanner, 153–155.

If this proposal is correct, it opens up a new way of looking at Thomas Aquinas' intention for the *Summa theologiae*. According to this interpretation, Thomas in the *Summa* is concerned with forming persons to exercise a certain cultural agency. If we are right, we will find evidence within ancient and medieval Christianity of practices of discovering and crafting a meaningful identity within the flow of life by appropriating and renegotiating the dialectic of human-centred and cosmos-centred meanings in given historical cultures. Although the empirical study of culture is a modern phenomenon, there are some indications that premodern peoples were reflectively aware of the role of human creativity in the constitution of their cultures. These indications are to be found in the practices of the ancient sciences of meaning, the *trivium*.

The Sciences of Meaning in the Ancient and Medieval Contexts

The recent publication of Marshall McLuhan's *The Classical Trivium*, his doctoral dissertation, has made his important study of the development of the disciplines of grammar, dialectic, and rhetoric, their relation to one another, and their role in the formation of education and culture in the West more widely available. This history argues that from antiquity "until the Cartesian revolution … . [L]anguage was viewed as simultaneously linking and harmonizing all the intellectual and physical functions of man and of the physical world as well."[20] The world itself was understood to be a book, "the lost language of which was analogous to human speech."[21] This "interfusion of language and physics" revolved around the doctrine of the *logos*. "The *Logos* or universal reason is at once the life and order which are in all things, and in the mind of man. When the Romans found it impossible to translate *Logos* by any single word, they therefore adapted the phrase *ratio et oratio* (reason and speech) … . It has often been pointed out how profoundly this doctrine of the *Logos* was received by Christianity."[22]

Awareness of the aesthetic and dramatic dimensions of meaning, and of their constitutive power, arises in the Greek world around 466 BCE in Sicily, shortly after a democracy replaced the rule of tyrants.[23] A man named Tisias

20 Marshall McLuhan, *The Classical Trivium: The Place of Thomas Nashe in the Learning of His Time*, ed. Terrence Gordon (Toronto, 2006), 16.

21 Ibid., xii.

22 Ibid., 22.

23 I follow here the reconstruction of George A. Kennedy; see Aristotle, *On Rhetoric: A Theory of Civic Discourse*, trans. George A. Kennedy (Oxford, 2007).

developed a method of writing judicial speeches on behalf of those suing to recover property confiscated under the pre-democratic regime. This method was marked by its awareness for the need to secure the good will of judges by appeals to aesthetic-dramatic dimensions of meaning. The Sophist Gorgias, who is perhaps best known from the Platonic dialogue that bears his name, came to Athens and combined his own approach to epideictic speechmaking with Tisias' method.

The rise of dialectic through the efforts of Socrates, Plato, and Aristotle presents a challenge to this art of rhetoric. Whereas Plato is wary of rhetoricians and rhetoric (for reasons related to his understanding of poetics, as we shall see below), Aristotle opts for an integration of rhetoric into wisdom. "Rhetoric is an *antistrophos* to dialectic," one of the methods used in all branches of knowledge.[24] An *antistrophos* is variously a coordinate, a counterpart, a correlate, a converse; as George Kennedy suggests, "in Greek choral lyric, the metrical pattern of a strophe is repeated with different words in the antistrophe." Aristotle recognizes that the control of aesthetic-dramatic meaning is part and parcel of the control of linguistic meaning, "of the various means of persuasion provided through speech, there are three species: for some are in the character of the speaker, and some in disposing the listener in some way, and some in the speech itself, by showing or seeming to show something."[25] Aristotle recognizes three basic kinds of speeches, the judicial, the epideictic, and the deliberative. He is particularly concerned with deliberative speech as an instrument for public decision making and community building and for the creation and furthering of civic friendship. Speech, as an act for creating public meaning, persuades because it communicates more than just linguistic meaning. It mediates the character and (genuine) practical wisdom of the speaker. It creates or communicates good will. It affects judgment by arousing or pacifying emotions, which for Aristotle are affective dispositions of the person which facilitate or prevent judgment and are rooted in a person's character.

Throughout his *Rhetoric*, Aristotle brings to the fore the link between linguistic and aesthetic-dramatic meaning in order to facilitate acts of meaning whereby persons and institutions constitute themselves. Chapter two of the second book is a sophisticated account of the basic emotions and how they are aroused or pacified. All of this, for Aristotle, must be always at the service of the common good and truth and thus requires genuine wisdom.

24 Ibid., 30.
25 Ibid., 38.

Cicero, like Aristotle, grounds rhetoric in genuine wisdom, going beyond the handbooks of rhetorical technique that proliferated in the ancient world, and especially in Rome during his lifetime. As he states through his "mouthpiece" Crassus in the dialogue *On the Orator*, genuine eloquence is more than rhetorical theory, "against these exponents of the science of rhetoric, who are exceedingly foolish persons, as they only write about the classification of cases and the elementary rules and the methods of stating the facts; whereas eloquence is so potent a force that it embraces the origin and operation and developments of all things, all the virtues and duties, all the natural principles governing the morals and minds and life of mankind, and also determines their customs and laws and rights, and controls the government of the state and expresses everything that concerns whatever topic in a graceful and flowing style."[26] The dialogue continues with a very interesting analysis of the relationship between language and the senses (chapter 25), the delightful effects of metaphor (chapter 39), the importance of rhythm for creating dignity and beauty (chapter 45), and more, including the significance of memory. Cicero is keenly aware of the psychological and spiritual power of language and its role in transforming the consciousness of the hearer and forming the character of both hearer and speaker.

By now, we can acknowledge – even if we have not yet explored this as fully as we will in the next chapter – that the thinkers of antiquity were aware in some meaningful sense that culture is a human construct and can vary. The sciences of meaning, particularly rhetoric, provided tools to deploy this power of meaning in its aesthetic and dramatic dimensions. Ancient and medieval Christians, including Thomas Aquinas, engaged their cultures purposefully with deliberate programs of transformation and implementation of Christian values in their cultures. How did Christian communities do this?

Ekklesia *and Culture: The Transformation of Human Meaning*

The French scholar Alain Michel has exposed the links that exist among Christian spirituality, culture, and beauty without, in doing so, assimilating Christianity to an aesthetic, a culture, or a philosophy.[27] Following Hans Urs

26 Marcus Tullius Cicero, *De oratore*, trans. E.W. Sutton and H. Rackham (1942; Cambridge, MA, 2004), 1: 61.

27 The key works of interest here are Alain Michel's *Les rapports de la rhetorique et de la philosophie dans l'œuvre de Ciceron: Recherches sur les fondements philosophiques de l'art de per-*

von Balthasar, Michel holds that beauty is central to Christian thought. His historical study shows that Christianity, while it certainly modified, transmuted, and converted the cultures it encountered, did not destroy them. Using a philological approach, he relies on identifying the particular use Christians made of the rhetoric, grammar, and philosophy of Greek and the Latin authors (particularly Cicero) for the composition of hymns and prayers. In this way, Michel brings to light the properly Christian aesthetic that flows from and shapes personal and communal spirituality.[28]

After Pythagoras' discovery that the cosmos could be understood mathematically and geometrically, music and geometry became particularly important to Greek thought, which enabled a particular understanding of poetry to flourish. Poetry is a musical knowledge that enables its practitioner to discover the harmony that obtains among beings. Harmony constitutes the image and model of justice. But this theoretical development needed to be reconciled with the prior heritage of Homer, whose poetry, far from breaking with the sensible and the dramatic, celebrates it, even when this involves portraying injustice and immorality. Homer himself provided the beginning of an answer: poetry is supplication of the gods, an act of worship. Whether intelligible harmony or supplication, poetry is understood by both Pythagoras and Homer according to what we have called "cosmos-centred meaning".

Faced with this heritage, which he receives through the lens of his commitment to dialectic and to "human-centred meaning", Plato argues for harmony against supplication. But the harmony he affirms contains a world-transcendent measure of integrity. For him, then, poetry is not knowledge; it is lying. Aristotle, who seeks to preserve poetry and rhetoric in some form, discovers the plausible. What is important in a poem is its measure, order, and balance; how the poet tempers the wondrous by the humane; how graceful and fitting one's imitation of the real is. Aristotle thus gives birth to a naturalistic

---

suader (Leuven–Dudley, MA, 2003), where he sets the foundation for his reading of ancient and medieval rhetoric in relation to culture, *La parole et la beauté: Culture et beauté dans l'hymnique chrétienne latine* (Paris, 1982), a survey of the rhetoric and poetics of the Western tradition from ancient Greece to the present day, and for our immediate purposes, *In hymnis et canticis: Culture et beauté dans l'hymnique chrétienne latine* (Louvain, 1976), a close reading of the poetics and rhetoric of the Latin patristic and medieval heritage in music and poetry. For a related discussion that makes more explicit use of Lonerganian categories, see my "Classical Rhetoric and the Control of Elemental Meaning," in *Meaning and History in Systematic Theology: Essays in Honor Robert M. Doran, SJ*, ed. John D. Dadosky (Milwaukee, 2009), 353–373.

28 Alain Michel, *In hymnis et canticis*, 10–15.

humanism where the harmony of nature anchors the harmony of culture.[29] *Pace* Plato's commitment to a world-transcendent measure of integrity, Aristotle establishes a new balance with the cosmos-centred meaning that understands the integrity of persons within their social order.

The heritage of Plato and Aristotle is communicated to the Latin world mainly in the works of Cicero, as we have seen. For him, as we shall see at greater length when we examine Aquinas' treatment of rhetoric in the *Summa*, rhetoric is the art whereby the hearts and minds of persons are transformed. Rhetoric's use of patterns of sound, affect, and imagery in eloquent speech is aimed at effecting a change in the hearer. This is possible because rhetoric, like all art, purifies and elevates aesthetic-dramatic meaning. But at the same time, Cicero affirms the role of philosophy and theoretical discourse in the life of wisdom. "As an orator, he seeks the plausible, as a Platonic philosopher, he distinguishes it from the true and attaches it to the probable. He affirms the virtues of speech, the exigencies of ideal beauty … . Cicero tries to harmonize the complementary exigencies of Platonism, Aristotelianism, and also of Stoicism and Epicurianism. In him better than anywhere else converge all the traditions that pagan thought produced in its history."[30]

Philo of Alexandria was an important model for Christians encountering pagan culture. The intersection of Judaic and Greek cultures in his writings exercised a profound influence on such a master Christian hymnologist as Ambrose of Milan. Philo was the first to appropriate the tools of Greek rhetoric for the interpretation of Scripture. In his understanding Greek allegory became Judeo-Christian typology. This way of proceeding, "even though it seems at first glance to leave too large a role to the imagination, will have an incomparable fecundity for many reasons: it will found all medieval reflection on symbol and language, determine both the importance given to language and the resolute will to interpret it by transcending it, to seek in all things the 'beyond' of the symbol."[31]

At this point, having set out the basic heritage which Western Christian literature – understood broadly as including poetry, homilies, prayers, and hymns – received from its historical and geographic context, Alain Michel traces the history of its development in great detail. I will select only a few specific cases that highlight the developments in this history. The first case is that

29 Ibid., 17.
30 Ibid., 22.
31 Ibid., 23.

of Saint Jerome as he translates the Scriptures. The text of the Vulgate has been hailed as a masterpiece of the renewal of Latin poetry, effecting a new balance between the "baroque" symbolism popular among Latin poets during the decline of the Western empire and the simplicity required by the Bible's divine subject matter and by the popular audience for which the Vulgate was intended. Jerome coined neologisms to translate the Hebraisms of the original text while also calling upon Virgil, Tacitus, Juvenal, Seneca, Cicero, and others for poetic and rhetorical strategies and language. For him, the profound originality of the texts meant that they cannot be reduced simply in translation to the Latin forms of the past. Neither did he want to erase the literary achievements of Latin culture. His project transfigured the cultural values of the pagans while adhering to the demands of the Scriptural text and its meaning. According to Jerome, "we find in the Bible, in much better version, all that the classical rhetoricians taught ... . The Bible equals and transfigures all of ancient poetry."[32] With the Psalms in particular, Homer's sense of poetry as supplication is transformed into the language of praise, changing even the music and metrical possibilities of Latin poetry.

One of the great figures in the development of a Christian poetics is Augustine of Hippo, and Michel spends much time examining his multiple achievements. Augustine's appropriation of the three classical rhetorical styles is of particular interest to this study. As a teacher of rhetoric, Augustine was quite familiar with Cicero's partition of styles into the simple, the temperate, and the grand. The simple style, free of ornamentation and ordered by its simplicity to the presentation of logical arguments, served for teaching. The temperate style, whose intent is to convince through delighting the hearer, became for Augustine the language of the sermon and of his mystical reflections on beauty. The grand style, highly ornate, and meant to evoke great emotions, was classically reserved for such occasions as the panegyric of the hero. In Augustine's hands, the grand style became linked to the outpouring of God's love, leading the hearer to conversion by the gift of tears. We have, with Augustine, the first intentional use of rhetoric as a means of inviting the person to a spiritual transformation by means of aesthetic-dramatic meaning. The classic example is the *Confessions*. The text opens with a discussion in simple style of the two wills; here, Augustine seeks to proceed only by demonstration. This is followed by the description of his struggles with chastity, and the style shifts to the temperate. In this discussion, there is a greater use of imagery, the rhythm

32 Ibid., 41.

of phrases becomes more musical, and Augustine "makes use of allegory (Continence herself appears to him) … . [The goal] is exhortative persuasion. But this is still not enough, and we witness the decisive moment of conversion, by the gift of grace. This begins with a storm of tears … ," which is captured in the grandest style.[33] Medieval authors, receiving this heritage, developed two tendencies. A simpler style, ascetic and more naturalistic, is placed in tension with a complex style using an imagistic language that links divine charity with profane elegance.

In his fifth-century poetry Boethius confronted the struggles of the now-Christianized Roman culture with that of the invading barbarians. The magnificent achievements of the Empire and the theoretical developments achieved by the Christian mind appeared as naught in the face of the violence of the Gothic invasions. In the midst of this, Boethius heard afresh the words of the Psalm: "The heavens are telling the glory of God, and all creation shouts for joy." Drawing from the highly imaged poetry of Virgil and his celebration of nature, Boethius rejoiced in the heavens and the stars, and the elevation of the soul engaged in praise of God through praise of them. For him, nature must be celebrated by the human spirit, because it is God's creation. Whatever happens to the achievements of mind and spirit, the cosmos will continue to bear witness to God. Christian poetry can rediscover the unity and greatness of the cosmos.[34] In order to announce the hope of the Gospel as urban culture fails, Boethius recovered "cosmos-centred constitutive meaning".

The Irish monastic artists and poets of the sixth century were faced with a very different crisis. These ascetics sought to preserve and communicate the spiritual and cultural achievements of the past for a society in which the institutions that had supported and fostered the growth of Roman language and culture had disappeared. The crisis in meaning which this occasioned appeared to them as a curse, a crucifixion that condemned the *ekklesia* to a slow and agonizing death by means of neglect. There is, instead, an explosion of creativity that is best seen in the violent expressionism of the decorative arts of Gospel books and other manuscripts of the period. But Irish poets and theologians also accomplished a radical transformation of language. In order to save their heritage, they drew from every available source of popular culture and ancient myth. They coined bizarre neologisms that survive in the theology of Johannes Scotus Eriugena, for example. They wrote natural poetry of incredible beauty

33 Ibid., 77.
34 Ibid., 104–105.

as they meditated on the ever-present violence of the ocean. The result was a radical reappropriation of "cosmos-centred meanings" that mediated the Christian past in a vivid and unique new way. The tempest and the deep met the crisis of a civilization that took the form of a crisis of language. [35] The literary creations of these authors "no longer serve the purpose of being understood by [non-Irish or non-lettered] others, but rather are intended as a language whereby the Irish *literati* can communicate with each other ... in order to conserve their science."[36] The religious culture of the day concentrated on itself in order to protect the linguistic and artistic heritage.

Our final example is that of the Carolingian Renaissance in the eighth and ninth centuries led by Alcuin. This renaissance, linked with Charlemagne's universalist aspirations for empire, was fuelled by Alcuin's rediscovery of Augustine's Ciceronian classicism with its sobriety and realism. Alcuin celebrated the human, and the nascent Romanesque art and architecture gave pride of place to the human figure. Though the political program dissipated quickly, the spiritual heritage of Alcuin set the Middle Ages on the course of an ongoing retrieval of "human-centred constitutive meaning". The renewal of the Church in Charlemagne's Europe required the reappropriation of classical learning (a common feature in the West) to express a new spiritual ideal. Pythagoras' ideal of beauty as harmony, for example, was retrieved as a principle for church architecture and the decoration of manuscripts. Alcuin recovered the links between the beautiful and the good and wrote a treatise *De rhetorica et virtutibus* that mediated this understanding to subsequent generations. For Alcuin, "all the corporeal and visible beauties are but analogues of the spiritual beauties, and love knows how to rise from the one to the other."[37]

The Mediation of Ekklesia *and Culture*

We can draw two further conclusions from the study by Alain Michel, along with our previous examination of the early Christian community. The first conclusion confirms the position of Robert Doran regarding the relation between Christian meaning and the dialectic of culture. "For theology to mediate between a cultural matrix and the significance and role of Christianity within that matrix is for it to mediate to the dialectic of culture, whether it be

35 Ibid., 107–109.
36 Ibid., 110.
37 Ibid., 120.

integral or distorted, the soteriological significance of Christian revelation."[38] In light of this, soteriology "is always relative to a prevailing set of constitutive meanings, and its particular form is always conditioned by these operative symbolizations. This is so because the experience of divine action that soteriology articulates is always an experience of deliverance from and beyond the constricting confines of these prevailing symbolizations."[39] Thus, the early community transforms its first-century Jewish heritage under the impetus of the person, life, work, and paschal mystery of Jesus the Christ. Augustine and Jerome affirm and yet transfigure their rhetorical inheritance, and Boethius announces hope in the face of the failure of "human-centred constitutive meanings" by affirming cosmos-centred symbols in new ways.

But this material reveals a further dynamic within the ecclesial task of self-constitution. As members of the Christian community seek to articulate their identity within a particular cultural situation, they both transform and are transformed by the sets of meanings and values they encounter. It is precisely by engaging, appropriating, affirming, correcting, and transfiguring the sets of meanings and values within the cultural matrix in which it finds itself that the *ekklesia* thus becomes itself and influences the cultural meanings and values of that situation. This is a genuine process of mutual self-mediation between the Christian meaning active in the community and the dialectic of culture – integral or distorted – that obtains for that concrete cultural matrix.

In this chapter we have explored how cultural practices and meanings proceed from acts of practical reason. In this light, a specific culture is the result of attentiveness to the dialectic of "human-centred" and "cosmos-centred" sources of meaning, of personal and political prudence, of justice, of temperance, of art, and of the absence of any one or other of these virtues. As such, specific cultures are both mediations of the past into the present and future and creative solutions to new challenges. They embody both success and failure to mediate or meet challenges creatively. As products of practical reason and its success and failure, they are a blend of the good and the bad. Whatever of the true, the good and the beautiful is present in them is expressed in actuality, in much the same way that substance is grasped only in the accidents that express it.[40] An empirical approach to culture under-

38 Robert M. Doran, *Theology and the Dialectics of History* (Toronto, 1990), 504.

39 Ibid., 509.

40 Bernard Lonergan proposes the following proportion: cultural values : social order :

stands that whatever is lasting and universal in a culture can only be grasped through its actual manifestation in an order of particular goods. Such an approach refrains from abstracting too hastily from the specific problems that had to be met, the conditions under which past achievement was appropriated and mediated forward, and so on.

Jesus of Nazareth is for the *ekklesia* that gathers around him and later gathers in his name a new source of meaning in history. He communicates this meaning in the process of working out his vocation, making of his life and career an authentic expression of his divine identity in human flesh, appropriating and transforming the practices and discourses of meaning available to him in first-century Judaism. This involves not only himself but also all the intersubjective encounters of his life, his use of both aesthetic and dramatic carriers of meaning, and his use, transformation, and affirmation of the language of the prophets, the Psalms and his everyday culture. This also involves the transformation of the religious and cultural elements he has inherited. This transformation affects the hearts and minds of his followers, as their world is transfigured by the new meanings into which Jesus initiates them, and this, in turn, prepares them in part for the radical transformation effected by the gift of Easter.

After Easter, the *ekklesia* experiences in a radical and definitive way the presence of the living Christ among them, along with the inner word of the gift of the Spirit, i.e., God's love poured into their hearts. This release of what we may call "soteriological meaning" becomes a force within the *ekklesia* whereby its members begin to exercise the same creative imagination that marked Jesus' human career, passion, and death. They take up the sets of meanings and values of first-century Judaism in a process of self-definition and self-discovery that constitutes a new mediation with the surrounding culture.

The crisis occasioned by the world mission precipitates a radical encounter with Greek culture that invites a further process of mediation between the *ekklesia* and the achievements and fissures of culture. We see perhaps more clearly here the elements of the dialectical reality of culture. Faced with the insistence of the Judaizers that belonging to Israel is necessary to salvation in Christ (belonging to the group as a measure of authenticity), for example, Paul exposes this demand as an overly "cosmos-centred" stance in his Letter to the Galatians (it would be a return to the world of the principalities and powers)

---

particular goods :: act : form : potency; see Bernard Lonergan, *De verbo incarnato* (Rome, 1961), 502–536.

and proposes instead the human consciousness of Christ (saved by the faith of Christ) as the measure of authenticity.[41] Under the impetus of soteriological constitutive meaning, the community discovers its renewed humanity under the new Adam and shifts the balance of the dialectic of culture towards "human-centred constitutive meaning".

This balancing and rebalancing of "human-centred" and "cosmos-centred" meanings, governed by the new meaning communicated by Christ, continues in every generation. Each social and cultural situation which forms the matrix within which the *ekklesia* lives, operates, and has its being invites a new mediation which discovers, validates, expresses, corrects, criticizes, transfigures, develops, or improves the sets of meanings and values of the culture even as it makes use of these to fulfill the task of ecclesial self-constitution. Past achievements of ecclesial self-definition and self-discovery become part of the inheritance which is appropriated and transformed under the light of soteriological constitutive meaning in every age. At times, the *ekklesia* gathered in council under the power of the Spirit sets boundaries that limit future acts of self-constitution and bring clearer definition to one aspect or other of the soteriological constitutive meaning that shapes the *ekklesia*. There is thus a play of constant and changing elements carried by aesthetic-dramatic, linguistic, and existential-moral embodiments of meaning.

Our study of certain moments in that unfolding history has shown the importance of rhetoric as the art and science which allowed Christian thinkers, pastors, and poets to mediate the intersubjective, aesthetic, and dramatic power of meaning during the patristic and early-medieval period. In the next chapter, we shall examine the role of rhetoric in the monastic and scholastic medieval traditions of poetry, worship, prayer, and teaching. This will allow us to take a closer look at Thomas Aquinas' appropriation and use of ancient rhetoric and poetics as a science of aesthetic-dramatic meaning.

41 This interprets "pistis Christou" as a subjective genitive. For an argument in favour of this controverted point, see Frank Matera, *Galatians*, ed. Daniel J. Harrington, Sacra Pagina 9 (Collegeville, MN, 1992); see also Greer M. Taylor, "Function of *Pistis Christou* in Galatians," *Journal of Biblical Literature* 85 (1966): 58–76.

CHAPTER THREE

Cultural and Pastoral Dimensions of Aquinas' Program

At the end of the last chapter, we found that rhetoric was for both ancient and medieval thinkers the science of aesthetic-dramatic meaning, and that it served cultural and civic purposes as well as being an instrument of personal formation. The purpose of this chapter is to explore this claim in greater depth as it applies to the Middle Ages and specifically to the work of Thomas Aquinas. I shall proceed in four steps: first, I will summarize the work of Mary Carruthers on medieval *memoria* and meditative practices. Then, I will retrieve the sociocultural shifts that transformed the world of the high Middle Ages along with the attendant shifts in spiritual and religious practice. I will close the chapter with a discussion of the transformation in theological pedagogy (the final step), after exploring in step three the key reform movements that converge in Thomas Aquinas' theological program.

Memoria *and Composition in Monastic Prayer*

Mary Carruthers has published a two-volume study of medieval meditative and cognitive practices from a rhetorical perspective. In *The Book of Memory*, Carruthers explores the *ars memoriae* as they were recovered and developed in the Middle Ages first in the monasteries and then in the schools. In *The Craft of Thought*, she examines the compositional practices that structured medieval monastic prayer before being appropriated and transformed by scholastic pedagogues.

In *The Book of Memory*, Carruthers proposes that the simple division between oral and written culture is insufficient to understand medieval and ancient literature. She proposes instead to think of medieval culture as a memorial culture, a culture in which the book is one of a number of supports for the remembering and retrieving of texts. Training one's memory in such a setting is the fundamental starting point of education. This is accomplished in the discipline of rhetoric, one of the three elementary language arts. It was not optional for someone to have a well-trained memory, because it is in memory that "one built character, judgment, citizenship and piety."[1] One inherits one's culture in one's memory such that rhetorical study becomes a primary instrument of socialization and inculturation. The training of memory was thus of moral and political concern to medieval people, as can be readily gleaned from the typical inclusion of questions on memory in treatises on ethics.

One remembers and becomes able to retrieve and manipulate the data of memory by creating and adding to a multiplicity of mnemonic schemes. These schemes, which are not always conceived of alphabetically (e.g., bestiaries) or architecturally (e.g., memory palaces), are heuristic rather than interpretative and intended to facilitate retrieval. Thus the importance of the distinction between natural and artificial schemes, which serve different purposes. A natural scheme is more helpful for retrieval when the material to be remembered has in itself (*ex parte rei*) a formal structure; an artificial scheme is more helpful for associating otherwise disparate materials.[2] As we shall see, part of Thomas' project in theology is to find and develop natural schemes that will be adequate to the mysteries he contemplates and teaches.

This concern for *adequatio* between schemes and things to be remembered raises a question of truth at the level of memory. *Adequatio*, in the phrase, "adequatio verbi et rei," which is similar to the definition of truth for Aquinas, embodies "what is basically a rhetorical view of the representational relationship between word and thing. ... *Adequatio* is a word of relationship, adjustment, fitting a word to what one wants to say ... [it] admits of many grades and degrees of approximation. ... [Being] a matter of more or less, [it] requires human judgment."[3] Because one is not born with this educational structure, and it cannot be gained passively, one must exercise one's will in the construction of an adequate memory, and thus one is making choices about one's present and future character. An "untrue" memory is false in two ways: it cannot recall accurately, and it prevents one from *being* true.

This is because of the nature of memory according to ancient and medieval theorists. The soul "is the whole complex of organization and functioning of a human being," and "mind is invoked to explain that aspect of its function relating to its ability to understand and acquire wisdom."[4] Images in the mem-

1 Mary Carruthers, *The Book of Memory: A Study of Memory in Medieval Culture*, Cambridge Studies in Medieval Literature (Cambridge, 2008), 9.

2 Ibid., 21.

3 Ibid., 28.

4 Ibid., 49.

ory are *affections*, meaning both that they impress the material of the brain and that they evoke feeling. "The nature of the memorial phantasm as *passio* or *affectio animi* is ... basic to the notion of trained memory as the *habitus* that perfects, indeed makes possible the virtue of prudence or moral judgment. ... [Each] phantasm is a combination not only of the neutral form of the perception but of our response to it (*intentio*). ... [T]he phantasm by its very nature evokes emotion."[5] The monk who remembered texts of Scripture for meditation divided the text into memorable bits and associated each bit with elements of personal observation, images, and affects roused by the text so as to fix the text in memory, not just as information but as a personal experience of some complexity and depth. The retrieval of such a text from memory necessarily also involved the retrieval of the images and affection one had associated with it.

In the twelfth and thirteenth centuries, one sees a proliferation of new memorial schemes, many of them proposed by teachers in the university, amongst whom the Dominicans are particularly present. This is in part due to the recovery of Aristotle's psychological and rhetorical treatises, but also, as we shall see in greater detail when we come to explore the shifts in pastoral ministry after the Fourth Lateran Council, because of the proliferation of texts to be remembered and the need of preachers to compose sermons for themselves instead of relying on collections of homilies published by the local bishop. Despite the shift in specific meditational practices and the new ends to which a trained memory must be put, "reading and memorizing were taught as they were in antiquity, as one single activity. ... [The] monastic understanding of what one does in reading ... not only persisted but became part of general culture in the thirteenth, fourteenth, and later centuries, for reasons that had as much to do with the moral value of *memoria* in meditation and prayer as with its utility."[6]

We shall see in the next chapter that the rise of cities and of the new merchant class introduced new cultural and social factors that placed strains on established patterns of public life. This in turn shifted the cultural purpose of education, increasing "people's needs and opportunities for speaking publicly to a variety of audiences both clerical and lay ... . Unlike in the earlier Middle Ages, when public oratory was the responsibility primarily of abbots and bishops ... the culture of the medieval university called for public disputations, sermons, and other forms of oral address on the part of all students as well as pro-

5 Ibid., 67–68.

6 Ibid., 101.

fessors … ."[7] Carruthers notes the prominence of Dominican teachers among those who provided adapted techniques of *memoria* better suited to the new situation.

Despite these shifts, or perhaps precisely because of them, the development of memory continued to be taught as a component of moral education, and continued to be tied to the activity of meditation and composition. "Merely to store memory by reading is an incomplete process without composition, for composing is the ruminative, 'digesting', process, the means by which reading is domesticated to ourselves."[8] This compositional work also exhibits continuity and change from the monastic to the scholastic context.[9] It is to this activity of composition, which Carruthers chronicles in *The Craft of Thought*, to that I now turn.

Carruthers proposes that monasticism is a "craft which is also a way of life." "The craft of making prayer continuously, which is the craft of monasticism [was called, by the early desert fathers] 'the memory of God' … . It recognizes the essential roles of emotion, imagination and cogitation within the activity of recollection … . Monastic meditation is the craft of making thoughts about God."[10] Monks developed their own art of memory and composition which, given their classical formation, shared features with Cicero's theories. This is why, when the Ciceronian practices and structures were revived in the thirteenth century, they seemed familiar to the culture. But the craft of composition was focused and redirected by the monks on tasks of literary invention intended to form citizens of the "City of God".

As we have already seen, pre-modern psychologies, which were rooted in rhetoric, understood the link between memory and affect. The storing of memories involves a kind of judgment that is not simply rational. Memories have *intentio*, a coloring that is "partly personal, partly emotional, partly rational and mostly cultural."[11] The monks associated *intentio* with "intensity" and the "creative tension" that enabled productive memory and compositional work to be done. Monastic composition is an activity of ordering and making one's life by ordering and making one's thoughts, structuring experience intentionally according to Christian patterns. This is a matter "not just of salvation but of

7 Ibid., 154.

8 Ibid., 192.

9 Ibid., 209–210.

10 Mary Carruthers, *The Craft of Thought: Meditation, Rhetoric, and the Making of Images, 400–1200* (Cambridge, 2000), 2.

11 Ibid., 15.

beauty and benefit, of *ornamentum* conceived of in the classical sense in which usefulness is merged with delight … . So the edifice of one's life … although created from stories available to all citizens, is also a fully personal creation … . The constant balance of individual and communal, *ethos* and *pathos*, is adjusted and engineered with the tools of rhetoric."[12] In this wider rhetorical context, the meaning of *ratio* is greatly enriched. In addition to the question of the truth-content of what is in our memories, *rationes* are the order, proportion, and measure that gather images together and relate them to each other in compositional work. These *rationes* are discovered and constructed by means of rhetorical techniques.

For monks, the processions and movements of the liturgy provided the key analogy for the mind meditating "its way through the sites of Scripture." This was "their essential conception of invention, the mind thinking … . Teachers of rhetoric … developed a concept to describe it, *ductus*."[13] *Ductus* is the flow of a composition, "the movement within and through a work's various parts," emphasizing "the conduct of a thinking mind on its way through a composition."[14] This movement can and should vary. The way should not always be smooth and easy, for some matters require that one work at them a bit. *Ductus* "emphasizes way-finding by organizing the structure of any composition as a journey through a linked series of stages, each of which has its characteristic flow … but which also moves the composition along" to its ultimate destination, its *skopos*.[15]

In this context of understanding, thinking, and meditation as a process of making thoughts that are stages on a journey, the great epistemological and religious vice is *curiositas*, undisciplined play with images that leads to mental crowding and confusion of images, to a lack of *rationes* ordering them. "[*Curiositas*] is a failure to pay attention, a vice of dilettantism, when we become so charmed by the play of our mental images that we lose our place and cannot remember what path they were supposed to mark."[16] The solution to this moral and spiritual problem is *conversio*, re-ordering and dis-placing our images, *converting* them, that is, turning them and disposing them in new networks of association. This is a kind of active forgetting by redefining associative paths.

12 Ibid., 21.

13 Ibid., 61.

14 Ibid., 78.

15 Ibid., 80.

16 Ibid., 94.

Conversion is a matter of memory, understanding, and will. It is also a matter of location, both location of self and location of images. One forgets one's sins by asking for forgiveness and changing one's *intentio* towards them: "what forgiveness changes is that *intentio*, the emotional direction ... towards the memory images that still exist in one's mind, including all those personal memories that make up 'my life'."[17]

All memories have *intentio*, but not all *intentio* is fruitful for the making of one's life as a citizen of the heavenly Jerusalem. The one who makes thoughts in prayer must monitor and modify the affective elements of memories. An important element of creating thoughts is *sollicitudo*, the carefulness or attentive mindfulness that promotes proper remembering and is a form of affective caring, which enters into the development of helpful *intentiones*. "One must feel, even deliberately create, emotion as part of reading" in order to "punctuate" (wound the memory with a *punctus* as one would a page one is writing on to line up letters properly) memories and keep them.[18] We thus see many medieval spiritual authors underlining how prayer begins in anxiety, with tears and great affective distress. "One remembers, not in a time of peace and tranquility, but in a context of strong emotion."[19]

Meditation in this context takes on the character of intense activity; the word *meditare* translates the Greek *meletein*, which "referred both to physical exercises, such as those soldiers do, and also to the memory exercises associated with learning to read and write. Such exercises were thought to shape the brain as athletics shape the body."[20] The notion of a spiritual exercise, so dear to Pierre Hadot, is rooted in this context. Meditation begins in "restlessness and compunction" and proceeds along a *ductus* "through the steps of inventive recollection to divine vision (if one's soul is prepared and God grants it) ... ." This understanding depends on "a model of thought as a restless, unceasing activity, requiring instruments, machines which can lift the mind and channel its movements, however variously, towards its destination, using as its primary tools its own images mapped out internally in mental pictures."[21] All of this is at the service of conversion and transformation, of receiving the shaping inheritance of the Scriptures and the liturgy, digesting it and following it, so that one makes of oneself (and is made into) a citizen of the heavenly Jerusalem.

17 Ibid., 95–99.
18 Ibid., 99.
19 Ibid., 103.
20 Ibid., 106.
21 Ibid., 221.

We can develop a better grasp of this rhetorical understanding of memory and thinking if we take a moment to notice how it translated into the architecture of the Middle Ages. Carruthers points out that the same basic instruments of thought led to very different ecclesiastical structures. Both Abbot Suger at Saint-Denis and Bernard of Clairvaux at Cîteaux wanted their buildings to serve inventive meditation. But Suger provided architectural *ducti* that are highly punctuated, full of surprises, and calculated to arouse feeling. Saint-Denis is like the writings of the Victorines whose urban context it shares. The heavy symbolism of the Victorines creates memorable structures and paths ready-made, as it were. Bernard "pared down the monk's oratory to an unadorned, moderately lighted, moderately sized *locus* variously subdivided into plain backgrounds marked off by the bays, the steps, the lights and shadows within."[22] Suger created elaborate *picturae* that shape meditation from the outside in, as it were; Bernard preferred to allow the monks to create their own images within the rhythm created by the repetition of light and dark, columns and bays, mnemonic "backdrops" of simple structures that can be filled in by the one meditating. The same rhetorical techniques were put to different uses, leading to different religious architectures. With this awareness of the flexibility of rhetorical tools brought to the fore, let us turn to the shift in pedagogical ideals from monastic to scholastic education.

Economic and Social Change in the High Medieval West

The end of the eleventh and the beginning of the twelfth centuries marked the start of a series of important socio-economic and demographic changes in Western Europe.[23] Substantial climatic shifts beginning in the 950s led to notable improvements in farm productivity and life expectancy. In northern France, technological developments also contributed to improving farm yields, which enabled farmers to survive on less land and in fact produce a surplus. Increasing political stability, as a result of the decrease in wars that was brought about by such mechanisms as the "king's peace" (introduced to protect individuals on errands for the ruler) and the "peace of God" (an important component in the

22 Ibid., 258.

23 For a summary of these changes, see David Nicholas, *The Evolution of the Medieval World* (New York, 1992). For an earlier and still relevant resource, see Marie-Dominique Chenu, *Nature, Man, and Society in the Twelfth Century*, ed. and trans. Jerome Taylor and Lester K. Little (Toronto, 1997).

Church's quest for *libertas ecclesiae*), fostered a growing network of local merchants and contributed to an increase in agricultural and artisanal trade between regions.

Significant changes in the fulfillment of feudal commitments also influenced the growth of an economy based upon trade. Lords increasingly accepted monetary payments from vassals in lieu of the more traditional obligations of labor. They then spent part of these revenues on mercenaries (knights) and created salaried standing armies. Many lords also began to tax the burgeoning agrarian economy as a more efficient means of collecting wealth than the previous gift-based methods. They supported the development of market towns and built mills for the grinding of flour, collecting fees or percentages of yield as payment for use of these facilities. With the influx of precious metals from the pillage of Muslim and Christian territories by Crusaders, it became possible to mint coins in greater quantity, which provided the final component for the rise of a monetary economy and removed one of the key barriers to international trade.

The manufacture of goods, which had been the purview of women and those who could not farm and had been a mainly artisanal activity, moved away from the home and shifted to market towns and urban centers, as the growth of trade and the development of international markets made specialization profitable. Towns that served as important ports on both river and sea particularly benefited from these shifts. As a result, the medieval city took on a greater importance in European life. "In 1200 most of the West was in the midst of a period of expansion ... . The most significant aspect of this demographic and economic expansion for the religious life of the time was the urbanization encouraged by the growth of trade and commerce, and the gradual transition to a profit economy based on money and banking rather than the gift economy that had characterized the early Middle Ages."[24]

Around the year 1000, medieval society understood itself as being tripartite: there were the *oratores* (those who prayed), the *bellatores* (those who fought), and the *laboratores* (those who labored).[25] The aforementioned shifts produced a new type of person, the urban dweller, who played new roles, faced new chal-

24 Bernard McGinn, *The Flowering of Mysticism: Men and Women in the New Mysticism (1200–1350)*, The Presence of God: A History of Western Christian Mysticism 3 (New York, 1998), 2–3.

25 For an excellent discussion of the political and socio-cultural dimensions of this self-understanding, see *Medieval Callings*, ed. Jacques Le Goff, trans. Lydia G. Cochrane (Chicago, 1990).

lenges, and represented a new set of forces in social and cultural life. The situation of the urban dweller was also a new spiritual reality that called for new pastoral intervention from the Church. "[T]he city, by its economy, its environment, and its ethic was destructive of family ties among the masses. Epidemics struck hard, solidarity was stretched to the limit, moral dangers lay in wait, the authority of the head of the family was endangered."[26] Money was the primary differentiating factor in the city, where revenues determined one's place in the hierarchy. Whereas in the early Middle Ages power had been expressed according to the relationship between *potens* and *pauper*, in the thirteenth century the dichotomy was perceived to be between rich and poor. This, in turn, affected the worldview of city-dwellers. The growing merchant class, the engine of urban development, was increasingly conscious of the challenge it presented to established feudal structures. It also began to feel the need for new ethical orientations and new rules of conduct. Urban preachers who attempted to respond to these needs have left behind sermons that bear witness to the new context and its internal paradoxes. For example, "[Berthold of Regensburg's] sermon on [the parable of the] talents contains an undeniable internal contradiction, a sort of tension between the traditional theocentric vision of the world and the vision of the world centered on Man, his aspirations and earthly interests, that had gradually taken form in the social consciousness of the burgher class. This picture of the world did not in any way negate the role of the Creator ... but it already included new potentials ... ."[27]

The growing influence of the merchant class on medieval society, particularly in the cities, led to a revolution in the cultural understanding and use of time. "Like the peasant, the merchant was at first subjected by his professional activity to the dominion of meteorological time, to the cycle of seasons and the unpredictability of storms and natural cataclysms ... . Once commercial networks were organized, however, time became an object of measurement."[28] The merchant needed to measure time accurately, in ever-smaller increments, if he was to keep an accurate account of profits, interest on loans, and other activities of his business. The advent of the mechanical clock, made possible by technological progress (itself fostered by mercantile need) revolutionized medieval urban life. Liturgical time, which had governed the days and seasons

26 Jacques Rossiaud, "The City-Dweller and Life in Cities and Towns," in *Medieval Callings*, ed. Le Goff, 139–179, at 148.

27 Aron Gurevich, "The Merchant," in *Medieval Callings*, ed. Le Goff, 243–283, at 256.

28 Jacques Le Goff , *Time, Work, and Culture in the Middle Ages*, trans. Arthur Goldhammer (Chicago, 1980), 34–35.

in the countryside, was replaced by the mechanized time of the work day, the cycle of fairs and markets, the time remaining on loans, and the time used to calculate interest.

These social, cultural, economic, and political changes, in turn, led to an explosion in medieval intellectual life. "Learning now had practical applications."[29] The growth of the monetary economy led to an increased need for literacy among merchants, as well as literate administrators in towns, churches, and courts. Legal scholars were required who could draw up contracts and run courts of law. The population shift to cities led to the decline of monastic schools in favor of urban cathedral schools. At the same time, the more secular goals fostered by urban culture, along with the explosion of interest in classical pagan literature among the increasingly sedentary courts of rulers, spawned a renaissance of interest in Latin texts and the development of a vernacular literature, particularly the poetry of courtly love. Established schools found themselves in competition with independent masters of arts, who taught grammar and philosophy but not theology. The traditional theological curriculum of the cathedral schools began to make more room for the arts. Guilds of masters and students formed to defend their rights and privileges against secular and ecclesiastical authorities.

Marie-Dominique Chenu has pointed out that, "The rise of new techniques both promoted and betokened a true discovery, an active discovery of nature; and man advanced toward self-discovery as he came thus to master nature … ."[30] This was the result of the increasing self-consciousness of the merchant class and its corresponding awareness of control over time and natural forces. Just as medieval thinkers began to absorb this momentous discovery of nature as a "dialogue partner" and as an object of study that could be understood by human reason and manipulated by human industry, the texts of Aristotle began to flood into the Latin West from the Arabic world. The teachings of "the Philosopher," rooted in rigorous observation and a respect for world-order as it is, fell on receptive ears.

The Evolution of Medieval Spiritual Life

The aforementioned shifts provided a pivotal setting for an enormous growth in religious fervor. "The resumption of trade and the growth of cities … and the

29 Nicholas, *The Evolution of the Medieval World*, 322.
30 Chenu, *Nature, Man, and Society in the Twelfth Century*, 39.

resultant specialization of labor by trades, brought about a new social mobility which led to mental and spiritual transformation. Man emerged from the indistinct mass in which he had languished."[31] A whole new class of Christians was emerging with its own pastoral concerns and challenges borne of its urban context. At the same time, the monasteries were re-evaluating their lifestyles, as well as their involvement in the active life. The writings of John Cassian were rediscovered, particularly his call to live the Reign of God uncontaminated. "Cassian defines as a diabolical illusion the call to convert others that persuaded monks to leave the community."[32] As the medieval economy became more structured by money, the riches of the monastery became a counter-testimony that eclipsed the monastic witness to the Reign of God. A new religious ideal emerged conditioned by, and responding to, changed cultural circumstances but understood differently by different groups within the Church: the ideal of the *vita apostolica*, i.e., the manner of living of Christ and the apostles.

For monks, *vita apostolica* meant a return to a more genuine and simpler *vita communis*. The reforms of Cluny and Cîteaux tended to separate monasteries from the world of education and preaching and promoted a stricter order of daily prayer and worship. For monastic reformers, the term *vita apostolica* "applied ... to the internal life of the first Christian communities which with their fraternal regimen prefigured and in a sense constituted the first monasteries."[33]

In contrast to a monastic understanding of the term, which implied a purification and a return to the roots of monasticism (at least to what was perceived to be its roots), the *vita apostolica* as it was understood by other groups represented a radical new challenge. "One of the most remarkable things about this new understanding of the *vita apostolica* .... is how rapidly the evangelical ideal ... spread to all levels of society .... As the twelfth century progressed, more and more laity were attracted to the evangelical rather than to the communal model of the apostolic life."[34] The evangelical understanding of the *vita apostolica* fostered a movement into the world and an embrace of the active life. This movement was centered on penance, preaching, and poverty and, while affirming the cultural turn to nature, recognized that God could be found

31 Le Goff, *Time, Work, and Culture in the Middle Ages*, 114.

32 Giovanni Miccoli, "Monks," in *Medieval Callings*, ed. Le Goff, 36–74, at 44.

33 Chenu, *Nature, Man, and Society in the Twelfth Century*, 206.

34 McGinn, *The Flowering of Mysticism*, 6.

by anyone anywhere. "Whereas the monastic view of God tended to reduce the truth and the causality inherent in things to little more than symbols or occasions of grace, and hence to reduce the use and enjoyment of things to a concession, the evangelical outlook allowed, and more than encouraged, the discovery of the laws of nature, an awareness of the demands of reason, and the value of social structures – all within the realm of grace."[35] Preaching took on new importance as a means of religious formation, and a new ideal of holiness developed which stressed knowledge of the Scriptures not as a means for personal sanctity alone but as a means of serving others. One grew in holiness, not merely by growing in personal knowledge of the Scriptures but by proclaiming their meaning to others.

The new evangelical ideal also stressed voluntary poverty as a counter-witness to the merchant's quest for profit. For many believers, including some merchants, the quest for profit could only be understood under the categories of usury and avarice. The way of life of the merchant class seemed to be a life of continual sin. "Among the principal criticisms leveled against the merchants was the charge that their profit implied a mortgage on time, which was supposed to belong to God alone."[36] The merchant's focus on profit and the laborer's dependence on wages represented many challenges to Christian self-understanding. For the most part, the only category under which Christian preachers could understand the merchant's vocation was that of greed. The merchant's behavior seemed to be predicated on a lust for monetary gain and power. Medieval sermons were full of "parables" of merchants who lose their souls in their quest for profit. The centrality of money and profit in urban life was met by the evangelical call to simplicity. This ideal proposed a way of life that emphasized earning one's bread by the labor of one's own hands, and distributing to the poor the profits that were not needed for simple living. At the extremes, many embraced voluntary destitution as an *imitatio Christi*. Such religious movements as the Waldensians, the *humiliati*, the "Poor of Christ," as well as such individuals as Francis and Clare, understood voluntary poverty as a form of asceticism that participated in the Passion of Christ.

From the eleventh to the thirteenth centuries Christian Europe witnessed a new emphasis on the humanity of Christ. This stress was connected to the new evangelical ideal of the *vita apostolica*, but it was also a response to the cultural interest in human autonomy and in nature. Important as well were the

35 Chenu, *Nature, Man, and Society in the Twelfth Century*, 228.
36 Le Goff, *Time, Work, and Culture in the Middle Ages*, 29.

liturgical and ecclesiastical reforms promoted by the pope and his curia. As emphasis was placed on the presence of Christ in the Eucharist through the efficacy of the priest among other liturgical reforms, women in particular turned to devotion to the Eucharist and the humanity of Christ as a way of prayer. "This form of meditation ... could be called a mysticism of the historical event ... . [It] manifests a more basic structure of religious consciousness that emerged into prominence and permeated the religious life of Western Europe in the later part of the Middle Ages."[37] As forms of worship changed and methods of prayer proliferated, and as the understanding of the Christian life expanded, both mystics and university-trained scholars became absorbed in the debates surrounding new moral dilemmas. Mystics such as Hadewijch of Antwerp agreed with theological scholars that it was not feelings of devotion that proved one's relationship to Christ but rather the practice of the virtues under the guidance of charity.

As we have noted, "urban activities multiplied moral dilemmas concerning the value of labor, profit, loans, wealth and poverty."[38] Urban life gave rise to other moral problems as well. Longer bachelorhood, necessitated by the longer periods required to establish oneself securely in the city, along with the increased availability of women, "raised questions concerning a sexual morality poorly adapted to new conditions of existence."[39] The poverty that appeared in cities as a result of mass migrations and the concomitant low employment as a result of economic shifts became a real strain on the Church's resources and a serious challenge to its ministry. "Faced with the people's growing discontent at the wealth of the church, of the nobility, and of the higher levels of urban society – a discontent that bred heresy – the church found it opportune to take the mendicant friars under its protection."[40]

There was also a growing awareness, fuelled by the arrival of peasants into the cities unprepared for the moral and spiritual challenges of urban life, that the official teachings of Christianity had not sunk deeply into the spiritual fibers of the average believer of any class. "[Many] peasant beliefs had their origins in the pre-Christian era or in non-Christian sources. Particularly on the

37 Ewert Cousens, "The Humanity and the Passion of Christ," in *Christian Spirituality: High Middle Ages and Reformation*, ed. Jill Raitt, Bernard McGinn and John Meyendorff (New York, 1987), 375–391, at 383.

38 Rossiaud, "The City-Dweller and Life in Cities and Towns," 151.

39 Ibid.

40 Gurevich, "The Merchant," 247.

parish level, the church was obliged to absorb many propitiatory rites, animistic practices and forms of sympathetic magic. The parish priest himself on occasion was not loath to practice magical arts … . Many church activities were connected in the peasants' minds with the returning cycles of agriculture."[41] Aron Gurevich has shown that this popular Christianity "had preserved vital links with the mytho-poetic and folkloric-magic consciousness" of pre-Christian Europe.[42] The religiosity of the mass of Christians, at least in its fundamental attitudes and behaviors, was not immediately affected by the shifts we have been tracing. "The increasing complexity in the parishioners' social composition, the growing numbers of burghers, merchants, tradesmen and knights, did not immediately lead to significant changes in these deeply rooted mental habits. They were shared by all strata of society, not just its lowest levels."[43] This religious mentality presented particular challenges to the Church's pastoral work. It equated the miraculous with the magical and venerated power, particularly "supernatural power capable of defending its own interests and protecting its clients;"[44] it blurred the distinction between good and evil, admitting of "good demons" who served humanity much in the way pixies and brownies had in pagan cultures; it "corporealized" the torments of hell, and "topographized" the relations between heaven, purgatory, and hell. It is not so much that, as some have tried to argue, Christianity was merely a veneer imposed on pagan beliefs and practices. People "behaved essentially as Christians."[45] It was more a question of a lack of differentiation of consciousness (in Lonergan's sense). "It was possible to destroy or discredit the old gods, but not to eliminate traditional habits of thinking, embedded as they were in the eternally repetitive cycle of agrarian life and linked with the many techniques of managing the matters of the world by way of magic."[46] Underlying these habits of thinking was a fundamental epistemological fact, namely that popular religiosity "reduced" the spiritual to the tangible, interpreting symbols literally and the abstract concretely. We can recognize here what Lonergan has called the first stage of meaning, where the common sense of the culture

41 Giovanni Cherubini, "The Peasant and Agriculture," in *Medieval Callings*, ed. Le Goff, 113–138, at 133.

42 Aron Gurevich, *Medieval Popular Culture*, trans. Jano M. Bak and Paul A. Hollingsworth (Cambridge, 1988), xv.

43 Ibid., 11.

44 Ibid., 49.

45 Ibid., 90.

46 Ibid.

remains unaffected by the discovery of *nous*.[47] This set of mental habits proved very resistant to many aspects of the Church's doctrinal and moral teaching, even as popular Christianity flourished in both cities and agrarian regions. The net effect of this popular religious mentality was often to bring the holy "down" into the secular, to domesticate it and rob it of its genuine ability to challenge the faithful in accord with the Gospel. This mentality went so far as to affect the patterns of preaching of reform-minded clerics. Their preference for *exempla* that discuss the punishment of usurers in graphic (and topographic) detail reveals the same material religiosity rooted in fear of power and a "corporealization" of the spiritual. Underlying this preaching is a systematic failure to grasp the concrete intelligibility of the Christian message. As a result, an understanding of this concrete intelligibility was displaced by the concreteness of natural cycles and popular fables.

The Transformation of Pedagogical Ideals

We have just surveyed the cultural shifts that characterized the twelfth and thirteenth centuries and the religious-spiritual developments connected with them. This summary has helped us articulate some important challenges to Christian life during this period: the need for a new personal morality for city-dwelling Christians, the development of a monetary economy with its attendant social injustices, the new relationship with creation characterized by distance from nature and an awareness of its manipulability, the growing interest in movements of evangelical life and in preaching, and a materialist popular religiosity resistant to the concrete intelligibility of the Gospel. We now turn to three particular movements that responded to these challenges. These movements, we will subsequently show, converge in Thomas Aquinas' theological praxis and find their most fruitful development there.

The Reforms of Lateran IV

The Roman pontiffs, beginning in 1123, had called councils primarily oriented to the reform of the Church and the promotion of *libertas ecclesiae*. The First Lateran Council ratified the Concordat of Worms and proposed several legal and moral reforms of the clergy. Lateran II was called to end schism in the Church and provided for several structural and moral reforms. The language of both councils, along with that of Lateran III, is legal in character: all three councils

47 Bernard Lonergan, *Method in Theology* (Toronto, 1990), 85–93.

promulgated "canons" of a practical order. The canons of Lateran III, in particular, were drafted by legal scholars of the highest ability. One senses that while these councils were aware of the hierarchical and social problems within the Church, they mainly tried to provide legal solutions to them. The one exception to this is the attack on usury that begins in Lateran II and continues in Lateran III. One easily perceives here the struggle of the Church to come to terms with the rise of the merchant class. "Nearly everywhere the crime of usury has become so firmly rooted that many, omitting other business, practice usury as if it were permitted, and in no way observe how it is forbidden in both the Old and the New Testament. We therefore declare that notorious usurers should not be admitted to communion of the altar or receive Christian burial if they die in this sin."[48] The Third Lateran Council pronounced the anathema against the Cathars and their defenders, and extended the indulgences and protections obtained through Crusading to those who would take arms against the southern French heresies.

Lateran IV strikes an entirely different note. "The fourth Lateran Council makes us feel what is so rarely to be sensed in the councils of the twelfth century, whether Roman or non-Roman: the immediate concern for pastoral care … . The council does not focus its attention narrowly on the reform of the clergy, but extends it also to the religious needs of the laity."[49] This becomes clear from the style of the council's decrees. The first document is a profession of faith, which is important for two reasons. First, it marks a crucial difference in the orientation of the council with respect to its three predecessors and their primarily legal and canonical orientation. The profession of faith signals a theological and pedagogical concern. Second, the profession of faith innovates in particular ways from previous conciliar doctrine, going beyond the mere need to combat the Trinitarian heresy of Joachim of Fiore, which would have required nothing more than a summary of earlier conciliar teaching, to propose a well-developed eschatology, to articulate the common labor of the Trinity in the effecting of the Incarnation, to enshrine the use of the term *transubstantiation*, and to offer a solid ecclesiology grounded upon the sacraments.

These achievements have been studied from numerous angles. Both Raymonde Foreville and Helena Tillman have indicated the conciliar fathers' debt

48 *Nicaea I – Lateran V*, ed. Norman P. Tanner, in *Decrees of the Ecumenical Councils* 1 (Washington, DC, 1990), 223.

49 Helena Tillman, *Pope Innocent III*, Europe in the Middle Ages: Selected Studies (New York, 1980), 189.

to the speculative theology of the masters of the school of Notre-Dame in Paris.[50] In this section, I would like to take up this point in terms of the council's pastoral orientation. The profession of faith's statement of a well-developed eschatology, for example, responds to, and tries to re-orient, popular religiosity. Whereas popular religious belief tended to understand the punishment of sinners as a function of power based on the common experience of the rule of feudal lords, the council's profession of faith affirms the belief in a particular judgment but articulates it in terms of the second coming of Christ. "He will come at the end of time to judge the living and the dead, to render to every person according to his works, both to the reprobate and to the elect. All of them will rise with their own bodies, which they now wear, so as to receive according to their deserts, whether these be good or bad … ."[51] The focus is not on an arbitrary exercise of power but on the justice of one's works. The conciliar emphasis on the authentic humanity of Christ and the endorsement of transubstantiation, along with the proposal of a sacramental ecclesiology, are also intended to instruct the faithful regarding the proper concreteness of Christian life, and thus to correct the misplaced concreteness of popular religiosity.

Lateran IV also innovates in terms of its response to the challenges of Christian living in the cities. Much has been made of the "paschal obligation" decreed by this council: "all the faithful of either sex, after they have reached the age of discernment, should individually confess all their sins in a faithful manner to their own priest at least once a year, and let them do what they can to perform the penance imposed on them. Let them reverently receive the sacrament of the Eucharist at least at Easter … ."[52] The priest receiving such a confession is instructed as follows: "[He] shall be discerning and prudent, so that like a skilled doctor he may pour wine and oil over the wounds of the injured one. Let him carefully inquire about the circumstances of both the sinner and the sin, so that he may prudently discern what sort of advice he ought to give and what remedy to apply, using various means to heal the sick person."[53] Canon 22 commands doctors to instruct their patients to see to the needs of their souls at a time of illness by calling for a confessor. Jacques Le Goff has shown how this endorsement of private confession and of the methodology

50 See Raymonde Foreville, *Latran I, II, III et Latran IV*, Histoire des conciles oecuméniques (Paris, 1965); also Tillman, *Pope Innocent III*.

51 *Nicaea I – Lateran V*, ed. Tanner, 230.

52 Ibid., 245.

53 Ibid.

of "penitentials" met the need to form the conscience of the merchant class and the growing urban populations.[54]

Lateran IV's tenth canon instructs bishops to appoint qualified persons to aid them in the work of preaching. The success of the mendicant preachers led by Fulk of Toulouse and Dominic had not gone unnoticed. The council understood, unlike its predecessors, that the heresies that had taken root in southern France were the result of religious ignorance and the scandalous witness of a rich and ignorant clergy. They thus endorsed the need for solid preaching by people living simply on alms. This realization is also at the root of many of the clerical reforms of this council. Canon 27, on the instruction of ordinands, is particularly interesting in this light: "To guide souls is a supreme art. We therefore strictly order bishops carefully to prepare those who are to be promoted to the priesthood and to instruct them, either by themselves or through other suitable persons, in the divine services and the sacraments of the church, so that they may be able to celebrate them correctly. But if they presume henceforth to ordain the ignorant and unformed, which can indeed easily be detected, we decree that both the ordainers and those ordained are to be subject to severe punishment … ."[55] Many of the other clerical reforms of the council strive to separate clergy and churches from the secular realm. Unlike the efforts of the previous Lateran councils, however, the concern here is not *libertas ecclesiae*, but rather that the holiness of holy things be preserved. This set of reforms, emphasizing the proper dress of clergy, the safekeeping of holy oils and the reserved Eucharist, and the removal of secular objects from within churches, is a response to the tendency of popular religiosity to "submerge" and dilute the sacred in the secular.

Lateran IV, then, represents an attempt to reform the Church, not so much structurally (though it does include certain structural measures), but catechetically and evangelically. Its focus on the *cura animarum* shows the influence of the Parisian theologians whose reforming spirit, as we shall see, led them to develop theoretical responses to pastoral questions. The council's agenda created the need for a new kind of pastor. "The demands made by the council upon the pastor implied a level of education of which the parish priests, in general, fell short. Not even the bishops, who in the practice of the early Church as well as in theory still were the pastors proper, were able sufficiently to ful-

54 See especially Jacques Le Goff, *Your Money or Your Life: Economy and Religion in the Middle Ages*, trans. Patricia Ranum (New York, 1990).

55 *Nicaea I – Lateran V*, ed. Tanner, 248.

fill the office of preaching and other pastoral duties, since they were overburdened with other tasks, and for other reasons ... ."[56] The demands of preaching, and of auricular confession as modeled by the council, created the need, not just for a learned clergy but for priests who were able to exercise practical judgment with a new kind of wisdom, had a view of the whole of doctrine, and could ask appropriate questions in unforeseen moral and doctrinal situations. While such aids as the penitentials partially filled this need, a more comprehensive solution was indicated. The council itself understood this, as can be seen from its call for the training of the clergy.

The Rise of the Dominicans

Marie-Dominique Chenu and William Hinnebusch have traced in great detail the origins of the Dominicans and their connection to the larger evangelical renewal in its mendicant expression.[57] This section assumes this previous scholarship as a general context and examines key characteristics of the Order of Preachers in light of what has been discussed in the previous sections of this chapter.

The Dominican movement had its origins in the urban preaching of Dominic and his companions against the Albigensian heresy (Catharism) in southern France. Dominican poverty was at the service of preaching, unlike the penitential poverty of the Franciscans. The Preachers' organization was itself modeled on new urban realities. "Early Dominicans acted in much the same spirit that drove townsmen to form guilds at the same time and in the same urban spaces ... . What guildsmen attempted to achieve as laymen within a new commercial environment, the followers of Dominic sought to realize as clerics within a new religious environment. Both presupposed the social consequences of urbanization ... and [both sought] to claim a relative freedom against inherited authorities."[58] The life and mission of the Preachers was particularly appealing to university students from whom they drew many of their recruits. "All these students ... functioned within a clerical culture but pursued learning in a social context that linked it mostly to preferment and ambition.

56 Tillman, *Pope Innocent III*, 190.

57 In particular, one should consult the masterly treatment in William Hinnebusch, *The History of the Dominican Order*, 2 vols. (New York, 1965).

58 John van Engen, "Dominic and the Brothers: *Vitae* as Life-Forming *Exempla* in the Order of Preachers," in *Christ Among the Medieval Dominicans*, ed. Kent Emery, Jr. and Joseph Wawrykow, Notre Dame Conferences in Medieval Studies 7 (Notre Dame, IN, 1998), 7–25, at 9.

Preachers offered a way to turn their high-spirited learning, their inner drive for *scientia* and understanding, to supernatural rather than strictly social ends, to the salvation of one's self and one's neighbour, the winning of human souls."[59]

This "urban" evangelical mendicancy produced a new ideal of holiness, which is reflected in the early documents of the Order. All medieval religious communities, including the Franciscans, relied on two formative sources: a rule to structure life in the community and a *vita* of the founder or of the archetypical patron of the community to inspire zealous living of that rule. The Dominicans, in addition to choosing an already established Rule, did not develop a *vita* of Dominic but rather relied on collected *vitae* of the first Preachers.[60] This reflects the revolutionary understanding of holiness operative in the Dominican community. "Unlike traditional monks or holy people, Preachers could regard their individual virtues as in some sense subsidiary to their mission .... In the entire monastic tradition since the Desert Fathers – and in Francis too – the mission was personal holiness. Outwardly directed missions ... only sprang from holy powers accrued by, or perceived as already present in, people of God. Dominic and his bishop from the beginning made virtue instrumental to the mission."[61] The new ideal of holiness led to a radical reordering of religious life. When he wrote the *consuetudines* that governed the Dominican way of living according to the Rule of Augustine, Dominic replaced both manual labor and *lectio divina* with lectures, study, and preaching.[62] From the beginning, "consecrated study" was constitutive of Dominican life. "Study and learning were the means to attain a sacred purpose – the salvation of men through preaching. In advancing that aim, they served simultaneously as instruments of personal sanctification for the friar. In the Dominican way of life they stood on a level with divine services and monastic observances strictly so-called."[63]

This practical reordering of the religious life with its emphasis on consecrated study is reflected in Dominican writings on the spiritual life. These texts tend to be unoriginal as far as their content is concerned, reflecting the writings of the Fathers and earlier medieval authors. What is new is both the intel-

59 Ibid., 17.

60 Ibid., 11.

61 Ibid., 20.

62 Hinnebusch, *History of the Dominican Order*, 46.

63 Ibid., 4.

lectualist interpretation that is given to these texts and the emphasis on a ministry of preaching as a means to one's personal growth in holiness.[64]

This does not mean that the Dominicans were mere academics. They were strictly focused on the *cura animarum* and sought to adapt the best means to effect the conversion of the other. "Preachers ... were to develop a sense not only for the right philosophical word with the learned or the right theological word with the heretic or the right rhetorical word with the crowd, but the right 'consoling' word – this is the most common term – to touch the soul of the troubled person."[65] Dominicans understood their learned preaching as a continuation of Christ's healing care of souls and knew themselves to be imitating the evangelical life of the early Church community. Portrayals of Dominic in early Dominican art bring this out clearly. The most common representation of Dominic connects him to "bread miracles."[66] In these images, " ... we see how the daily routine of the common meal in the refectory is transformed into a miraculous event, in which Dominic offers a parallel for Christ, praying at the start of the communality of the Last Supper, and his friars ... assume the role of the apostles."[67] This *conformitas* between Dominic and Christ, as it reflects the Preachers' self-understanding as a community that practiced an *imitatio apostoli*, grounded a whole way of life within which learned preaching found its place: "Dominic appears in Dominican art as the agent of Christ, not his imitator ... . Christ's position among the medieval Dominicans was, indeed, unique. But the visual sources also suggest that the founder of the Order might approach a Christ-like role – not through suffering and *compassio* but by gathering his friars around him to live the apostolic life."[68]

This particular relation to Christ is evident in Dominican preaching. The Dominicans preached Christ as a model to be imitated in his human deeds and favored *exempla* taken from the New Testament rather than the more common *exempla* fables that found their origins in popular life and mythology. Jesus, as the Incarnation of truth, was the concrete embodiment of Christian teaching

64 See in particular Simon Tugwell, "The Spirituality of the Dominicans," in *Christian Spirituality: High Middle Ages and Reformation*, ed. Raitt et al., 15–31, at 16 and 26–27.

65 van Engen, "Dominic and the Brothers," 18.

66 Joanna Cannon, "Dominic *Alter Christus*? Representations of the Founder in and After the *Arca di San Domenico*," in *Christ Among the Medieval Dominicans*, ed. Emery and Wawrykow, 26–48, at 35.

67 Ibid., 36.

68 Ibid., 39.

both moral and dogmatic.[69] This emphasis on the concreteness of Jesus Christ will play a great role, as we shall see, in Thomas Aquinas' theology.

It is easy to understand, then, why the Dominicans were particularly well-suited to meet the demands of Lateran IV and to respond to the needs of "an inquisitive, curious, active, expanding, city-dwelling population."[70] The various elements of Dominican spirituality which we have reviewed also help us to grasp the Dominican understanding of the preaching office in the Church. "The Church delegated the Order of Preachers to preach and teach sacred truth … . The teaching intended was not the restricted kind performed by the modern professor, but teaching in its early Christian and medieval sense. It was almost interchangeable with preaching. It was the task of instructing the people with authority in the doctrines of the faith. 'Doctor' in this sense is very close to 'preacher.' Teaching included the priest who taught the faith from the preacher's chair and the scholar who expounded it in his books."[71]

The University of Paris

We have already alluded to the general shifts in educational needs that were spawned by the rise of the merchant class and the development of urban centers. The period between the years 1000 and 1200 also saw a decrease in the importance of monastic schools as reforms in the monastic orders led to the closing of schools and as the population shifted away from rural areas towards the cities. The "increased employment opportunities for educated men outside the Church" meant that "many students, even though they were generally accorded the same legal privileges as the tonsured clergy while they were at the schools, did not belong, or aspire, to even the lowest grade of minor orders … . Clerics by legal status but usually lacking the accountability or the obligations of the clergy, scholars collectively represented a new and distinct social group, one that did not fit neatly into existing categories."[72]

It has been amply documented by a number of historians that as the number of students in Paris grew, discipline problems also increased: housing was not readily available, masters did not have proper venues for classes, and the

69 Richard Newhauser, "Jesus as the First Dominican? Reflections on a Sub-Theme in the Exemplary Literature of Some Thirteenth-Century Preachers," in *Christ Among the Medieval Dominicans*, ed. Emery and Wawrykow, 238–255, at 244.

70 Hinnebusch, *The History of the Dominican Order*, 54.

71 Ibid., 56.

72 Stephen C. Ferruolo, *The Origins of the University* (Stanford, CA, 1985), 206.

authorities frowned on the various conflicts that marked scholastic life, such as the strikes and violence by which students sought to improve their lot. At the same time, masters were convinced that the education offered in the schools was crucial to meeting the needs of the time. They also held themselves responsible for protecting their students from the authorities and for disciplining the wayward. The guild [*universitas*] of masters and students in Paris was formed to address all these situations. "The scholars in Paris formed a single guild because despite the diversity of subjects they studied or taught, they considered themselves involved in a common endeavor, the pursuit of knowledge and truth. They thought of education as vital to the general improvement of society … . The university they formed was a product not so much of narrow professional self-interest as of a higher educational ideal and a commitment to reform."[73]

This sense of vocation fit well with the general societal perception of the purpose and character of the university. "Three basic characteristics were thought to distinguish this new educational institution from other types of schools. First, it was an enduring and autonomous corporate body [like other guilds, but dedicated to study] … Significantly, this pursuit [of knowledge] was regarded not as a private vocation but as a public activity. The common endeavor of members of the guild was not so much independent study and research as teaching and learning … . The second basic characteristic of the university was an emphasis on the sharing and transmitting of knowledge," and finally, "[third] in contrast to other schools, the university was not specialized either in its constitution or in its goals."[74]

Despite this growing commitment to reform, the shifts in educational emphasis and the new kind of student attending the university prompted a number of public criticisms, both external and internal to the university. The environment of the university could foster a self-serving ambition among both masters and students. Rightly or wrongly, Peter Abelard has always been considered the archetype of the kind of scholar who allows personal interest to get in the way of higher values. The monastic critique of the schools and the university often fastened on this aspect of university life. William of Saint-Thierry's *Speculum fidei* is a good example of this criticism. William suggests an important distinction between what human beings can do and what God must do. Human beings can transmit, in conformity with doctrine and under the guidance of ecclesial institutions, the content of faith, which is accessible to

73 Ibid., 5.

74 Ibid., 4.

all, but only the Holy Spirit can give the truth which this content tries to express, along with the pious assent to that truth.[75] Education seeks to increase devotion and love of God. It ought to issue forth in deeper charity.[76]

This criticism was not restricted to monastic circles. A growing body of internal critics, particularly alumni of the schools who were in public life in the Church and in society, were alarmed at what they saw there. John of Salisbury,[77] considering the schools, believed that "rather than carefully searching for truth by systematically examining the opinions of the ancient philosophers, [scholars were] selecting doctrines and models of conduct on the basis of whim alone. The primary blame [belonged] to the masters, whose excessive verbosity and useless disputations deceive rather than assist students in their search for truth."[78] John also believed that the purpose of education is the fostering of charity.[79] The purpose of knowledge is to serve as a solid foundation for the cultivation of virtue. "The true and unique security of life is when the mind, enlivened by the Spirit, is enlightened by the knowledge of things and is kindled by the love of honour and the cultivation of virtue. Knowledge precedes the cultivation of virtue because no one can faithfully seek that of which he is ignorant ... ."[80] Public service requires a life of virtue and well-honed practical skills. "Just as eloquence, unenlightened by reason, is rash and blind, so wisdom, without the power of expression, is feeble and maimed. Speechless wisdom may sometimes increase one's personal satisfaction, but it rarely and only slightly contributes to the welfare of human society."[81] Ultimately, it is a question of the service of God. "Unless one refers what he knows to the service of God, his knowledge is not only of no benefit, but even becomes a handicap. For it is futile to know many things, if the one thing which is the most necessary of all, and is made manifest through understanding creatures, be lacking ... . The pagan philosophers were thus occupied. [As St. Paul shows] while boast-

75 William of Saint-Thierry, *Le miroir de la foi (Speculum fidei)*, ed. and trans. Jean Déchanet, Sources chrétiennes 301 (Paris, 1982), 139.

76 Ibid., 123.

77 Other "internal" critics of the university whose texts have survived are Peter of Celle and Peter Comestor.

78 Ferruolo, *The Origins of the University*, 136–37.

79 John of Salisbury, *Policraticus*, trans. Cary J. Nederman (New York, 1990), 161.

80 Ibid., 15.

81 John of Salisbury, *Metalogicon*, trans. Daniel D. McGarry (Gloucester, MA, 1971), 10.

ing of their wisdom they fell into foolishness, since they failed to return thanks to the author of [all] good things."[82]

The reforming masters who championed the formation of a guild, along with the external and internal critics of the university, were slowly articulating a new ideal for the scholar. Within the larger context of the emergence of this new, more general, ideal, the theologians teaching at Paris were busy trying to address the new pastoral problems arising from increased urbanization and the need to improve preaching. "Although far fewer in number than the masters of arts, the theologians had greater prestige in the schools owing both to the status of their subject and to the fact that their tenure was usually longer … . Among the theologians who taught in Paris during the formative years of the university, many were concerned … with practical and moral matters, many of which bore directly on education."[83] Of particular importance was the large body of clerics assembled under master Peter the Chanter in the late-twelfth century, a group to which John of Salisbury belonged. This group of scholars, along with endorsing the monastic critique of the university, is responsible for the honing of the scholastic method and for a very fruitful application of it to the moral challenges of the day. As John Baldwin has shown, they were also influential in developing the curriculum and pedagogy of the faculty of theology and articulating an ideal of holiness which this pedagogy sought to serve.[84]

This reform, aside from influencing the Fourth Lateran Council, resulted in the peculiar pedagogical method used by the masters of theology, which has been so carefully studied by Palémon Glorieux.[85] A careful review of some of his findings will help us to understand the ideal that emerged from the reforms promoted by Peter the Chanter and his circle. The student of theology spent seven years in the faculty, during which time he was required to "regularly attend all the lessons given in the school by the biblical and sentential bachelors and by the master; attend the discussions and exercises which took place in the afternoon; be present for all the acts of the faculty and the university held out side of his college, namely all ordinary and special disputations, and the inau-

82 Ibid., 269.

83 Ferruolo, *The Origins of the University*, 184–85.

84 John Baldwin, *Masters, Princes, and Merchants: The Social Views of Peter the Chanter and His Circle* (Princeton, 1970).

85 Palémon Glorieux, "L'enseignement au moyen âge," *Archives d'histoire doctrinale et litéraire du moyen âge* 35 (1968): 65–186.

gural sessions of both bachelors and masters; attend all religious exercises, namely masses, sermons, processions, etc."[86] This combination of methods served a particular set of values: the evaluation of knowledge, the importance of effective communication of ideas, the application of knowledge to new problems and situations (disputations), and the participation of masters and students in the life of the Church.

The role of the master of theology included three sets of responsibilities. He should communicate a clear, solid, substantial, and coherent doctrine to which his students will be able to refer in their future teaching and preaching; he should form his students to the task of reflection on, and personal assimilation of, the sacred page and teach them to express themselves well; finally, he should challenge them to preach and teach the Gospel message, not as abstract speculation but as a message for life and truth.[87] Corresponding to these three sets of responsibilities, the master had three basic sets of tools at his disposal: *lectio*, by means of which doctrine was passed on; *disputatio*, to teach the skills of dialogue and reflection, as well as to promote personal expression; *praedicatio*, to safeguard theology's character as sacred science.[88] The faculty of theology by means of these exercises intended to "former des clercs ouverts aux problèmes théologiques,"[89] who could receive the *sacra pagina* "reverenter et amanter."[90]The masters of theology together with the other masters of the University of Paris believed that education was central to social, ecclesial, and moral reform. They knew that this reform required a new kind of clergy, able to grasp the whole of theology and apply theological knowledge to new problems in a responsible and methodical way, and able to participate in the preaching that was so central to the spiritual life of the Church.

86 Ibid., 95. Translation mine.
87 Ibid., 106.
88 Ibid.
89 Ibid., 107.
90 Ibid., 109. In a series of important studies exploring the thought and praxis of such figures as Robert Grosseteste, William of Pagula, William Duranti, and John of Freiburg, as well as the education of the Dominican *fratres communes*, and Boniface VIII's constitution *Cum ex eo*, Leonard Boyle has shown how closely the content of these exercises adhered to contemporary pastoral concerns; see his essays collected in *Pastoral Care, Clerical Education and Canon Law, 1200–1400* (London, 1981).

The Convergence of Three Reform Movements

It should be clear that these three reform movements interacted in a number of ways. Lateran Council IV endorsed the Dominican way of life and recognized in the Friars Preacher individuals who could successfully put the Council's program into action. The theology of the Parisian masters informed the perspectives and decisions of the bishops at Lateran IV. The Dominicans drew much of their early membership from the universities. Beyond these historical interactions, however, there is a deeper convergence of ideals which must be highlighted briefly.

All three movements sought to promote a new ideal of holiness as a remedy to the Church's struggles. Lateran IV called for the formation of a clergy able to exercise practical judgment rooted in a grasp of the whole of doctrine in order to interpret Scripture faithfully within the Church by solid preaching and to form the consciences of the faithful by asking appropriate questions in unforeseen moral and doctrinal situations. The Dominicans promoted just such a life of learned preaching, whereby personal virtue was no longer an end in itself but an instrument for mission. For Dominicans, consecrated study was a constitutive part of a formation that fostered the ability to find the right consoling word to comfort the faithful. The Parisian masters put knowledge at the service of God in a life motivated by charity, creating a pedagogy that awakened a search for truth and led the student to receive the Scriptures with love and reverence.

Lateran IV and the Dominican movement were both concerned with the catechetical and theological renewal of the faithful who were enmeshed in the materialist tendencies of popular religiosity. Lateran IV relied on the teaching of the Parisian theologians to develop a corrective to popular religiosity and mandated annual confession as an instrument for the development of conscience. It also sought to protect the sacred from dilution in the secular. The Dominicans distanced themselves from the tales and fables that shaped popular preaching, preferring concrete examples from the New Testament so as to keep the Gospel "unadulterated." They also understood themselves to be called to teach the doctrines of the faith alongside the bishops.

Finally, both the Dominicans and the Parisian masters found in the discipline of the schools a set of tools whereby the new ideals of holiness could be made real. The scholastic turn to theory promoted an understanding of the whole of doctrine from first principles, and classroom exercises, particularly disputation, inculcated the skills for a successful active life of preaching and pastoral care.

CHAPTER FOUR

Literary and Rhetorical Tools of the *Summa theologiae*

Thomas Aquinas received the license to teach on his own authority from the Chancellor of the University of Paris by papal decree in 1256 at the same time as Bonaventure, although it would take almost another year before both were formally recognized in the faculty of theology. Forty-one years had passed since the Fourth Lateran Council and since a papal charter had promulgated the first formal guidelines for the *universitas* of masters and students residing at Paris, thus giving official recognition to the new institution. Additionally, fifty-three years had passed since the beginning of Dominic's preaching in southern France and thirty-five since Dominic's death. The age of Peter the Chanter was over, and the theological fervor that had driven the reforms of the Parisian schools had given way to emerging disputes concerning the extent to which masters and students in the Faculty of Arts could treat theological topics, as well as confrontations between the masters as a body and the bishop and chancellor of Paris. The well-known dispute between the secular masters of theology and the mendicants that had erupted in the early 1250s had reached a precarious settlement with the exile of the secular master William of Saint-Amour from Paris, but Bonaventure and Aquinas were caught in its aftermath, thus causing the pope to mandate their inception into the faculty of theology. The Dominicans had flourished, were well established in most urban areas of Europe, and numbered many important theologians in their ranks including several prominent secular masters of theology who had taken the Dominican habit. The program mandated by Lateran IV was being implemented with varying degrees of success, using pastoral strategies that conflicted with the deeper concerns of the conciliar bishops. The years after the council had seen an explosion of *summae confessorum* which, while they offered guidance to confessors, did little to foster the wisdom needed to form consciences in new urban circumstances. Similarly, the dissemination of approved collections of sermons met the need for sound catechesis of the faithful but also hindered the development of a clergy able to interpret the sacred page reverently and with charity.

Thomas Aquinas involved himself in all of these currents and historical trends as consultant, teacher, preacher, and polemicist. By studying the writings which reflect these immediate involvements in the life of the Church, his position with respect to the converging ideals and goals already summarized becomes clear. The letters, homilies, class notes, and polemical writings of Aquinas are rarely tapped for an understanding of his theology; in this context, they can guide our understanding of his theological contribution in its proper historical context, and thus provide an enriched reading of the classic texts that have historically been seen as more important and influential.

Aquinas the Theological Consultant

A number of Thomas Aquinas' letters are responses to enquiries from bishops, other theologians, and even lay people who wanted advice on issues of conscience or on pastoral and doctrinal problems. Aquinas' answers are sometimes chiding and sometimes compassionate but always instructive. They provide a wealth of knowledge about his position on the issues of his day, and a number of them are relevant for a contextual understanding of his theological approach.

Thomas wrote *De articulis fidei et sacramentis ecclesiae* in response to a request by Leonard, archbishop of Palermo, sometime between 1261 and 1270.[1] The bishop had requested a *memoriale*, or abridged treatise, on the articles of faith and the doubts that can arise with regard to them, as well as a short treatment on the sacraments and the errors relative to them.[2] This task, writes Aquinas, comprises the whole of theology, and would be too onerous to complete. Thus, Aquinas provides a short definition of each article or sacrament and importantly what errors should be avoided.[3] Although Hyacinthe-François Dondaine has indicated that the list of errors comes from Augustine's *De haeresibus*,[4]

1 Jean-Pierre Torrell, *Initiation à saint Thomas d'Aquin, sa personne et son œuvre* (Fribourg, Suisse, 1993), 513.

2 Thomas Aquinas, *Opuscules*, ed. M Védrine, M. Bandel, and M. Fournet (Paris, 1857), 532.

3 "Et qui errores sunt circa quemlibet eorum vitandi." "[A]nd which errors are to be avoided with respect to each one." Thomas Aquinas, *Opuscule* V (translation mine).

4 This comment comes from his preface to Thomas Aquinas, *De articulis et Ecclesiae sacramentis [ad Archiepiscopum Panormitanum]*, ed. H.-F. Dondaine, Opera omnia iussu Leonis XIII P.M. edita 42 (Rome, 1979) 207–257.

Thomas treats them as very much present in his own day. They are not merely problems for the past. As Félix Vernet writes in the *Dictionaire de théologie catholique*, "Presque tous les auteurs du moyen âge ont vu [in the Cathars] les successeurs directs des anciens manichéens."[5] Thus, to list these errors does not simply catalogue what people have believed in the past but warns the bishop who has care for souls in the present day. For Thomas, knowledge of the theological past has immediate pastoral uses in the present. Far from being a sign of his lack of historical awareness, his list of errors indicates his sensitivity to contemporary concerns and his understanding of the theologian's primary role as an interpreter of Scripture, which is especially evident when he follows each error listed with a Scriptural quotation that corrects it. Thus, the list of errors with respect to the uniqueness of God begins with the error of those who hold that there are many gods, in response to which he quotes the first commandment.[6] This criticism responds to the functional animism of popular religiosity, which included the worship of powers and belief in demons. The second error listed is that of the Manicheans, which was the common medieval condemnation of the Cathars.[7] The third error is that of the Atropomonsites, who make God corporeal, which is precisely the failure of the materialist popular religiosity of Aquinas' day.[8]

Thomas' concern with pastoral consequences is also apparent in the brief letter titled *Responsio ad lectorem Bisuntinum*, which he sent to his Dominican confrère Gérard, who was a lecturer in theology at the convent in Besançon. Gérard's questions seem, at first glance, rather fanciful, until we realize that they are inspired by the *exempla* which medieval preachers were so fond of using. The star which appeared over the stable in Bethlehem, was it shaped like a cross? Was it shaped like a man? Was it shaped like a crucified man? And did the small hands of the infant Jesus create the stars? Did the Virgin, seven times a day, suffer the pain of the sword which Simeon predicted for her?[9] One can hear in these questions the tales used by some preacher to make a moral point in a sermon. Aquinas' answers vary from the indulgently playful to the outright scolding. To the first three, he replies that while John Chrysostom reports

5 F. Vernet, "Le Catharisme" (1910), in *Dictionaire de théologie catholique* (Paris, 1903–1972), 2: 1997–1999, at 1998.

6 Thomas Aquinas, *Opuscules*, 533.

7 Ibid.

8 Ibid.

9 Ibid., 132–34.

having heard similar stories, he had found no evidence for them and had recommended they not be spread as gossip. Aquinas makes the same recommendation, adding that "non enim decet praedicatorem veritatis ad fabulas ignotas divertire."[10] He is less gentle with the story about Mary's suffering: "Nec aestimo hujusmodi frivola esse praedicanda, ubi tanta suppetit copia praedicandi ea quae sunt certissimae veritatis."[11] Neither case is blameworthy, though there is danger of scandal to the faith of the people. Thomas is more indulgent with the case of the infant Jesus' hands. We can imagine the preacher who, seeking to make the Incarnation more concrete for popular religiosity, thought of this simple paradox as a helpful device. Aquinas uses the question as an opportunity to review the principle of the *communicatio idiomata*, leading Gérard to understand that the most proper expression is that "this little child, who has small hands, created the stars." Again, he reminds Gérard of the danger of exciting heresies or creating scandal by using such seemingly inoffensive stories: "non sunt autem in talibus quantum fieri potest, simplicium animi sollicitandi."[12] Aquinas' concern is always for the well-being of the faithful and that the truth of the Gospel carries its own ability to convince. Fables and *exempla* inhibit this truth by catering to either the credulity or the materialistic religiosity of the people.

Aquinas' commitment to the truth of the Gospel and particularly to its conciliar expression is evident in his commentary *Super primam et secundam Decretalem*, written in response to a request from the archdeacon of Todi, who sought to better understand the profession of faith of Lateran Council IV, as well as that council's condemnation of Joachim of Fiore. The profession of faith is carefully explained, item by item, with all the resources of the theologian, "qui visiblement en prend à coeur la richesse doctrinale plus que la conjoncture historique."[13] Again, Aquinas lists classical errors. Where we expect him to mention the Cathars, it is the Manicheans who appear. In his explanation of the second decree of Lateran IV, he explicitly makes the link

10 "[N]either is it fitting for a preacher of the truth to be diverted towards such unknown fables." Ibid.

11 "I do not think such frivolities ought to be preached, when there are so many sure truths to be taught." Ibid.

12 "As much as possible, we must not disturb simple souls." Ibid.

13 Thomas Aquinas, *Super Decretalem [Expositio super primam et secundam Decretalem ad Archidiaconum Tudertinum]*, ed. H.F. Dondaine, Opera omnia iussu Leonis XIII P.M. edita 40E (Rome, 1968), 1–53, at 6.

between Joachim of Fiore and the teaching of the Arians: "unde manifestum est quod Joachim in errorem Arianorum incidit, licet non pertinaciter… ."[14]

Aquinas confronts the materialistic religiosity of his contemporaries in the very interesting *De sortibus*, on the use of lots. The letter was written to his friend Jacques of Tonengo, in the context of Jacques' disputed election as bishop. Another cleric had been elected; the cathedral chapter had split in two and the factions intransigently refused to negotiate. Because the Holy See was vacant on account of the pope's recent death, the two factions decided to resolve the situation by drawing lots. Jacques asked Thomas if this was legitimate. Aquinas carefully assesses the issues.[15] In particular, he takes pains to separate human freedom from natural processes, trying to pull apart what materialistic religiosity naïvely holds together. He points out that while God remains free to use lots to reveal God's will, in general human beings use them in ways that are superstitious and against the Gospel. First, he writes, it is evident that any use of lots that involves pacts with the devil are barred to the Christian. Second, any use of lots that attributes to things powers they do not have is empty superstition. While it is possible to use lots if it is a question of putting one's faith in God, nevertheless one can sin in four circumstances: if one has recourse to lots without necessity; if, even in a case of necessity, lots are consulted without proper respect and devotion; if one intends to use the knowledge for personal gain and for earthly objectives; if one seeks, by means of lots, to make a decision which ought to come only by divine inspiration. Though one ought not elect a bishop by drawing lots, since this is the purview of the Holy Spirit, it is better to use lots in cases of disputed elections rather than subjecting the people of God to painful divisions. Aquinas concludes, however, that if something is to the advantage of the faithful, the Holy Spirit will eventually reveal it.

Aquinas' work as a theological consultant reveals a deep concern for the truth of the Gospel and a belief in the immediate pastoral effectiveness of doctrine and careful reasoning. He rejects the use of fables as *exempla*, and is at pains to break the material religiosity of his contemporaries. Finally, he is deeply aware that "errors" against faith are actual options for believers in the present, and exhorts his correspondents to be aware of them as a pastoral challenge.

14 "[A]nd so it becomes clear that Joachim had fallen into the error of the Arians, though without obstinacy… ."

15 Thomas Aquinas, *Opuscules*, 525–548.

Aquinas the Preacher and Catechist

According to Louis Jacques Bataillon and Jean-Pierre Torrell, there are authentic texts extant for nineteen of Thomas Aquinas' Sunday sermons. At least twelve of these, in Torrell's careful estimation, were delivered in Paris; some of the others may have been given in Bologna and Milan. These sermons, while interesting in their own right, do not illustrate particularly well Aquinas' concern for the issues that interest us in this study. In 1272 Aquinas was residing in Naples and teaching theology at the university there. The prior of San Domenico in Naples had appointed him, possibly as early as 1260, preacher general for the region, an office he held until his death in 1274. In this capacity, Aquinas co-ordinated all Dominican preaching activity in the "entire geographical area throughout the church year."[16] It is in this context that he took responsibility during Lent of 1273 for a series of *collationes* on the Apostles' Creed. Nicholas Ayo calls these *collationes* "sermon-conferences"; they were "rather longish and patterned more on the thirty-minute retreat conference of our own day than on the Sunday homily."[17] These sermon-conferences were preached daily in the parish church of San Domenico Maggiore in Naples to large groups of lay Catholics. "These are catechetical instructions for adults, and typically they were not simplistic, short, or question-and-answer in format. Quite likely they were given in the evenings, when more time could be devoted to a leisurely sermon-conference."[18] These *collationes* show Aquinas in his best form as preacher and catechist and illustrate his typical methodology for forming lay Catholics.

Thomas follows the section on God's providence and governance (part of the instruction on the first article of the Creed) with a discussion of why certain people believe in many gods. Four reasons are given: the weakness of the human intellect stuck in materiality, human adulation of lords and kings, inordinate affection for family and relatives, and the malice of the devil. These four principles echo Lateran IV's critique of materialistic religiosity. Aquinas recognizes that people are misled. "Although not intending so in their hearts, they do show by their deeds that they believe in many gods."[19] The talks are intended for a popular audience, and the language is simple and straightfor-

16 Thomas Aquinas, *The Sermon-Conferences of St. Thomas Aquinas on the Apostles' Creed*, trans. Nicholas Ayo (Notre Dame, IN, 1988), 2.

17 Ibid., 1.

18 Ibid., 5.

19 Ibid., 31–33.

ward, but the analysis remains sophisticated both theologically and sociologically. Aquinas challenges his hearers to move forward and makes serious demands on their intellect and will. Part of the solution to popular religiosity, he believes, is to make speculative theology intelligible to them. It is in this light that we ought to understand Aquinas' insistence that we are in God's image "not as body but as incorruptible soul, having free will."[20] Far from proposing a dualism between body and soul, this insistence is therapeutic, a corrective to popular religion. "Therefore we ought to have dominion and preeminence over things, and be in submission, in obedience, and in service toward God."[21]

Thomas' discussion of the phrase "And in Jesus Christ ..." achieves two tasks. He proposes the psychological analogy for the Trinity as a lived spiritual reality, which leads to frequent meditation on the Word and brings it into action.[22] This second task is the ideal of the evangelical reform movement from which the Dominicans sprang. Aquinas offers Mary as an example of evangelical Christian living. There are here no legends and myths, only Scripture. In offering the psychological analogy of the Trinity, Aquinas once again shows his commitment to *scientia*, i.e., knowledge arising from first causes or reasons, as an antidote to the materialism of popular religion. Thus, Thomas did not restrict *scientia* to advanced theological students.

Aquinas suggests that there are spiritual benefits to a proper understanding of the doctrine of the Incarnation. By such an understanding, one knows what God has done and can cooperate with what God is *actually* doing in the Incarnation. Our faith is confirmed by God's very self in Christ; our hope is raised; charity is enkindled; we have a truer grasp of our own dignity.[23]

The *Compendium theologiae*, another interesting catechetical text, was written over a long period of time. Begun in 1265 at the request of Reginald of Piperno, Thomas' *socius*, it remained unfinished when he died nine years later in 1274. In this short work, we discover "un Thomas inhabituel ... . Il est soucieux de simplicité et de brièveté ... . Il prend ainsi très honorablement place dans la série des 'abréviateurs' de la doctrine chrétienne qui n'ont cessé de jalonner les siècles."[24] Thomas desires to imitate the Word who, "though con-

20 Ibid., 43.
21 Ibid.
22 Ibid., 47–53.
23 Thomas Aquinas, *Sermon-Conferences on the Apostles' Creed*, 61–63.
24 Torrell, *Initiation à saint Thomas d'Aquin*, 240.

taining all things within his immensity, willed to become small. This he did, not by putting aside his greatness, but by taking to himself our littleness. No one can say he is unable to grasp the teaching of heavenly wisdom ..."[25] embodied in Christ.

The first point of interest for us concerns the overall structure of the *Compendium*, which is the same as that in the profession of faith promulgated by the Fourth Lateran Council. Aquinas chooses to follow St. Paul's teaching on the theological virtues of faith, hope, and love, and thus organizes the text in three sections, one for each virtue. "[T]he first thing necessary is faith, by which you may come to a knowledge of the truth. Secondly, hope is necessary, that your intention may be fixed on the right end. Thirdly, love is necessary, that your affections may be perfectly put in order."[26] The ordering is pedagogical and seeks to cooperate with the order of God's heavenly wisdom revealed in Christ. The *Compendium* teaches from reasons and causes and not from authority. Clearly, Thomas believes that this pedagogical strategy applies to all believers.

Our second point concerns the section on faith. Thomas makes a twofold distinction. "All the knowledge imparted by faith turns about these two points: the divinity of the Trinity and the humanity of Christ. This should cause us no surprise: the humanity of Christ is the way by which we come to the divinity."[27] Thomas discusses this simple division in a number of other texts, notably in *de articulis fidei* and in the *collationes* on the Apostles' Creed, both of which we have already reviewed, but here he exploits it to be the basis of a systematic treatment of doctrine that fulfills the pedagogical expectation created by his introduction to the text. Like the other works that we have examined, in the *Compendium* Thomas shows his preference for *scientia* and theory as a way to work against the materialism of contemporary religion.

Aquinas the Polemicist

Thomas Aquinas' reception of the license to teach as a university master occurred in the context of the dispute between secular clerics and mendicant friars at the University of Paris. The secular master William of Saint-Amour published a wide-ranging and scathing theological condemnation of the men-

25 Thomas Aquinas, *Light of Faith: The Compendium of Theology*, trans. Cyril Vollert (Manchester, NH, 1993), 3.

26 Ibid., 4.

27 Ibid., 5.

dicant life and particularly of the presence of mendicants in a university. Monks ought to be in monasteries and not in the *saeculum*. Those who seek worldly honors cannot be true religious. The efforts of William and his followers met with enough public success that Aquinas responded to them in his *Contra impugnantes Dei cultum et religionem*, the first of eventually three polemical works against the criticisms concerning religious mendicancy by secular masters. It remains a model of public theological reflection and reveals Aquinas' understanding of his own and the Dominican order's mission in theological education.

Aquinas writes at the beginning of his treatise that certain "perverse men" have discredited the mission of true religious by their "counsels full of trickery." These men seek to prevent true religious who can, by their word and example, bring to fruition in others the perfection to which these religious make profession and who "nolentes quaedam astruere, per quae eorum status totaliter destruitur, et redditur nimium onerosus et vituperabilis, subtrahento eis spiritualia solatia et corporalia onera imponentes."[28] These critics threaten the perfection of the mendicant orders in seven ways. First, they make every effort to take away from the mendicants both study and *scientia*, so that, reduced to this state, it will be impossible for them to resist the opponents of truth or to find the Spirit's consolation in Scripture. Second, they wish to exclude the mendicants from the company of students so that their life becomes an object of contempt. Third, they wish to prevent them from preaching and hearing confessions. Fourth, they wish to impose manual labor on the mendicants so that they would come to a disgust of their life and not be able to take care of confessions and preaching. Fifth, they attack the perfection of the mendicants and blaspheme against holy poverty. Sixth, they hold back alms and food from those whose lives are professed to mendicancy and use their power to prevent others from giving such alms and food. Seventh, they defame in their speech and in their writing the reputation of the saints.[29]

Although Thomas likely inflated some of these accusations, particularly the last few, for rhetorical effect, there are interesting similarities between Thomas' understanding of the mendicant mission, some of the characteristics

28 "[R]efuse to build up those things which would destroy their state, and [these men] would take away from them [the religious] spiritual consolations and impose corporeal burdens." Thomas Aquinas, *Contra impugnantes Dei cultum et religionem*, ed. H.-F. Dondaine, Opera omnia iussu Leonis XIII P.M. edita 41A (Paris, 1969), 522.

29 Ibid., 522–524.

that we have noted of the reforms of Lateran Council IV, of the Dominican movement in its infancy, and of the early theological masters at the university. There is a strong commitment to study as part of the spiritual consolation of Dominican life and to teaching as a way of bringing spiritual perfection to others, which both Lateran IV and the early Dominican movement hoped to do. In this context one purpose of *scientia* is to find the Spirit's consolation in Scripture. Thomas knows that students at the university are a fertile source of recruits for the Dominican order and that these same students find in the Dominican life something attractive. Thomas displays a strong commitment to the ministries of preaching and hearing confessions, and in this way he conforms to the reform program of Lateran IV.

Thomas presents a more positive and constructive view of the mendicant's mission at the university. Service of the divine in the world requires a person who lives only for God. The ministry of confession is of this kind, "quae fit per doctrinam."[30] Indeed, the best teachers are those who more fully understand divine matters by means of contemplation. The proper end of vowed religious is first to contemplate, and thus, by this very fact they are particularly apt to teach.[31] We hear in this not only an echo of the Dominican *tradere aliis contemplata* and a new theology of religious life, but also a new theology of ministry in conformity to the demands of Lateran IV. Ministers of the church ought to preach and teach from *scientia* attained in contemplation, the contemplation that comes from study rather than monastic *lectio*. To teach, writes Aquinas in the next passage, is a spiritual work of mercy: "militia spiritualis quae utitiur armis spiritualibus, scilicet sacris documentis ad errorum impugnationem."[32] Later in the document, Aquinas explicitly places the Dominican mission in the context of Lateran IV's decree *inter coetera*, which encouraged bishops to take on helpers for preaching and confessions.[33] He notes the incapacity of most priest-pastors to fulfill this mission of preaching and forming consciences.[34]

Those who work for the salvation of souls, writes Aquinas, ought to shine by their life and their *scientia*; and yet, one would be hard put to find a large enough number of such ministers to place them at the head of all of the parishes

30 Ibid., 536.

31 Ibid.

32 "[S]piritual warfare which uses spiritual arms, that is, holy lessons/examples to combat errors." Thomas Aquinas, *Contra impugnantes*, 537.

33 Ibid., 586.

34 Ibid., 593.

in the world. Because of the lack of lettered men, it has not been possible to fulfill the decrees of the Fourth Lateran Council, which mandated that there be in every metropolitan church a few persons who could teach theology.[35] Nevertheless, religious, with the help of God's grace, have been fulfilling this function to an extent greater than that envisaged by the council. Thus, it is advantageous to establish a religious community in which there are learned men who, dedicated to study, can come to the assistance of those who cannot study because of lack of time.[36] Here, Aquinas is placing himself firmly in the reform line of both the council and the early masters of theology at the university, proposing a ministry of teaching that is a service of, and participation in, the mission of the Church.

This point is developed at greater length, with a more nuanced theological justification, in the *De perfectione vitae spiritualis contra pestiferam doctrinam retrahentium homines a religionis ingressu*, which was written over a decade later in response to renewed attacks by secular masters at the university. In this work, Thomas shows that the ministry of teaching, preaching, and hearing confessions is the perfection of the bishop, who is constituted in the Church under Christ as a mediator between God and people.[37] Insofar as he is established as the servant of all people, the bishop must be the first in contemplation, in order to draw from God's bosom what he must give to others.[38] Religious share in this ministry of the bishops, and by their vows are obliged to serve under the bishops in all things that have as their end the salvation of souls, such as preaching and hearing confessions.[39] The lifestyle of preaching religious, then, is a participation in and service of the ministry of the bishop, who is the preeminent preacher, teacher, and confessor in the Church.

Aquinas' polemical writings proved an effective counter-measure against the attacks of the secular masters. For our purposes, they have also been a fruitful source for bringing to a more explicit level Aquinas' commitments as a theologian in the Church. We are now in a position to complete this initial study of Aquinas by looking at those texts where he reflects explicitly on his ministry as a teacher in the classroom.

35 Ibid., 595.

36 Ibid., 596.

37 Thomas Aquinas, *De perfectione vitae spiritualis contra pestiferam doctrinam retrahentium homines a religionis ingressu*, ed. H.-F. Dondaine, Opera omnia iussu Leonis XIII P.M. edita 41B (Rome, 1969), 91.

38 Ibid.

39 Ibid., 92.

Aquinas the Teacher

Aquinas' gave his inaugural lecture as a new master of theology between 3 March and 17 June 1256, shortly after he had been granted the license by the chancellor of the university in February of that same year, although it would still be some months before he was formally admitted into the faculty of theology because of the aftermath of the quarrel with the secular masters. In this lecture Aquinas presents his initial understanding of his new ministry as master of theology. The tenth question on the nature of the teacher in his disputation *De veritate* ("on the truth") also comes from Aquinas' first regency in Paris (1256-1259). The first and third quodlibets, which concern the role of study and teaching with respect to pastoral ministry, come from his second Parisian regency (1268-1272). These texts represent ten years or so of reflection on the mission and function of theological education.

Thomas' inaugural lecture or *principium* is clearly inspired by pseudo-Dionysius: "in the world of the spirit just as much as that of the body, God acts through intermediaries. It is thus in the transmission of wisdom: it is first poured out upon the intellect of the teachers ... and from there, by their ministry, it bathes the minds of listeners with its waves of heavenly light."[40] The lecture begins with Psalm 103:13: "Watering the earth from his things above, the earth will be filled from the fruit of your work." Thomas likens the teacher to the mountain which receives the rain from heaven and from which streams of water flow into valleys. Teachers "can only communicate wisdom in a ministerial role, and so the fruit of the mountains is not ascribed to them, but to the works of God."[41] Aquinas' choice of a Dionysian-style idiom of participation is not accidental. It serves to highlight the nature of theological teaching as a ministry of God's Word. *Sacra doctrina* is elevated in three ways: in its source, which is God; in its subtle content, which transcends human reason and is revealed by the Holy Spirit through teachers learned in the text of sacred Scripture; in its sublime goal, which is eternal life.[42] Thus "what God requires is ministers who are innocent ... , intelligent ... , fervent ... , and obedient."[43] In a key passage of the *principium* Thomas links the three functions of the medieval master of theology, namely preaching, teaching, and disputing, to the text of

40 Torrell, *Initiation à saint Thomas d'Aquin*, 75. Translation mine.

41 See *Albert and Thomas: Selected Writings*, ed. and trans. Simon Tugwell, The Classics of Western Spirituality (New York, 1988), 359.

42 Ibid., 356.

43 Ibid., 359.

Titus 1:9.[44] His invocation of this passage is deliberate. This verse refers to the virtues of the one who ought to be chosen as *episkopos*. Even here, Thomas understands the ministry of the theologian to be inseparable from that of the bishop.

The disputed question "on the teacher" from the collection *De veritate* also reflects this participatory understanding of the work of the master of theology. James Collins points out that "as a theologian, St. Thomas regarded sacred doctrine as the supreme instance of the teaching office. Every human effort at communicating new knowledge to others shares, in some manner, in the central aim of education: the humanistic and religious aim of perfecting man's grasp of truth and thereby his participation in the knowledge and life of God himself."[45] The teacher, says Thomas, is like the doctor, who heals not principally but through the activity of nature: "a man is said to cause knowledge in another through the activity of the learner's own natural reason, and this is teaching."[46] God alone teaches principally and interiorly. All human teaching is effective only because of the light of reason implanted in us by God.[47] One key aspect of any teaching is that it has two "subjects": the material being taught and the person who is taught. Teaching thus shares in both the contemplative and active lives. It is a function of contemplation with respect to its material and of the spiritual works of mercy with respect to the person.[48] It is imperative, then, that the teacher be a contemplative, one who receives God's wisdom.

One might expect that after ten years or so of teaching, Aquinas would have had less lofty ideals with respect to the study and teaching of theology. Yet the first and third quodlibets are remarkable for their continuity with his earlier reflections. In the second article of question 7 of the first quodlibet, we find this instructive analogy: "And so in the spiritual edifice, those who are particularly concerned with the care of souls by ministering the sacraments or any other particular means, are like manual laborers; the principal laborers are the bishops, who govern and command in what manner the preaching of their

44 "He must have a firm grasp of the word that is trustworthy in accordance with the teaching, so that he may be able both to preach with sound doctrine and to refute those who contradict it."

45 Thomas Aquinas, *The Teacher, the Mind: Truth, Questions X and XI*, trans. James V. McGlynn (Chicago, 1962), xvi–xvii.

46 Ibid., 17.

47 Ibid., 18.

48 Ibid., 56.

official ought to be ordered; and so it is properly said that the *episcopos* is the 'overseer.' Similarly, doctors of theology are like principal laborers, who study and teach in what manner the care of souls ought to be undertaken."[49] In question 4, article 1 of the third quodlibet, Aquinas teaches that the one who gives the license to teach imparts a share in authority. The one who receives the license "receives only the opportunity to communicate … . To communicate the knowledge that one has is laudable, and belongs to charity according to Wisdom 7:13: 'I learned without guile and I impart without grudging;' and in 1 Peter 4:10, 'Like good stewards of the manifold grace of God, serve one another with whatever gift each of you has received."[50] The holiness of the teacher lies in uniting knowledge with charity; by this means, he or she avoids the spiritual dangers of holding the magisterial chair.[51]

The Service of Sacra doctrina

The socio-economic shifts of the late-twelfth and early-thirteenth centuries created new pastoral challenges for the Church as cities grew in size and cultural importance. The new relationship with nature, which technological developments made possible, liberated people from dependence on natural cycles, brought about a new awareness of the natural world as an "other" to be manipulated, and created a context for the reception of the works of Aristotle. All of these forces combined to expose the lack of penetration of the Gospel into popular culture and the materialistic basis of popular religion.

In response, new and charismatic forces within the Church emphasized the *vita apostolica* as a model of Christian life. The humanity of Christ became a focus of piety for both the mystics and the new preaching orders, opening up the possibility of a preaching that emphasized the authentic concreteness of the Gospel as a response to the misplaced concreteness of popular religiosity. Three key movements built upon these *charismata*: the evangelical reforms mandated by Lateran IV, the learned preaching in poverty espoused by the Dominicans, and the theological reforms of the Parisian masters. These three movements created a new ideal of priestly ministry, the holiness of which depended

49 Thomas Aquinas, *Quaestiones quodlibetales* 1.7.2, ed. R. Spiazzi (Turin, 1949) (my translation).

50 Thomas Aquinas, *Quaestiones quodlibetales* 3.4.1, ed. Spiazzi (my translation).

51 Ibid.

on cultivating a wise understanding of the whole of Christian life and doctrine rooted in Scripture. This wisdom was ordered to preaching and the hearing of confessions as instruments for the deeper conversion of the faithful.

Thomas Aquinas, as master of the sacred page, appropriated these cultural and pastoral realities and adopted a praxis that made theology an instrument of conversion, both for the theologian and for those he served. He sought to direct the attention of his students, and of the faithful whom he taught in his preaching and catechesis, to the Gospel. He was profoundly aware, as we have seen, of the perils of misplaced pastoral strategies that replaced the concrete intelligibility of scriptural narratives with fables and myths as *exempla*. He also knew that the theological errors of the past continued to be actual pastoral challenges in the present. In particular, he was committed to finding correctives to the materialism of the popular religiosity of his day. To this he opposed *scientia* or knowledge from first causes. *Scientia* is placed at the service of the Gospel to help the faithful and the clergy achieve the proper grasp of the whole of Christian truth called for by Lateran Council IV. This commitment to *scientia* implied a commitment to proper spiritual pedagogy, as we saw in Thomas' *Compendium theologiae*. This *scientia*, however, is the fruit of contemplation, which is the proper end of vowed religious, who therefore are eminently suited to teach the things of God. This teaching is a participation in the ministry of the bishops, who are themselves instruments of the saving *sacra doctrina* revealed by God in Christ. It calls the Dominican master of the sacred page to a holiness that unites knowledge with charity.

Thus, Thomas Aquinas' intellectuality, so often noted by commentators, is a choice to participate in the corrective process initiated by God through the twelfth-century evangelical renewal. It is a decision to function at the level of the dialectic of culture and the dialectic of the subject by promoting "human-centred constitutive meaning" at a time when "cosmos-centred meaning" played too great a role in popular religiosity. He did this by adopting an ideal of *scientia* that promotes the theoretical differentiation of consciousness and orients the person according to the concrete intelligibility of the Christian message. Theology is thus both a content and a praxis. With this basic understanding as a guide, let us now turn to his discussion of wisdom and of *sacra doctrina*.

Aquinas' pastoral and catechetical praxis reveals a notion of *sacra doctrina* as both a content and a task. The teacher of *sacra doctrina* participates in the revealing activity of God in Christ. Here, I will establish whether this notion of *sacra doctrina* informs the content and structure of the *Summa theologiae*, and what consequences, if any, this has for the interpretation of the text.

Reforming Pastoral Education

After spending almost fourteen years in Cologne and Paris and then two more years in Naples, Thomas was sent in 1261 to Orvieto to take up the position of conventual lector. There he was responsible for the instruction of the *fratres communes* in pastoral and biblical theology, an instruction which Leonard Boyle has shown was markedly practical.[52] It is likely at Orvieto that he began to be dissatisfied with the Dominican system of education, which, while it sought to promote the development of those theological skills that served preaching and the hearing of confessions, tended to teach moral and sacramental theology apart from dogmatic and systematic matters.[53]

In 1265 the chapter of the Roman province of the Dominicans assigned Thomas Aquinas to the convent of Santa Sabina in order to begin a personal *studium* in theology. This experiment in Dominican theological education was the initial setting for the writing of the *Summa theologiae*. At Santa Sabina Thomas developed his own curriculum.[54] In the first year, he chose to lecture on the first Book of the *Sentences* of Peter Lombard, which treats the triune nature of God as well as the doctrine of creation. This choice signals Thomas' radical departure from the typical Dominican curriculum and his desire to set the teaching of moral theology on a wider doctrinal base.[55]

But who were Aquinas' students? Leonard Boyle maintains that this experiment is only remotely connected to the eventual development of intermediate level provincial *studia* in theology. The students drawn from the convents for Aquinas' project at Santa Sabina were simply promising young *fratres communes*. Michèle Mulchahey, departing slightly from Boyle's position, understands the experiment to be more closely aligned with later developments, when "student friars who had distinguished themselves in their study of both logic and natural philosophy could move into their province's intermediate theology stream ... . The more immediate function of a provincial theology studium was to form lectors for the province's lower schools."[56] While she agrees with Boyle that Thomas' *studium* was not a full-fledged *studium provinciale*, she believes it represented an attempt to provide a more solid theological

52 Leonard E. Boyle, *The Setting of the* Summa Theologiae *of Saint Thomas*, Etienne Gilson Series (Toronto, 1982), 4.

53 Torrell, *Initiation à saint Thomas d'Aquin*, 174–175.

54 Boyle, *Setting of the* Summa Theologiae *of Saint Thomas*, 11.

55 Torrell, *Initiation à saint Thomas d'Aquin*, 211.

56 M. Michèle Mulchahey, *"First the Bow is Bent in Study...": Dominican Education Before 1350*, Studies and Texts 132 (Toronto, 1998), 277.

education for those who had responsibility to teach in the local convents. In terms of this study, it does not matter whether Aquinas taught students preparing to be conventual lectors or a more general constituency. In either case, the goal of the *studium* was clearly pastoral. Thomas was training either teachers of pastoral theology or actual practitioners.

It is for these students, then, that Aquinas began the *Summa theologiae*. The *Prima pars* was developed as a direct result of Thomas' teaching at Santa Sabina. After trying to teach from the *Sentences* for a year, he abandoned this enterprise and began his own summary of theology with its own proper order. It is likely that the material of the *Prima pars* from question 45 onwards represents classroom material.[57] Thus, the "beginners" of the prologue of the *Summa* are promising young *fratres communes* and not, despite the complexity of the material, advanced students at a *studium generale*.

Torrell points out that only in the light of this historical context can the pedagogical concerns of the *Summa theologiae* be properly understood.[58] If we look at the terms used to describe the intended audience for the *Summa*, we can find additional support for this claim. The prologue opens with a pair of contrasting phrases: the doctor of Catholic truth ought not only *provectos instruere* but also *incipientes erudire*.[59] Thomas distinguishes between the proficient (*provectos*) and beginners (*incipientes*) and between two ways of teaching them: *instruere* and *erudire*. *Instruo* is literally to construct or erect, i.e., to build. It is instruction in the sense of "informing."[60] *Erudio* is literally to "unrude," i.e., to bring into culture. This means to educate in the sense of "bringing up from immaturity" or enlightenment.[61] While it is true, given the historical evidence, that Aquinas' students came to him with some basic formation acquired from the conventual schools and from the routines of personal and liturgical prayer that punctuated the Dominican day, the contrast between these two pairs of words, *provectos* and *incipientes* and *instruere* and *erudire*, as well as Thomas' clear option for a particular term of each pair, suggests that the complexity of the *Summa* is not aimed at experts but serves the pedagogical purpose to "unrude" beginners.

"Propositum nostrae intentionis in hoc opere est," writes Aquinas, "ea quae ad Christianam religionem pertinent, eo modo tradere, secundum quod con-

57 Ibid., 280–94.

58 Torrell, *Initiation à saint Thomas d'Aquin*, 211–12.

59 Thomas Aquinas, *Summa theologiae* prologus.

60 Roy Deferrari, *A Latin-English Dictionary of St. Thomas Aquinas* (Boston, 1986), 538.

61 Ibid., 352.

gruit ad eruditionem incipientum."[62] The key phrase in this passage is *eo modo tradere*. The original Blackfriars translation rendered *tradere* as "to treat of," which suggests the production of a treatise. But the more obvious translation is "to hand over, to pass on, to transmit," which aligns the phrase with the theological understanding of "tradition."[63] The difference in meaning and emphasis is significant. Our intention in this work, writes Aquinas, is to transmit whatever belongs to the Christian religion in a way suited to the education of beginners. This understanding corresponds with what we have already examined concerning Aquinas' conception of the activity of the teacher in the Church and suggests a pedagogical concern.[64] This concern is reflected in the phrase *secundum ordinem disciplinae* in the next paragraph,[65] which preserves a salutary ambiguity. It refers to the proper order of the subject matter and also to the pedagogical order that corresponds to it. Aquinas establishes this order so that the souls (*animis*) of pupils (*auditorum*), as distinct from readers (*lectorem*), will not be wearied.

Implementing a Pedagogy: Thomas Aquinas' Rhetoric and Poetics

In the previous chapters we carefully traced the developments that led from monastic to scholastic pedagogies of the spiritual life, to uncover Aquinas' particular appropriation of these ideals. In this context, how did Thomas put the tools of ancient and monastic rhetoric at the service of his pedagogical program? How did he understand the role of practices for crafting thoughts and making memories in his intellectualist context?

Mary Carruthers' careful study of the notion of *memoria* allows her to read the biographical account prepared by William of Tocco as a record of Thomas Aquinas' practices of recollection and composition. What is important is not the accounts of miracles or even the insistence on the holiness of Aquinas' life, but the number of instances where Aquinas' prodigious memory is mentioned, and the kinds of behaviours either recorded by Reginald of Piperno, Thomas' *socius*, or related to Tocco by other witnesses. Carruthers begins by cataloguing some

62 Thomas Aquinas, *Summa theologiae* 1 prologus.
63 Deferrari, *Latin-English Dictionary of St. Thomas Aquinas*, 1046.
64 Liam G. Walsh makes a similar point in his "The Divine and the Human in St. Thomas' Theology of the Sacraments," in *Ordo Sapientiae et Amoris: Hommage au professeur Jean-Pierre Torrell*, ed. Carlos-Josaphat Pinto de Oliveira (Fribourg, Suisse, 1993), 321–352, at 327–328.
65 Thomas Aquinas, *Summa theologiae* 1 prologus.

basic elements that emerge from a careful reading of the texts: the need for social isolation during times of composition, the great efforts of concentration, the ability to dictate up to four or five separate works simultaneously, the importance of the *littera inintelligibilis*, the shorthand notes occasionally used by Aquinas, and the noticeable absence of such shorthand notes for the later works. She includes in her analysis the famous episode of a dinner with the king of France, at which Thomas suddenly exclaimed in the middle of the meal, "That settles the Manichees! Reginald, get up and write," as if he were still in his cell.[66] At this point the king summoned secretaries to take down Thomas' dictation. There are a number of clues in this story to Thomas' compositional habits. Thomas is described as distracted from the meal, intensely concentrated on other matters – which turn out to be the response to be given to Manicheanism. There is the moment where the *res* emerges, and Thomas is ready to dictate.

Carruthers also notes an incident connected with the composition of the literal commentary on Isaiah. At a certain point, Aquinas found himself unable to settle a point of interpretation. Reginald, who had stayed up and was in the next room, overheard Thomas talking as if to a number of other persons, their various voices emerging inchoately. Suddenly, the other voices fell silent, and Aquinas came to the door, and told Reginald to begin taking dictation, which he gave as if he were reading a page from a book.[67] This incident can be dismissed as an instance of hagiographical exaggeration, or it can be interpreted naively as in instance of unmediated vision or visitation. If one reads it with an awareness of compositional habits, one begins to notice several interesting items in the story. First, Aquinas' use of audible speech and *murmuratio* to aid recall, a standard memorial practice. Next, it is possible to grasp in the plurality of voices the possibility of Aquinas actually speaking in these different voices, "acting out" the roles of his various interlocutors to stimulate recall and understanding, another common compositional practice. Carruthers suggests that Aquinas' statement that his conversation had been with Peter and Paul be taken seriously and interpreted as connected with these memorial behaviors. At no time need we deny the supernatural character of these events; nevertheless, understanding them in light of memorial practices helps us grasp them as instances of graced encounter mediated by common cultural practices. We gain

66 Mary Carruthers, *The Book of Memory: A Study of Memory in Medieval Culture*, Cambridge Studies in Medieval Literature (Cambridge, 2008), 5.

67 Ibid.

a richer understanding of those moments recorded by Thomas' secretary Evan, when Aquinas would fall asleep dictating and continue dictating in his sleep, if we grasp the kind of clarity and obviousness captured in the *res* once achieved. There was no need to think through the argument, but simply to "read it off" the *res*: "What Evan took for sleep may have been an extreme form of Thomas' concentration. Or perhaps we should credit the story as told; since the matter had been worked out beforehand in Thomas' memory, perhaps a kind of mental 'automatic pilot' took over in times of extreme fatigue."[68] To give another example of the benefit of reading Thomas' work with an awareness of memorial and compositional practice, the structure of the *Catena aurea* evinces the standard practices of *divisio* and recall of authorities based on mnemonic techniques.

Carruthers examines another episode of note in the biographical records: Thomas' difficulty when writing on Paul's epistles. Dismissing his secretaries, Thomas fell to the ground and prayed with many tears and much agitation until what he sought was given to him. That Thomas prayed is not, for our purposes, the interesting point, but that his prayer took the form of the worrying of his emotions to aid recall is. This is not calm and serene prayer. It is prayer with great agitation. Again, we see traces here of compositional and recollective practices: "A modern scholar similarly stumped would go to the library or thumb through notes. By such transports of fear, Thomas ... expected to stimulate [his] memorial [library]."[69] There is evidence, then, that Thomas made use of the recollective and compositional practices of his day. This is important to keep in mind if we are to grasp the nature of a text like the *Summa* for three reasons: it gives us warrant to seek out traces of these recollective and compositional practices in the written text; it helps us be more precise about the nature of the text of the *Summa* as a pedagogical and memorial aid; finally, it helps us grasp how such highly evolved structures as we hope to uncover in the *Summa* could come to be and could be held in one mind ahead of the dictation of the text, which, even for a mind as great as Aquinas', can seem a prodigious feat if we are not aware of the memorial practices which ground these structures.

Helpfully, Aquinas has explicit teaching on memory, rhetoric, and the crafting of thoughts. His commentary on Aristotle's *De memoria et reminiscentia* reveals that Aquinas actively retrieved the monastic tradition but through the lens of the pseudo-Ciceronian *Rhetorica ad Herennium*. He stresses the impor-

68 Ibid., 7.

69 Ibid., 202.

tance of frequent meditation to assist ease of recollection: "... frequent meditation of those things which we sensed or understood preserve their memory so that one recollects well the things seen or understood. Meditation is nothing other than considering things many times as an image of things previously apprehended and not only in themselves, which mode of preserving pertains to the formality of memory."[70] The cause of recollecting is the order of movements by which impressions of what we apprehend are left in the soul, an order of movements which is either natural (from the thing itself) or from custom, "such that one is accustomed to the fact that the second movement follows the first in the majority of instances."[71] This ordered movement forms a *ductus* through the material one retains. A proper *ductus* is the result of performing four key tasks: reducing to some order what one wishes to retain; applying the mind profoundly and intently, i.e., with *sollicitudo*, to these things; frequently meditating on them in their proper order; always beginning to recollect from the starting point.[72] This starting point ought to be more universal, "that from which one is wont to be moved to divers things."[73]

Question 49 of the *Secunda secundae*, on the parts of prudence, reproduces and summarizes the various elements of memorial practice we have observed in monastic prayer under the rubric of the *Rhetorica ad Herennium*. One who seeks to remember must select images that both fit the ideas to be remembered and are somewhat out of the ordinary, since this arouses affect and facilitates recall, must create an order that facilitates movement from one idea to the next, must remember and craft thoughts with *sollicitudo*, so that they will be more deeply imprinted on the soul (here Aquinas changes the pseudo-Ciceronian *solitudo* – silent aloneness – to the monastic *sollicitudo*), and must meditate on these things frequently so that they can be easily remembered.[74]

In the *Summa theologiae* Thomas places particular emphasis on the *ordo doctrinae*, and this involves a particular *ductus* that governs his literary composition of the text. Olivier-Thomas Venard has studied carefully the poetics of the *Summa* and the art that governed its composition, thus re-establishing the link between the intellectual and memorial dimensions of the text. Literary pro-

70 Thomas Aquinas, *Sentencia libri De sensu et sensato cuius secundus tractatus est De memoria et reminiscencia* 3.348, ed. R.-A. Gauthier, Opera omnia iussu Leonis XIII P.M. edita 45.2 (Rome–Paris, 1985).

71 Ibid., 5.360.

72 Ibid., 5.371.

73 Ibid., 6.379.

74 Thomas Aquinas, *Summa theologiae*, 2–22–2.49.1.

duction, Venard points out, was a daily fact of Thomas' life. Thomas lived the interpenetration of composition and contemplation that set the spiritual practices of the Middle Ages apart from later movements. What we know of Thomas' actual compositional practices, particularly from William of Tocco's biography, shows us how Thomas performed monastic forms of crafting thought as part of his compositional practice: prayer with tears, the recall of authoritative "voices" stored in memory, and the frequent recourse to collections of sayings to nourish meditation, leading to a disposing of self for graced contemplation of the divine mysteries. These practices find their way into the order and content of the *Summa*, particularly in objections and *sed contra* which often serve as triggers for a fuller recall.

Venard also explains that scholastic texts were produced by a sensibility finely balanced between the Romanesque taste for baroque symbolism and the Gothic preference for conceptual clarity and simplicity. "To read or write a conceptual discourse with a symbolic mentality is to read or write it in its operative dimension, and not as the clotted result of some past meditation now ended."[75] Thomas' symbolism, as a result of his turn to theory, is very pure, very high, and very spare. The image is often latent, but it is there, and its presence governs the memorial *ductus* that orders the text.

Thomas chooses a specific poetics for the text of the *Summa*. The clarity, transparency, and spareness of the text promote an adequation of the form of the text to the matter of the divine mysteries. This personal choice corresponds to Thomas' act of faith. Because God has chosen to speak the language of human beings, a discourse on God is now possible, which ought to be shaped by God's initial speech. This is the force of Aquinas' notion of *sacra doctrina* whereby the human teacher participates in God's teaching activity in the church and in the world. Three basic rhetorical principles govern the poetics of the *Summa*: the principle of *determinatio*, the principle of *clarificatio*, and the principle of causality. Working together, these three principles shape the *ductus* of the *Summa*.

Determinatio

Thomas always seeks to determine the limits, to achieve greater precision. This is a question of communicating the form, which is the essence of the subject matter. This requires a language that is itself chosen with care. Citing Henri-Dominique Gardeil, Venard points out that the words Thomas adopts to

75 Olivier-Thomas Venard, *Thomas d'Aquin, poète théologien I: Litterature et théologie – Une saison en enfer* (Geneva, 2002), 44 (my translation).

render precise this aspect of reality are themselves carefully determined and delimited.[76] The *ductus* of the *Summa* orders a process of searching for precision; this is not a Promethean quest to contain revelation within a system but to constantly push human thinking forward. Thomas' precision incorporates a moving viewpoint, and a term left less determined at the beginning of the *Summa* will be more precise after a certain route has been traveled through the text. Although Thomas always speaks formally, this is accomplished with great suppleness. The horizontal *formaliter loquitur* is joined to the verticality of analogical discourse, the discourse which helps the mind rise to supernatural mysteries. The principle of *determinatio* is also responsible for the great care Thomas puts into *divisio textus*, which in the *Summa* is achieved by the different levels of prologues. Determining the correct division of the text is part of determining the accurate meaning to be investigated by means of the *quaestio*. To get this division wrong, thereby conflating meaning by conflating elements of the mystery, would falsify the adequation of the text to the real and prevent the proper shaping of the person by the mystery under investigation.

Clarificatio

The compositional practice of clarification seeks to make the text manifest and transparent to its own point even in its structure and materiality. It is part of Thomas' commitment to participating in the manifestation which the Incarnation is. Venard refers to a classic text on this question, Erwin Panofsky's *Gothic Architecture and Scholasticism*, which he initially gave as the Boniface Wimmer lectures at Saint Vincent College in 1948. In these lectures, Panofsky had recourse to the principles of Gothic architecture to explain the scholastic concern for what he calls "manifestation". The earliest flying buttresses did their work of bearing loads without decoration and without calling attention to themselves. Over time, however, they develop a unique decorative presence which communicates visually their structural role. A similar concern is evident in the practice typical of Gothic architecture whereby the structure and proportions of the central nave and the aisles are projected onto and made visible by the proportions and decorations of the façade of the church. The goal is to reveal, to make transparent: "[A Gothic architect] would have taken it for granted that the primary purpose of the many elements that compose a cathedral was to ensure stability .... But he would not have been satisfied had not the membrification of the edifice permitted him to re-experience the very processes of architectural composition .... To him, the panoply of shafts, ribs, buttresses,

76 Ibid., 169.

tracery, pinnacles, and crockets was a self-analysis and self-explication of architecture."[77] The same is true of the scholastic mind: "… the Scholastic mind demanded a maximum of explicitness. It accepted and insisted upon a gratuitous clarification of function through form just as it accepted and insisted upon a gratuitous clarification of thought through language."[78]

This principle commits Aquinas to certain compositional practices. He works and reworks the arrangement of terms in sentences to maximize their sound quality and semantic efficiency. He seeks a "natural order," i.e., what "sounds" right to the ear. "The connection of words in the sequence of sounds they represent also retains Thomas' attention; this mimics on the plane of language the fittingness that intelligence grasps on the plane of beings themselves, by the succession of units of sound, the play of volume and timbre, by the use of homoteleutons [repetition of words containing the same syllable], or of figures of derivation."[79]

Thomas is also concerned with the unity and coherence of sentences, preferring short simple sentences arranged for effect ("punch"), where emphasis is directed to maximizing the expressivity of the final word or words on the question. He shows a sensitivity to the sentence as a melodic enunciative and thematic argumentative unity. He works to create an organic unity that will appeal to the memory even as it shapes the making of thoughts. The principle of *clarificatio* also leads him to the use of internal cross-referencing by means of *analepses* and *prolepses*, to make explicit the returns backward and the leaps forward which the *ductus* of the composition requires of thinking.

Causality

Causality, for Thomas, is an expression of the self-diffusiveness of the good whereby beings reflect the fruitfulness of their Creator. It guides his poetics on two levels. It is the foundation of *representatio* on the metaphysical level (I can have an image because it is an effect of a cause), and it grounds our participation as created intelligences in the creating Intelligence, since it is our own *inventio* that creates within the world an expression of the order the Creator established in the cosmos. Bonaventure's theological symbolism, deployed in an abstract register, is grounded by Thomas in the concrete world of substances by the principle of causality. By deploying horizontal and analogical causalities, Thomas reconciles and harmonizes texts and elements from the tradition; causality thus serves a hermeneutical purpose.

77 Erwin Panofsky, *Gothic Architecture and Scholasticism* (New York, 1957), 58–59.
78 Ibid., 59–60.
79 Venard, *Thomas d'Aquin*, 176.

Venard suggests that within this rubric Thomas' use of etymology is especially noteworthy. In his rhetoric Cicero teaches that to know the exact definition and derivation of words gives one the ability to exploit their "internal energy," i.e., the power of the particular attributes of names. This power resides in the disposition which the deployment of symbol and wordplay, as well as image and association, all of which medieval etymology involves, can create in the hearer or reader. Etymologies are causative of affect and image and dispose the student to accept more readily what is proposed for understanding and judgment.

Conclusion: Spiritual Formation and the Rhetorical Imagination

Thomas Aquinas is one of the last theologians to have become a saint precisely as a theologian. The study, appropriation, and communication of *sacra doctrina* is a service to the church and her members as they seek to craft their identity in every age. This crafting of a Christian identity in worship and life engages Christians in the culture of their day and in a process of mutual self-mediation that both appropriates and transforms the constitutive meanings whereby members of a culture discern a direction in the flow of life and choose a form of life that best expresses the truth of the Gospel. In Aquinas' day, the received form of Christian living was failing to meet the challenges of rapid urbanization and the growth of early capitalism. Catholic pastoral care in the face of the failure of material religiosity and the rise of new questions of social and marital ethics required the appropriation of a more human-centred set of constitutive meanings. Aquinas proposes a scientific approach to theology that promotes a conversion to a more theoretical and intellectualist stance that orders the formation of pastoral agents able to interpret Scripture on their own authority in unforeseen situations, agents who are also able to hear confessions with a wisdom that is truly their own even as it participates in God's Wisdom at work in the Church and the world. Corresponding to this intellectualist project is a rhetoric and poetics that favor a certain kind of formation of the imagination and memory even as they make use of classic rhetorical devices to propose certain tasks to be undertaken by the student as he or she reads.

In the second part of this book, we will explore the specific rhetorical pathway that guides the student through the *Summa theologiae* on this journey of conversion. We move, then, from general historiographical and historical considerations to the text itself, in order to bring into immediate relief the concrete elements of Aquinas' spiritual pedagogy.

CHAPTER FIVE

The Spiritual Pedagogy of the *Summa theologiae*

The *Summa theologiae* was developed as a result of Thomas Aquinas' teaching at Santa Sabina. After trying to teach from Peter Lombard's *Sentences* for a year, he abandoned this enterprise and began his own summary of theology with its own proper order. Jean-Pierre Torrell points out that only in the light of this historical context can the pedagogical concerns of the *Summa theologiae* be properly understood.[1]

The Character and Methods of Sacra doctrina

A growing body of scholars has been reexamining the meaning and role of the phrase *sacra doctrina* in Aquinas' theology.[2] *Sacra doctrina* emerges from these studies as a complex idea that joins an objective dimension, namely the content that is taught, to an active dimension, namely the various practices and tasks of the teacher who transmits the teaching.[3] In his studies on this concept as wisdom Mark Johnson has profoundly developed our understanding of the objective dimension of *sacra doctrina* as "God's knowledge in our frail minds." I propose here to explore the complementary aspect of *sacra doctrina* in its active dimension, as the pedagogical praxis of the wise teacher transmitting what he

1 Jean-Pierre Torrell, *Initiation à saint Thomas d'Aquin, sa personne et son œuvre* (Fribourg, Suisse 1993), 211–212.

2 Mark Johnson provides an excellent bibliography of these studies in an early footnote to his article "God's Knowledge in Our Frail Minds: The Thomistic Model of Theology," *Angelicum* 76 (1999): 25–45, at 28; see also Eugene Rogers, *Thomas Aquinas and Karl Barth: Sacred Doctrine and the Knowledge of God* (Notre Dame, IN, 1995), for its understanding of the Scriptural and Christological character of *sacra doctrina*, as well as Jean-Marc Laporte, "Christ in Aquinas' *Summa Theologiae*: Peripheral or Pervasive?" *The Thomist* 67 (2003): 221–248.

3 Jean-Pierre Torrell, *Saint Thomas d'Aquin, maître spirituel* (Fribourg, Suisse, 1996), 2–11.

or she has received from God. This entails being attentive to the rhetorical clues embedded in the text of the *Summa*.

God uses a variety of methods to teach humanity and on account of this so does *sacra doctrina*. In question 1 of the *Prima pars*, Aquinas notes two key methods, argumentation and metaphor, both of which have scriptural warrant.[4] These two basic methods account for a range of concrete methods used by God in Scripture, all of which represent God's *manuductio* of human beings in accordance with God's revelation. Medieval pedagogy recognized five kinds of *manuductio*: sensible examples, less universal propositions which students could judge from what they already knew, similitudes, opposites, and trust in a teacher's authority.[5] All of these are present in Scripture, and all, therefore, can be used in the enterprise of *sacra doctrina*. Thus, in article 8 of the first question, Aquinas shows how argumentation is used to proceed from a more basic proposition (Christ's resurrection) to a more remote one (our bodily resurrection). His response to objection 2 in the same article is careful to sort out the kinds of authority and their pedagogical status. In articles 9 and 10 of this question Thomas outlines the usefulness of metaphor in providing similitudes and opposites. Aquinas points out that God can also use things to signify other things. The supreme kind of sensible example finds its ultimate expression in the Incarnate meaning of Christ's conception, birth, life, ministry, passion, death, resurrection, and exaltation at God's right hand.

Thus, we can expect to find in the *Summa theologiae* not only causal explanations but also examples, comparisons, oppositions, images, proportional relationships, analogies, and more. Many of these are signaled in the text by some form of the term *convenientia* (fittingness or appropriateness). Gilbert Narcisse's masterful study has shown that these arguments from fittingness are not merely descriptive but are ways of expressing the aesthetic-dramatic intelligibility of the relations between certain mysteries.[6] They express the *rationes Dei* embodied in historical events or incarnate meanings (especially in Christ). As Aquinas points out in articles 9 and 10 of the first question, while such forms of "argumentation" may be weak when they are rooted in human wisdom, as part of God's *manuductio* in divine revelation they are supremely effective. They cor-

4 Thomas Aquinas, *Summa theologiae* 1.1.8 and 1.1.9.

5 Marie I. George, "Mind-Forming and *Manuductio* in Aquinas," *The Thomist* 57 (1993): 201–213, at 205.

6 Gilbert Narcisse, *Les raisons de Dieu: Arguments de convenance et esthétique théologique selon saint Thomas d'Aquin et Hans Urs von Balthasar* (Fribourg, Suisse, 1997).

respond to the concrete intelligibility whereby things in God's wisdom explain other things.

In his work on the *Summa contra Gentiles*, Thomas Hibbs has shown that the pedagogy of that work is determined by the interplay between dialectic and narrative, and that certain progressions in the text, while logically incomprehensible, make perfect sense as narrative progressions or dramatic reversals borrowed from Scripture. "What makes the notion of narrative legitimate, indeed inescapable, is not a diminished appreciation or deconstruction of the metaphysics of the *SCG*, but a proper understanding of it. Thomas' peculiar appropriation of the neo-Platonic motif of the *exitus-reditus* highlights the contingency of creation, in its origin and its endurance ... as an unfolding of divine providence, creation is a sort of narration ... a setting forth, an exposition, a telling or relating ... . [Scripture, in addition,] is a narrative that divides and organizes the whole of time in relation to its transcendental beginning and end."[7] Thus the overall logic of the *SCG* is narrative in the strong sense, not abandoning logic or causal explanation, but combining it within the "divine comedic" framework of the biblical narrative as a whole.[8] Because of this, "progress in the reading of the text ... is possible only on the condition of docility to its pedagogy ... . [Without] the active participation of the reader 'all that is before us is indeed nothing but a book.'"[9] Mina Ofilada highlights this aspect in the *Summa theologia* and understands that the *exitus-reditus* scheme is "a pedagogical manner of comprehending the Christian life ... . The very pattern or structure of his theology, and the way he comprehends it, is for St. Thomas the same pattern or path of the Christian life,"[10] which is to participate in the patterns of salvation history. Thus, the text of the *Summa theologiae* is not only *materially* a spiritual theology (as shown by Torrell),[11] but

7 Thomas S. Hibbs, *Dialectic and Narrative in Aquinas: An Interpretation of the "Summa Contra Gentiles"* (Notre Dame, IN, 1995), 7.

8 Ibid.

9 Ibid., 4.

10 Mina M. Ofilada, "The Role of the Teacher as a Condescending Mediator as Viewed from Aquinas's Notion of *Sacra Doctrina* and Its Bearing on the Nature of the Theological Enterprise," *Angelicum* 77 (2000): 373–396, at 383.

11 The term "spiritual theology," which I will continue to use throughout this chapter, is an anachronism, since for Saint Thomas all theology is a spiritual enterprise. Nevertheless, our contemporary situation is such that we need to be reminded of this fact, since for us, theology is often distinguished according to the pair dogmatic-spiritual, a distinction that continues despite the renewal of theology in the *ressourcement* and after Vatican II; see Torrell, *Saint Thomas d'Aquin, maître spirituel*.

also a spiritual theology in its *form*, as a spiritual pedagogy or a series of "spiritual exercises" designed to engage the student and lead him or her to an encounter with divine truth in Christ.[12]

The Structure and Dynamic of the Summa

The State of the Question

To call the *Summa* a spiritual pedagogy in its *form* is to suggest that it is not a static and closed system but rather a dynamic and systematic progression that links together the various truths of the Christian faith. It is also to direct attention to its structural elements.[13] An initial narrative reading of the *Summa*, such as that proposed by Albert Patfoort, shows that in contrast, for example, to Bonaventure's salvation-historical sequence of Father-Son-Spirit in his *Breviloquium*, Aquinas' presents the sequence of Father-Spirit-Son in the *Summa*. This raises the question of the Son's centrality to the *Summa*'s order.[14]

In order to respond to that question, various scholars have proposed different accounts of the theological structure of the *Summa*. One set of proposals conceives the *Summa*'s plan as "concentric". Michel Corbin, working from the texts of the prologues, articulates a broad concern within the *Prima pars* for God and God's work, namely creation; the *Secunda pars*, which concerns the ambit of creation, focuses more narrowly on human beings and their work, namely acts leading to beatitude; the *Tertia pars*, which concerns humanity, looks at Christ and his redemptive work, which leads to the glory of the blessed.[15] Erik Persson offers a second proposal, based upon work of Yves Congar on Thomas' commentary on the *Sentences*, and focuses on modes of presence from the more general (in creation: *Prima pars*), through God's special presence by grace (*Secunda pars*), to the unique presence of God to Christ in the hypostatic union (*Tertia pars*).[16] Jean-Pierre Torrell develops a third proposal from a

12 At least three authors use the term "exercise" to describe Thomas' pedagogy: see Gilles Emery, "Le traité de saint Thomas sur la Trinité dans la *Somme contre les Gentils*," *Revue Thomiste* 95 (1995): 5–40, and David Burrell, *Exercises in Religious Understanding* (Notre Dame, IN, 1974); to these two published works should be added the recent work of Matthew Levering.

13 Laporte, "Christ in Aquinas' *Summa Theologiae*," 221–248.

14 Ibid., 226.

15 Ibid., 226, 228.

16 Ibid., 227, 228.

retrieval of the notions of image and resemblance as they are used in *Summa*. Human beings are the image of God in the widest sense according to their capacity to know and love (*Prima pars*); they are image in a more particular way in their graced acts of knowing and loving (*Secunda pars*); this image comes to its fulfillment in the blessed, who know and love God perfectly (*Tertia pars*).[17] Each of these proposals has strengths and weaknesses and account for different features of the text's structure and dynamic. What emerges from a study of these proposals is an awareness of Christ's place in the *Summa* as structurally central, even if a linear reading from beginning to end seems to "de-center" him. Jean-Marc Laporte suggests the image of a cone, placing Christ at the peak of the development. When the cone is viewed from above, Christ is seen to be the center point of the development, around which the broader and more preliminary considerations arrange themselves concentrically.[18]

An alternative to understanding the plan of the *Summa* as concentric is the set of proposals that build on Marie-Dominique Chenu's retrieval of the neo-Platonic *exitus-reditus* scheme. These proposals understand the *Summa*'s plan to be cyclic. Properly understood within a Thomist framework that preserves God's freedom and removes all necessity, these proposals remain helpful in emphasizing and preserving the dynamic and salvation-historical character of the *Summa*'s order.[19]

The place of Christ throughout the *Summa* can also be studied from the perspective of the creeds, because Aquinas' ordering of theological *loci* seems to reorder them according to the creeds. Thomas' systematic ordering of the articles of faith into two groups emerges from a careful study of his treatment of them in the *Secunda secundae*. There are those that pertain to God and those that pertain to the Incarnate Word. Aquinas finds the Scriptural justification for this reordering in Hebrews 11:6 and John 17:3. It should be noted that this is also the basic order that he follows in the *Compendium*.[20] A comparison the two shows that Aquinas "corrects" the order by placing Christ in a more salvation-historical position in the *Summa*.[21]

This focus on the creeds and on the systematic grouping of theological *loci* leads to questions about Aquinas' methodology and its role in contributing to the final order of topics in the *Summa*. Aquinas wants to proceed from first

17 Ibid.
18 Ibid., 231.
19 Ibid., 233.
20 Ibid., 234–236.
21 Ibid., 239.

principles, which is the proper method of science, but theology by definition cannot be a pure Aristotelian science because it treats contingent events. Aquinas thus reformulates the notion of Aristotelian science according to the demands of *sacra doctrina*. The order of the *Summa* emerges as a progression from more general and universal articles of faith to more particular and contingent ones.[22] Jean-Marc Laporte suggests, however, that there is also present in the *Summa* a performative dimension that makes Christ foundational as the source of the revelation under examination.[23]

This rapid survey of contemporary accounts of the structure of, and dynamics in, the *Summa* yields some important insights. The core of these insights is that Christ's role in both the content and the performative dimension of the *Summa* is pervasive. Christ is present at the beginning of the text as revealer and teacher. Christ is also at the climax, the narrative peak and center, of the progression of that same order.

A Rhetorical Approach

To speak of "pedagogy" is to evoke a discourse that seeks to have an effect on those it addresses. It also indicates techniques of ordering and presenting materials which are intended to make the material not only intelligible but also easier to appropriate. We have already seen under the umbrella of *manuductio* five such techniques. The medieval pedagogue had other pedagogical tools which he found in such sources as Aristotle's *On Memory and Remembering* and Cicero's *On the Orator*. The various techniques for *inventio* (finding the most appropriate argument), *dispositio* (how to order the arguments according to a plan), and *elocutio* (the set of literary and stylistic techniques related to the writing of a discourse) all contributed to the composition of a meaningful text. The art of rhetoric which governed the use of these techniques by the teacher also structured the reception of material by the student. In addition to techniques for teaching in the classroom, there corresponded techniques for remembering and training the memory, as Mary Carruthers has recently shown.[24] All of these techniques were understood by medieval thinkers within the context of moral psychology and

22 Ibid., 242–243.

23 Ibid., 246.

24 The work of Mary Carruthers is of great assistance for understanding the role of rhetoric in medieval thinking and writing; see especially her *The Book of Memory: A Study of Memory in Medieval Culture*, Cambridge Studies in Medieval Literature (Cambridge, 2008).

epistemology. For example, Aquinas' treatment of the parts of prudence in the *Secunda secundae* of the *Summa theologiae* makes this amply clear.[25] In order to grasp the pedagogy of the *Summa* as spiritual, we must be attentive precisely to these rhetorical elements, and we must remember that they seek to affect memory, understanding, and judgment as the primary activities of a person.

The two most elementary forms of pedagogy used by Aquinas in the *Summa* are the textual divisions of the prologue and the article (which is in reality a *quaestio disputata*). The prologue signals the *divisio textus* of the subsequent text. The *divisio,* as Carruthers has shown, is given so that the student can create the memorial structures within which the *res* will be remembered. As the author announces in his prologue the plan of what is to follow, he also suggests links to be made between the elements of the *divisio*. Each question of the *Summa* has a prologue. Generally, these few lines of introductory text enumerate the list of articles simply. On rare occasions, however, they express the logical sequence between one or two particular articles in the series. "Examples of this kind invite the reader to labour to discover the logic of the series of articles for himself, and from this the specific importance of each article."[26] In other prologues Thomas recalls what has already been studied in order to announce what lies ahead. From the various levels of these prologues, then, we can discern not only the structure of what is to come, but also the effect Aquinas wants to achieve in the student. The prologues also govern the grouping of interpretive units. They delimit the beginning and end of sets of questions and order questions in relation to each other. Thus, they set doctrines and notions in relation to each other, thereby affecting the meaning of these very doctrines and notions. By being attentive to these prologues, we interpret the text more faithfully, and we overcome groupings and structures imposed by later editors and commentators.

The articles of the *Summa* have many stylized features which commentators have studied closely.[27] It is especially important to notice one feature which

25 Thomas Aquinas, *Summa theologiae* 1–2.49.1.

26 Albert Patfoort, *La Somme de saint Thomas et la logique du dessein de Dieu* (Saint-Maur, 1998), 18. Translation mine.

27 Consult, for example, the classic study of F. Blanche, "Le vocabulaire de l'argumentation et la structure de l'article dans les ouvrages de saint Thomas," *Revue de Sciences Philosophiques et Théologiques* 14 (1925): 167–187, as well as Marie-Joseph Nicolas' introduction to Thomas Aquinas, *Somme théologique*, ed. Albert Raulin (1984–1986; repr. Paris, 1999–2004), 1: 58–60, and Marie-Dominique Chenu, *Toward Understanding Saint Thomas*, trans. A.M. Landry and D. Hughes (Chicago, 1964).

editors and translators often obscure in their rendering of the text of the *Summa*, namely the title of the article.[28] Thomas often employs a short phrase, which usually begins *videtur quod*, to propose a position opposite to that announced in the prologue of the question, which provides the list of articles. There is sometimes an important shift between the way an article is first announced in the prologue and the way it is introduced in its title. In his study of the *Summa* Albert Patfoort provides a number of examples for this phenomenon, of which we mention only one. In the prologue to question 103 of the *Prima pars* Thomas announces that in article two of the question he will ask "quis sit finis gubernationis mundus." In the title of article 2, however, he writes "Videtur quod finis gubernationis mundi non sit aliquid extra mundum existens."[29] By this strategy Thomas signals an important shift in perspective that leads the reader forward from an initial supposition. The shift may be the result of new insights reached in the articles that have gone before within the same question, or it may introduce a perspective relevant to the appropriate solution of the problem at hand. In any case, the title of the article is often an important rhetorical indicator of Aquinas' pedagogical objective.

Another important pedagogical feature of the article, one that is often missed when one is not aware of the importance of memory in medieval pedagogy, is the *sed contra*. It has often been noted that the *sed contra* signals the basis for Thomas' *respondeo* in any given article, even on those rare occasions where he limits or corrects the position outlined in the *sed contra*. But the *sed contra*, properly understood, does much more. It is a metonymic device, where the "part" that is cited calls the student to retrieve from trained memory the "whole" of the *res*, whether the source be Augustine, Aristotle, sacred Scripture, or some other authority. The *res* that is retrieved from memory functions as an enriching interpretive context for the *respondeo*, as Eugene Rogers has shown in his *Thomas Aquinas and Karl Barth: Sacred Doctrine and the Natural Knowledge of God*. This act of retrieval also structures previously known material into the framework of *sacra doctrina* promoted by the *Summa*, thereby transforming the student's knowledge of, and orientation to, the *res* under examination. What was previously known according to the order of a *catena* or *florilegia* is now reappropriated according to the *ordo doctrinae*.

For Thomas, the refutation of error translates into two pedagogical strategies. The first is the choice of the disputed question as a basic literary unit. The

28 Note well: this is *not* the headline inserted in bold text by subsequent editors.
29 Patfoort, *La Somme*, 20.

second, and more significant, is the consideration of historical errors and heresies as a means of illuminating orthodox teaching.[30] What is at stake here is *not* the mere refutation of error, "but at a deeper level the attempt to grasp its pattern, its dynamic and its interior logic, so as to comprehend it and face it on its own terms, and in this way make manifest the truth of the Catholic faith."[31] Thus, the refutation of error forms the basis of a pedagogical exercise which corresponds to Thomas' insight that historical heresies and errors remain actual spiritual options for believing Christians.[32] The truth is better possessed when it includes the knowledge of where those who are in error go awry. A great example of this technique is found in article 1 of question 27 of the *Prima pars*. In his response (*respondeo*) Thomas begins his explanation for the notion of processions in God by first listing the errors of Arius and Sabellius. He then analyzes these positions according to the fundamental error of understanding they both commit (both understand procession on the analogy of an external act) before explaining the proper analogy, which is from an act that terminates within the agent. The *Tertia pars* with its concern for the Incarnation, is another important locus of this pedagogical strategy, which is particularly useful when core doctrines are at stake.

Aquinas also employs two kinds of textual references, *analepsis* and *prolepsis*. *Analepsis* is an appeal to what has already been said, i.e., a "backward look" in order to create either a narrative or a causal link with the material at hand. *Prolepsis* appeals to something that will be explained later but is necessary in some way to understand the material being considered. Both of these techniques depend on the structures for memory created by the student. Aquinas is signaling to the student that particular elements in his or her structure must be retrieved and that a link must be created between the present material and

30 A profound study of the importance Aquinas attached to the refutation of error in the work of the theologian can be found in the third and fourth chapters of René-Antoine Gauthier, *Thomas d'Aquin, Somme contre les Gentils: Introduction* (Paris, 1993). Starting from Gauthier's insights, Gilles Emery has recently produced a series of excellent articles studying Aquinas' use of heresies and errors in his trinitarian theology: see his "Le photinisme et ses précurseurs chez saint Thomas," *Revue Thomiste* 95 (1995): 371–398; "Saint Thomas d'Aquin et l'Orient chrétien," *Nova et Vetera*. 4 (1999): 19–36; and "Le traité de saint Thomas sur la Trinité."

31 Emery, "Le traité de saint Thomas" 17. Translation mine.

32 I am very grateful to Gilles Emery, OP, for his help in clarifying this point, which was confirmed in a conversation with him on 5 June 2001, in his office at the University of Fribourg, Switzerland.

the elements indicated. An example of *prolepsis* can be found in the first question of the *Prima pars*, where the text appeals to the relation between grace and nature, which relation is only explained at the end of the *Prima secundae*. Thomas' use of *prolepsis* is more than a shortcut. It often will call to the reader's mind the lived reality, e.g., Christ encountered in Scripture or the sacraments, the rhythm of daily worship and prayer, or a key image from the liturgy or the spiritual tradition, that forms the basis for an orthodox response to the problem at hand, but which will be explained fully in its proper place in the *ordo disciplinae*.[33] A classic example of *analepsis* occurs in article 7 of question two in the *Tertia pars*. Aquinas sends the student to question thirteen of the *Prima pars*, where he had initially outlined the basic solution to the relation between God and creatures. This earlier solution becomes the template according to which the student grasps the intelligibility of the relation between the Word and his human nature in the Incarnation. Such textual crossovers, both backwards and forwards, indicate an interpretive strategy to be followed by the student.

Closely related to this technique of textual crossover is that of repetition. Aquinas repeats key terms or ideas in different sections of the text. There are both continuities and discontinuities in this repetition, such that the full meaning of the term or idea only emerges at the very end after the student has successfully "navigated" the process by which the intended meaning emerges. The notion of *verbum* is developed in this way in the text of the *Summa*. There can also be repetition of key analytical tools, for example the use of the pair knowledge-will. It first serves as a major distinction within God's operations and later becomes the basis of the analogy by which processions can be understood to occur in God. This pair also serves to sort out the various operations involved in human choice, and then it serves as the principle of distinction between the theological virtues and immediately after, the cardinal virtues. It distinguishes the two major sets of perfections in the incarnate Christ, until finally, it serves as the basis for sorting the fruits of the various sacraments. Along the way, it has helped define the nature of beatitude. Each repetition slightly modifies the previous use that is made of the pair, so that its full analytical capacity is known only at the end of the *Summa*.

On at least two occasions Aquinas presents his material in a strictly narrative fashion, following the order of a particular biblical account. The first such occasion is found in the questions concerning the six days of creation during his

33 Patfoort, *La Somme*, 16.

examination of the doctrine of creation,. The second is in the second part of Thomas' Christology in the *Tertia pars*. In the first case, Aquinas distinguishes between three works of God, namely *creatio* properly speaking, the work of *distinctio*, and the work of *ornatio*. These three works are related to each other narratively according to the biblical account of the six days of creation. The causal links between them are thus dramatic and temporal, as opposed to strictly logical. At these points, Aquinas is bringing to light the concrete intelligibility of Scripture. We must therefore be attentive to the narrative elements in the text, not only in these two explicit cases, but in cases where, as we shall see, the narrative element is more structural than material.

The last major rhetorical element to be examined in this study concerns the use of arguments from *convenientia*. "Fitting", writes Bernard Lonergan, "is said of something that is intelligible in the proper sense of the word and yet not necessary as to either its existence or its essence, something that, in a theological context, cannot be perfectly understood by us in this life."[34] By means of arguments from *convenientia*, a theologian can inquire into those contingent theological mysteries that are "rooted in divine wisdom which orders all possible beings," which God has freely chosen "in order to manifest his divine goodness."[35] Gilbert Narcisse has shown the epistemological, metaphysical, and theological import of these aesthetic-dramatic arguments. By their very nature, these arguments are also rhetorical strategies. Additionally, Gilles Emery[36] has shown the link between these arguments and what, in the *Summa contra Gentiles*, Aquinas calls the use of credible and probable reasons to console the faithful and develop their faith.[37] These arguments appeal to religious sensibility, to memory and feeling, and make use of these mechanisms to trigger understanding.

Thomas deploys such a strategy in question 1 of the *Tertia pars* on the fittingness of the Incarnation. The second article of this question concerns the Incarnation's suitability for redeeming humanity. Justifying his response

34 Bernard Lonergan, "The Notion of Fittingness: The Application of Theological Method to the Question of the Purpose of the Incarnation," in *Early Latin Theology*, Collected Works of Bernard Lonergan 19 (Toronto, 2011), 483–534, at 483.

35 Ibid., 519.

36 Emery, "Le traité de saint Thomas," 7.

37 Thomas Aquinas, *Summa contra Gentiles* 1*: God*, trans. Anton C. Pegis (Notre Dame, IN, 1975), 9.54.

according to the third chapter of the Gospel of John, Aquinas states in the *sed contra* that whatever saves us is *de facto* necessary for our salvation. According to Thomas' response, this necessity is of a particular kind. The Incarnation is not necessary for our restoration in an absolute sense, because God could have chosen any of a myriad of ways to save us. It is necessary, however, "quod melius et convenientius pervenitur ad finem." Aquinas then offers ten reasons for this, five of which are from the perspective of our progress in the good and five from the perspective of our withdrawal from evil. Without going into the particulars of these reasons, it emerges that in each case the Incarnation is more suited to our restoration because it is more appropriate or bears greater fruit. In some cases, Thomas' explanations adduce material from earlier in the *Summa*. The series of reasons from the perspective of our progress in the good builds upon certainty of faith, greater hope, deeper love, Christ as model to imitate, and the Incarnation as the greatest participation of humanity in divinity. Thus, in his answer, Thomas presents reasons that correspond to the sequence of treatises from the beginning of the *Secunda secundae* to the present treatise on the Incarnation. Each reason of fittingness appeals to the fulfillment of material previously considered and gathers it in the "climax" of the Incarnation, thereby transforming it and bringing it to its fullness of meaning.

A Test Case: God in the Prima pars

Until recently, it was thought that Thomas treated God in two ways in the *Summa theologiae*, *de Deo uno* and *de Deo trino*. These two treatises were thought to be self-sufficient, and they were understood to correspond roughly to what can be known about God according to unaided human reason and then according to revelation. Generations of students of Aquinas studied the treatise *de Deo uno* in philosophy and *de Deo trino* in theology. In addition, the consideration of God properly speaking was thought to end at question 43 because question 44 begins an examination of the nature of creation. Scholars interested in a more theologically responsible interpretation of the *Summa*, however, have proposed that there is one continuous treatment of God incorporating both *de Deo uno* and *de Deo trino*. Various reasons are proffered to support this stance. A careful look at the rhetorical clues in the text sheds important light on this debate.

An initial reading of the various prologues in the *Prima pars* allows us to disengage the general construction of the argument. The structure of this part can be presented in the following schema:

The consideration of God will be threefold (*Prima pars*)
[according to God in God's self] (qq2–43)]
"that which belongs to the divine essence" (qq2–26)
whether God is (q2)
in what manner God is, or rather, in what manner God is not (qq3–13)
in what manner God is not (qq3–11)
of God's simplicity (q3)
of God's perfection (qq4–6)
of God's infinity (qq7–8)
of God's unchangeableness (qq9–10)
of God's oneness (q11)
in what manner God is known to us (q12)
in what manner God is named by us (q13)
that which pertains to God's operating (qq14–26)
the operations remaining in the operator (qq14–24)
of God's knowing (qq14–18)
of God's willing (qq19–21)
that which belongs to both (qq22–24)
the operations proceeding to exterior effects:
of divine power (q25)
of divine *beatitudo* (q26)
"that which pertains to the distinctions among Persons in God" (qq27–43)
of the proceeding of divine Persons (q27)
of relations of origin (q28)
of the divine Persons (qq29–43)
taken together (qq29–32)
of each particular Person (qq33–38)
of the Person of the Father (q33)
of the Person of the Son (qq34–35)
of the Word (q34)
of Image (q35)
of the Person of the Holy Spirit (qq36–38)
insofar as He is called Holy (q36)
insofar as He is called Love (q37)
insofar as He is called God's Gift (q38)

the persons in relation to ... (qq39–43)
... the divine essence (q39)
... the properties (q40)
... notional acts (q41)
... each other (qq42–43)
[according as God is the first principle and final end: the proceeding of creatures from God (qq44–119)]
the producing of creatures (qq44–46)
the distinctions among creatures (qq47–102)
in general (q47)
of good and evil (qq48–49)
of spiritual and corpreal creatures (qq50–102)
purely spiritual creatures, i.e. angels (qq50–64)
purely corporeal creatures (qq65–74)
the creature both corporeal and spiritual, i.e. humans (qq75–102)
the preserving and governing of creatures (qq103–119)

This schematic presentation shows clearly how the various prologues organize the material into units. A number of general observations can be made from this picture of the rhetorical structure of the *Prima pars*.

The prologue to question 2 provides many of the basic indications for the structure of the *Prima pars*. It is important to keep in mind that the prologue signals the *divisio textus* which the student is expected to perform and that this *divisio* creates an ordered structure in memory whereby elements are distinguished and related. In the prologue to question 2 Thomas distinguishes between "Dei cognitionem, quod in se est" and "quod est principium rerum et finis earum."[38] This is the basic division that governs the whole *Summa* even as it signals its unity. Like the patristic authors before him, Aquinas is concerned with God, whether his consideration centers on God in God's very self or on God revealed in the *magnalia Dei*. There is a sense in which the whole *Summa* is one consideration of God, and the threefold division of the work into considerations of God, of human beings in their movement towards God, and of Christ as the concrete way into God is inscribed within this fundamental unity, the pedagogical implications of which we will consider later in more depth. According to the prologue, the *Prima pars* is a lengthy consideration of God articulated in

38 Thomas Aquinas, *Summa theologiae* 1–2 prologus.

three moments, "consideratio autem de Deo tripartita erit": (1) "ea quae ad essentiam divinam pertinent, (2) "ea quae pertinent ad distinctionem Personarum," and (3) "ea quae pertinent ad processum creaturarum ab ipso."[39]

The pedagogical continuity between these three moments is supplied by the prologues that correspond to the beginning of each. According to the prologue to question 2, the matter to be treated between questions 2 and 26 falls under the notion of God's essence, i.e., God's existence, God's manner of existence, and God's operations are all considerations under this broad category. This is important because God's essence or nature is one part of the conciliar definition of the Trinity. Thus, Thomas has already begun the consideration of God as defined by the Council of Nicaea. This consideration, as both Josef Pieper and David Burrell have shown, is mainly "therapeutic," that is, it seeks to correct by means of the *via negativa* mistaken notions of God's existence, God's unity, and God's operations, as well as establish the basis for Aquinas' use of analogy as a form of theological understanding.[40] Thus, question 2 itself does not begin with "whether God exists," but rather with "whether the statement 'God exists' is self-evident." This is a properly biblical starting point, "The fool says in his heart, 'there is no God'" (Ps. 14:1).

At first glance, the prologue to question 27 does not appear to give much help to our argument. It should be noted, however, that the very first sentence juxtaposes the unity of essence to the Trinity of Persons. The text of the first article depends on the theology of the names of God first discussed in question thirteen. Aquinas' response makes no sense unless the student already possesses a properly analogical understanding of knowing and willing in God. The prologue to question 14 had introduced the two distinctions Aquinas employs. First, there is a distinction between two kinds of operations, "quae manet in operante" and "quae procedit in exteriorem effectum." Second, within those operations that remain in the operator, there is a further distinction between intellect and will.[41] Intellect and will are first discussed within the questions on divine operations, which form part of the consideration of the divine essence, beginning at question 14 (on the intellect alone), then at question 19 (on the will alone), and finally at question 22 (on the intellect and will taken

39 Ibid.

40 The reader will find an excellent discussion of these matters in Burrell, *Exercises in Religious Understanding*; see especially the chapter on Aquinas, beginning at page 80. We will revisit the pedagogy of the *via negativa* later in this chapter.

41 Ibid., 1.14 prologus.

together). This pair reappears in question 27 within the analysis on the divine persons, specifically as part of the psychological analogy for understanding how there can be processions in God. The material on intellect and will does not enter directly into the analogy (or at least most of it does not), but it is the necessary background for understanding the analogy precisely as an analogy, that is, for grasping that the notion of intellect and will in God is different from the notion of intellect and will in us. There is thus an important continuity in difference between the first and second moments of the tripartite consideration of God.

The prologue to question fourteen also introduces the distinction between operations that remain in God and operations that terminate in effects outside of God. It further specifies this distinction as one between God's intellect and will and God's power. Thomas uses the *divisio* in this case to create a structure by which the student distinguishes and relates two elements under one heading of operations. The consideration of persons in God depends on and enriches the discussion of operations that terminate in God. It reaches a climax at question 43 with a consideration of the missions of the Son and Spirit, which reintroduces the question of operations that terminate outside of God. The prologue to question 44 restates the notion of procession, this time applying it to creatures: "Post considerationem divinarum Personarum, considerandum restat de processione creaturarum a Deo." The relation between the consideration of Persons in God and the consideration of the procession of creatures out of God is mapped onto the relation between God's intellect and will and God's power. Thomas' examination of the procession of creatures, then, depends on and enriches his consideration of God's power in the first moment of the tripartite consideration of God. This link has already been prepared by Aquinas' discussion of the name *Verbum* as it is applied to the Second Person. In article 3 of question 34 Thomas asks whether the name *Verbum* implies a relation to creatures. He answers that because God's Word is expressive of God's unrestricted act of understanding, by which the Father understands both himself and all things in himself, then that one Word is expressive, not only of the Father but of all creatures. Because God's knowledge is both cognitive and operative with respect to creatures, as Aquinas has already shown in q.14 a.8, then the Word is both expressive and operative of creatures. The Word is thus at the centre of a continuous movement from the consideration of God's nature through the consideration of the Persons to the consideration of creatures.

Aquinas composed, then, not three treatises but one consideration of God that takes up the entire *Prima pars*. A clearer understanding of this is provided in Thomas' treatment of God in question 2, which culminates in the third article, "utrum Deus sit." Much has been written concerning the famous five proofs, whether they are an attempt to prove God's existence, or whether they are an attempt to find *rationes* to understand what it means to say "God". For the purposes of this study, we will focus on the *sed contra* to this question. Thomas quotes Exodus 3:13. God says "Ego sum qui sum."[42] Unsurprisingly, Thomas' choice of biblical authorities is never accidental,[43] although scholars have often disagreed about the meaning and importance of certain quotations. In the past, scholars suggested that Thomas understood this verse from Exodus according to a Greek metaphysical framework to be a philosophical proclamation of God as the source of Being, i.e., as Being itself. This argument, however, is to be found only in the third of the five proofs in Thomas' response. Other interpreters, aware of this fact, explain that the five proofs are reducible to the third. Such an interpretation imposes a singular meaning to the Scriptural phrase, reducing its meaning to "Ego sum: 'qui sum'," and reading article three of question two from the perspective of q.13 a.11, "utrum hoc nomen 'Qui est' sit maxime nomen Dei proprium."

If we place this article in the context of the question as a whole, however, a different meaning emerges. The first article asks whether God's existence is self-evident. The answer is no, because fools can deny it (Ps. 14:1). While the proposition "God exists" is self-evident in itself, it is not evident to us. By the end of the article, the student has learned that the question is not whether God exists, since this proposition is self-evident; rather the question is how to come to understand God's existence, and move from foolishness to wisdom. The second article of this question establishes what kinds of arguments might move us from foolishness to wisdom in this specific case. Because we cannot know God's essence, we can only know God from God's effects, i.e., creation, grace, and revelation. It is this strategy that Thomas implements in the third article. It may seem strange that Aquinas employs five proofs to make this straightforward point, especially because in question 13 he will comment and expand on only one of the five arguments. It is precisely this rhetorical use of repetition that is important. The five ways to prove God's existence repeat the same pattern of thought and the same intellectual progression from dependent realities

42 Ibid., 1.2.3 sed contra.

43 See, for example, Jean-Pierre Torrell, *Initiation*; also Eugene Rogers, *Thomas Aquinas and Karl Barth*.

to an independent reality.[44] Aquinas proposes that God's existence in light of God's revelation to Moses is absolutely not dependent on created things or values and therefore free in this sense. This is, in fact, a rather sophisticated grasp of the text of Exodus, where God's name is a kind of reflexive word play: "I am who I am"; "I will be who I will be"; and "I cause to be what I cause to be" are all possible translations.[45]

As a model of consistency, Aquinas interprets the biblical phrase in the same way in question 13 article 11 as he does in question 2 article 3, and he therefore does not understand the biblical phrase simply according to the ontological demands of ancient Greek philosophy. It should be noticed that question 13 article 11 follows the metaphysical enterprise that Thomas began in question 3. After ten questions, the understanding of the reader has been changed, and new considerations have been raised, especially in question 8, "de existentia Dei in rebus." Aquinas had not yet determined God's proper existence in things in question 2. Further, a close reading of question 13, article 11 reveals an interesting nuance in the reply to the first objection. The objection states that God's name is incommunicable, but that "Qui est" is communicable and thus inappropriate. In the reply, Aquinas takes up the metaphysical interpretation according to which "Qui est" signifies Being itself. But then he suggests that the Tetragrammaton is the most appropriate name for God, "quod est impositum ad significandam ipsam Dei substantiam incommunicabilem, et, ut sic liceat loqui, singularem." The Tetragrammaton, for which the Latin phrase "Ego sum qui sum" is a rendering that emphasizes precisely God's incommunicability and singularity as well as God's independence or "ungraspableness," is offered here as more appropriate than the metaphysical "Qui est," thus preserving a wider perspective. The third article of question 2, then, must not be interpreted in a restricted sense, but as a kind of prelude to the strategy of the next eight questions, in which Aquinas systematically cuts any links by which reason might "bind" God to created beings.

Indeed, beginning with question 3, Aquinas' exercise of the negative way (*via negativa*) continues to intensify but with an interesting variation in pattern. The pattern of movement from general to particular leads back to a consider-

44 One is reminded of the technique of giving points for meditation in the *Spiritual Exercises* of Hildegard of Bingen or of Saint Ignatius of Loyola. The points enter into the same matter from different perspectives, inviting the person who is praying to repeat the same journey by different paths.

45 John J. Collins, *Introduction to the Hebrew Bible* (Minneapolis, 2004), 112.

ation of creatures at the end of each question. In each case, Aquinas seeks to establish what is the proper understanding of God's relation to creatures relative to the particular aspect examined in the question. Thus, in the last article of question 3 Thomas establishes, against three key errors regarding God's simplicity, how God can be the being of things. In the last article of question 4 concerning God's perfection Aquinas argues how precisely creatures can be said to resemble God. The last article of question 6, on God's goodness, establishes how things are good in relation to divine goodness. Question 8 in its entirety examines, in light of the infinity of God established in question seven, how an infinite God can relate to finite creatures. Question 10 establishes the proper relations between God's eternity, the angelic *aevum*, and created time. Question 11 concludes with the consideration of how God's unity relates to the unity of created things. It becomes apparent that even within what is ostensibly a consideration of God in himself, Aquinas has not abandoned the consideration of creatures. The basic notions which will serve to explain the doctrine of creation in the third moment of the consideration of God are introduced in the first moment. This is another kind of 'continuity in difference'. Aquinas establishes the proper basic relations between God and creatures in the first moment and brings them to explicit fruition in the third moment of the *Prima pars*.

This rapid survey of structural and rhetorical elements provides new perspective on the question of what constitutes the consideration of God in the *Prima pars*. By noting continuities between the various questions of the first part, we have challenged the belief that there are two treatises on God and a separate treatise on creation. Additionally, we have seen a developmental relationship between the various elements and teachings of the *Prima pars*, such that earlier notions are not to be understood only in themselves but as preparatory to later questions and arguments. Undoubtedly, this interpretation is not exhaustive of the possibilities for an analysis of Thomas' text, but it shows the benefits of taking into account the rhetorical clues in the text. Most importantly, we have highlighted the careful *manuductio* by which Aquinas seeks to move students from foolishness to wisdom through a structured series of exercises.

The Summa *as a Whole*

Let us turn now to the question of the structure and dynamic of the *Summa* as a whole, and ask whether there are rhetorical clues in the text that can further our knowledge of its spiritual pedagogy. We begin by discerning the basic rhetorical structure of the "argument" from the relevant prologues.

sacra doctrina: whether it is; what it is; in what manner it is (1.1)
the exposition of this doctrine (1.2–119; 2; 3)
  of God (1.2–119)
    in God's self (1.2–43)
      that which pertains to the divine essence (1.2–26)
      that which pertains to the distinctions among Persons (1. 27–43)
    that which pertains to the proceeding of creatures from God (1.44–119)
  of the movement of the rational creature into God (2)
    of the final end of the human creature (1–2.1–5)
    of human acts (1–2.6–114; 2–2)
      in general (1–2.6–114)
      in particular (2–2)
  of Christ who, as human, is our way into God (3)
    of Him as Saviour (3.1–59)
      the mystery of the Incarnation in itself (3.1–26)
      the things done and suffered by Him (3.27–59)
    of His sacraments, from which salvation flows (3.60ff)
    of eternal life, the end to which we attain through His resurrection

This structure clearly brings out the tripartite division of the *Summa*. As Jean-Marc Laporte has argued, the structure has two poles determined by the two basic data of Christian revelation according to the Letter to the Hebrews and the Gospel of John, God and Christ.[46] God is the first principle and most universal datum of revelation, while Christ is the most particular and concrete. The whole *Summa* in this light is a long progression to understanding Christ. Everything that goes before the *Tertia pars* is at the service of the understanding of the one particular and contingent fact that God became human, which has particular consequences for human salvation. Within this progression from universal to particular, Thomas has managed to preserve the historical order of revelation: God, creation, governance of creatures, the Law, grace.

A careful reading of the prelude to question 2 leads to a further insight. The phrase "ad huius doctrinae expositionem intendentes," which sets out the tripartite division, is preceded by the statement " … . principalis intentio huius sacrae doctrinae est Dei cognitionem tradere, et non solum secundum quod in se est, sed etiam secundum quod est principium rerum et finis earum, et spe-

46 Laporte, "Christ in Aquinas' *Summa Theologiae*," 221–248.

cialiter rationalis creaturae ... ." This suggests the following tripartite division, which is slightly different from the one we saw before:

Of God (the whole *Summa* from 1.2 onwards)
- In God's self (1.2–43)
- As the principle of all things (1.44–119)
- As the end of all things (2 and 3)
  - The movement of the rational creature into God (2)
  - Christ, who as human is our way into God (3)

According to this scheme, the whole *Summa* treats only God under three aspects: *in se*, as *principium rerum*, and as *finis earum*. This final consideration is twofold, in general and in particular, i.e., in Christ. Our point here is not to deny the obvious, but rather to highlight an important connection between the text of the *Summa* and other medieval texts of theological and spiritual formation. It was a commonplace during the Middle Ages to think of progress in the knowledge of God as occurring in three moments of contemplation of God's resemblance: first, in the consideration of the *vestigiae Dei* in creatures; then in the *imago Dei* (or *imago ad imaginem*) in human beings, that is, in their spiritual nature; then in the *Imago*, that is, in Christ. Some authors also added a fourth moment, the consideration of God in God's self.[47]

This three- (or four-) fold consideration of God was taken from the writings of Augustine, particularly his *De Trinitate*. Augustine also distinguishes between the image of God in us from our spiritual nature and the image of God in us as reformed by grace. Anselm of Canterbury in the *Monologion* uses this doctrine of image and resemblance to develop his doctrine of the Word as Archetype of created beings and their unity in Being. Hugh of Saint-Victor, betraying a more Dionysian influence, structures the degrees of resemblance of creatures to God in a hierarchy of progress into God. This journey back to God is, for him, a *manuductio* that leads to our own growing in resemblance to God, i.e., to our deification.

Bonaventure, however, in his *Itinerarium mentis in Deum* proposes the most systematic account of the progress into God via the consideration of creatures. He sets forth a six-fold process: first, the consideration of the vestiges of God in the distinction and ordered multiplicity of beings; second, the consideration

47 Paul Lamarche, "Image et ressemblance" (1971), in *Dictionnaire de spiritualité* 7 (Paris, 1932–1995), 1402–1472.

of the vestiges of God in the origin, development, and end of beings; third the consideration of the image of God in the spiritual nature of the human soul; fourth, the consideration of the image of God in the soul reformed by grace; fifth, the consideration of the unity of God through God's primary name, which is Being; finally, sixth, the consideration of God as Triune through God's name of Good. These six steps of the *Itinerarium mentis* lead to a mystical encounter with Christ – God and human – who has been the way but is now the resting place. This account, as a narrative of progress in the Christian spiritual life, is one possible systematization of the elements inherited from Augustine by medieval theologians. It should not be surprising then that Aquinas' theology makes use of these same elements of a narrative of progress into God.

Aquinas explicitly comments about this tradition in the first four chapters of the second book of his *Summa contra Gentiles* where he introduces the consideration of creatures. In the first chapter, Thomas establishes that meditating on the things God has made leads us to a deeper knowledge of God, because a consideration of the effect can help us understand the nature of the cause. Then, in the second chapter ("That the consideration of creatures is useful to the edification of faith"), he offers four reasons in support of this enterprise. The first three reasons continue the argument of chapter one: we grow in admiration for the Divine Wisdom, since the work produced by the maker's art resembles that art itself, we grow in awe of the divine power, which awakens reverence for God in our hearts, and our hearts are inflamed with love of God's goodness. The fourth reason is different: the consideration of creatures establishes us in a certain resemblance of the divine perfection. Specifically, the result of this consideration in the light of divine revelation is a certain resemblance in us to the Divine Wisdom.[48] It is clear from this section of the *Summa contra Gentiles* that Thomas knows the tradition of the consideration of creatures as a way into God both by knowing God in creatures and by growing in resemblance to God.

A closer look at the major prologues in the *Summa theologiae* reveals a similar awareness and application of this ancient Christian tradition. The prologue to the *Secunda pars* offers some important clues. "Since, as Damascene states, human beings are said to be made in God's image, in so far as the image implies 'an intelligent being endowed with free-will and self-movement', [and] now that we have treated of the exemplar, i.e., God, and of those things which came forth from the power of God in accordance with His will, it remains for us to

48 Thomas Aquinas, *Summa contra Gentiles 2: Creation*, trans. James F. Anderson (Notre Dame, IN, 1975), 30–32.

treat of His image, i.e., human beings, inasmuch as they too are the principle of their actions, as having free-will and control of their actions ... ." Aquinas shows in the prologue that he understands the two particular terms "God - human beings" as a function of the pair of general terms "exemplar - image", so that God is to the human being as exemplar is to image. The term "image" is particularly important here, as can be gathered from its triple repetition. This notion is relational in the sense that an image necessarily implies an exemplar. This means that although we are no longer considering the exemplar itself, nevertheless, insofar as we are considering human beings under the formality of "image", we continue to enrich our grasp of the exemplar. We are seeing the exemplar in the image.

We should also note Aquinas' use of *ad imaginem*. Human beings are made "to the image" of God. The prologue here is summarizing the content of question 93 of the *Prima pars*, the title of which reads: "Deinde considerandum est de fine sive termino productionis hominis, prout dicitur factus ad imaginem et similitudinem Dei." Here, Aquinas first introduces the distinctions and terms that become important with the *reditus* that begins in the *Secunda pars*. There is an image of God in us, but it is not a perfect image, because the likeness between God and ourselves is not one of equality. Only the First-Born possesses such equality and can be properly termed *Imago Dei*. We are *imago ad imaginem,* which signifies our approaching to God's likeness as from a distance. The image is found in everyone insofar as we all possess a natural aptitude for understanding and loving God, but it is in some in a more developed way insofar as they habitually know and love God, which is the conformity of grace. Above all, it is in the blessed in heaven, who know and love God perfectly by the likeness of glory. The image, which is according to the Persons of the Trinity and thus makes the psychological analogy possible, is thus best differentiated into image and similitude. The *imago* is in us according to nature; the *similitudo* is the expression and perfection of the image in grace and glory. *Similitudo,* writes Aquinas, belongs in a particular way to love of virtue, because there is no virtue without love of virtue. *Similitudo* in this particular sense is linked to habit and virtue, which are considered in their concrete particulars in the *Secunda secundae* under the conformity of grace established by the theological virtues. There is then a progression from the *Prima pars* to the *Secunda secundae*, from exemplar to *imago ad imaginem*, and to *similitudo* under grace.

The notion of exemplar occurs in question 44 article 3, in which Thomas established that God is the primary, exemplary cause of all things. In the *corpus* of this article, he refers explicitly to the way in which the work of art reveals the nature of the artisan. Thus, he understands God as an exemplar in two ways: (1) as the exemplary cause of all creatures and (2) as the one whom humans imitate by their knowing and willing. This means, if we reverse the order, that creation reveals God in two ways: (1) in the showing forth of the Divine Wisdom in all things and (2) in human beings in particular, as knowing and choosing creatures. Our sequence, then, is now God as exemplar, God considered in the vestiges, God considered in the *imago ad imaginem*, and God considered in the *similitudo*, which is wrought by the gift of grace.

Aquinas considers in an explicit sense the third element of the medieval pedagogy (the consideration of God in the *Imago Dei*, i.e., in Christ Incarnate) within his Christology in the *Tertia pars*. In order to fully prove this position we begin not in the *Tertia pars* but in the *Prima pars* at question 35. At this point in the text, Aquinas treats the Second Person of the Trinity *in se*, following his examination of the Second Person as *Verbum* of the Father. He conceives of the Second Person of the Trinity as the *Imago Patri*, and establishes that to be the image of the Father is proper to the Son. He distinguishes in the response to the third objection in article two between two ways of being in God's image. "In the first sense the Son is the Image of the Father; in the second sense human beings are called the image of God; and therefore in order to express the imperfect character of the divine image in us, we are not simply called the image, but 'into the image' … ." This important text contrasts the Son and human beings according to the more general pair of terms *imago* and *imago ad imaginem*. This points towards the same kind of relationship between the second and third elements that we saw in the more general Christian tradition.

If we turn now to the beginning of the *Tertia pars*, we come to the question of the fittingness of the Incarnation. According to the *sed contra* of the first article, it was most fitting that God became incarnate, because as John Damascene says, it is by the mystery of the Incarnation that God's goodness, wisdom, justice, and power are most completely revealed. In the *corpus* of this question Aquinas shows that the Incarnation is the highest communication of God's goodness to a creature and therefore a most fitting expression of God's nature.[49] This is, of course, exactly the language he used in the *Summa contra Gentiles*. The Incarnation, compared to the other expressions of God's nature, is the most fitting and most complete.

Thomas makes the link between the *Imago* and the *imago ad imaginem* even more explicit in the prologue to the *Tertia pars* and its analepsis to the *Secunda*

49 Thomas Aquinas, *Summa theologiae* 3.1.1 corp.

pars. He recalls the consideration of beatitude and the vices and virtues. Previously, his consideration culminated in the particular states of life within which we can live the vices and virtues, the highest and most perfect of which was the mixed life of contemplation and action. As we saw, by preaching and ministering to the faithful, one shares with others what one has received, thus participating in the communication of the good by following Christ and imitating him.[50] The practice of the virtues *in via* finds its most perfect expression in the imitation of Christ. Aquinas, then, quite reasonably continues the consideration of theology in the *Tertia pars* by treating the exemplar we seek to follow, Christ Incarnate.

Therefore, the *Summa* contains a threefold progression of elements. God is known in all creatures (*vestigiae Dei*); God is known in human beings (*imago ad imaginem* and *similitudo*); God is known in Christ (*Imago* and Incarnate). Aquinas' use of the tradition is marked by his realism. He abandons the Augustinianism of his predecessors, who saw creatures as mere symbols of God, in favor of the affirmation of the autonomous existence of creatures in relation to God. This leads to a reversal of the order of progression that we find, for example, in the *Itinerarium mentis* by Bonaventure. As Gilles Emery has noted with respect to the *Summa contra Gentiles*, the doctrine of the image and of resemblance is not, as in the tradition, a point of departure but rather a point of arrival.[51] Instead of proceeding from creatures and by moving away from them reaching God, Aquinas begins with God and moves towards the various ways in which creatures resemble God: as *vestigiae Dei*, as *imago ad imaginem*, as *similitudo*, and in the Incarnation of the *Imago*, Jesus Christ. Because human knowing, as embodied creatures, is tied to experience, our consideration of creatures enriches our consideration of God. We know God most concretely and fully, and are therefore most in God's image, when we have traveled the whole path of the *Summa*. This is the importance of the prologue to question 2 of the *Prima pars*, in which Thomas understands the consideration of creatures to be the consideration of God as first principle of things and as final end, especially of rational creatures.

There is, then, a narrative structure in the *Summa*, the climax of which is the consideration of Christ whom we seek to imitate and who is our most perfect way into God. In order to know Christ (and therefore have our most intimate encounter with God), however, we must first have knowledge of how

50 See, for example, 2–2.184.3 ad 1, and 188.7 corp.

51 Gilles Emery, "Le traité de Saint Thomas," 22.

human beings reach God in general (and therefore encounter God as final end). Furthermore, in order to properly know God as final end, we must first know him as first principle through a consideration of the production of creatures. Finally, in order to know him as first principle, we must have some knowledge of him in himself.[52] We participate most in Divine Wisdom when we have traveled the entire path of the *Summa*, such that we know God *in se*, then as first principle, then as final end, and then in Christ. Thus, the consideration of Christ is the climax of a narrative of progress into God whereby the student of theology is transformed by Divine Wisdom and is thus enabled to preach and hear confessions as one of the wise who participate in *sacra doctrina*.

Conclusion: Reading the Summa *as a Spiritual Pedagogy*

Aquinas' decision to abandon the teaching of Peter Lombard's *Sentences* during his experimental *studium* at Santa Sabina, along with the related decision to begin reorganizing the material of theology for his *Summa theologiae*, indicates a clear commitment to pedagogy. This is further confirmed by the overall prologue of the *Summa* itself, which states clearly that the purpose of the work is to "unrude beginners," and to bring them into the horizon of Catholic culture and learning. Reading the *Summa* means being actively engaged by the *manuductio* of *sacra doctrina*, participating actively in the pedagogical process by which God leads us to salvation.

A study of the practice of *sacra doctrina* in the text of the *Summa* has confirmed this notion and has deepened our understanding of the pedagogical dimension of the text. *Sacra doctrina* is the human participation in all its facets

52 Henk Schoot has noted this same narrative structure ands shown its relation to the Word quite clearly: "... all human naming of divinity is tied to the Word Incarnate in that both consist of a union between God and humanity. These unions are ordered hierarchically. In fact, these unions that are analyzed as mixed relations are capable of providing us with an elucidating overall structure of Aquinas' *Summa Theologiae*. Aquinas adduces the model of a mixed relation in discussing the names of God, in discussing the Trinitarian missions, in discussing creation, in discussing grace, in discussing the hypostatic union and in discussing the sacrament of the Eucharist ... ." Schoot unfortunately focuses only on the activity of naming God, which is, for our own purposes, a mechanism within the pedagogy. Henk J.M. Schoot, *Christ the 'Name' of God: Thomas Aquinas on Naming Christ*, Publications of the Thomas Instituut te Utrecht n.s. 1 (Leuven, 1993), 197.

of preaching, teaching, forming others through the sacraments and pastoral care in God's revealing activity, which is ordered to our salvation. Without God's *doctrina*, we could not learn the end to which we are ordered, and without knowledge of that end, we could not achieve it. This *sacra doctrina* is anchored in the person of the Word, God's Wisdom Incarnate. The Word, therefore, is not merely the content of *sacra doctrina* but also its structuring principle.

There is a need, in light of this, to understand better the dynamic nature of this structure and to capture the way in which the structure "works" on the student, that is, the way in which the structure promotes a process of learning and transformation. In order to bring out this pedagogical dimension of the text, such that we can overcome our modern tendency to think of a work of theology as a content divorced from its form or purpose, we have explained some of the rhetorical devices that were available to masters of theology in the thirteenth century and which are at work in the *Summa*. Aquinas' pedagogy is embodied in this rhetorical dimension of the text, by which the content is structured into a dynamic series of "spiritual exercises." To this end, the doctrine of God in the *Prima pars* was employed as a "test case". This "test reading" showed the rich possibilities of bringing to light the pedagogy of the text for the understanding of Aquinas' theology.

Finally, a preliminary reading of the various major prologues of the *Summa* has shown the links between its pedagogy and the common narrative of personal spiritual development which Aquinas shared with his contemporaries. It has also shown Aquinas' freedom in restructuring that narrative according to his own theological and spiritual commitments. One of these key commitments is to the humanity of Christ, which leads Aquinas to place Christology at the climax of the spiritual pedagogy.

CHAPTER SIX

The Incarnate Word as the Destination of a *Ductus*

From the previous chapter it is clear that the entire *Summa* is ordered according to a fourfold narrative structure. Although he borrows this structure from contemporary theological pedagogy, Thomas Aquinas modifies it in two key ways. First, he corrects its neo-Platonic assumptions so that the specificity of Christian theology as rooted in the Incarnation takes on greater importance. In this way, Thomas achieves in the *Summa* a rich theological understanding of the concrete intelligibility of the particular and the historical. Second, he places the Incarnation at the climax of this structure, unlike the general metaphysical contemplations of God one and triune that crown such works as Bonaventure's *Itinerarium mentis in Deum*. In this chapter I will consider the pedagogical structure and dynamic adumbrated in the last section of chapter five and explore it in greater detail, bringing to light its Christological basis. In order to make this point more clearly, we will first turn to Aquinas' lectures on the Gospel of John (*Lectura super Ioannem*), in which he deals explicitly with the progression from vestige to Image. The remainder of this chapter will comment on Aquinas' pedagogical use of the various rhetorical devices at his disposal in order to show the Christoformity of the spiritual pedagogy of the *Summa*, or more precisely, the manner in which, as is the case with the *Lectura super Ioannem*, the Word is the "structuring principle" of *sacra doctrina*.

The Lectura super Ioannem

Thomas Aquinas begins the *Lectura super Ioannem* with a series of eight lectures on the first fourteen verses of the Gospel (this is roughly equivalent to what Scripture scholars recognize today as John's prologue), rightly recognizing that the shape and content of the Gospel are contained in these verses as in a kind of theological overture.[1] According to Thomas, the purpose of John's Gospel is to show the divinity of the Incarnate Word. To this end, the text falls into two unequal sections: the prologue and the rest of the Gospel. The prologue treats mainly of Christ's divinity; the rest of the Gospel records what the Incarnate Word did and suffered in the flesh. It is in his study of the prologue that Aquinas deals explicitly with the fourfold pedagogy.

John begins with a treatment of Christ's divinity at verse one: "In the beginning was the Word ... ." This is followed at verse three with an analysis of the Word's power: "All things came into being through him ... ." The final section of the prologue, says Thomas, deals with the saving power of the Word in the Incarnation, beginning at verse fourteen: "And the Word became flesh and lived among us ... ." It is these last two divisions that are of particular interest.

In Lecture 1 Aquinas seeks to understand the first two verses of John's Gospel according to the psychological analogy for the Trinity. He shows how the procession of the Second Person, understood as the generation of a Word according to the psychological analogy, brings to light the twofold expressiveness of the Word in God. The Word expresses both the Father's self-understanding and, in that self-understanding, the Father's understanding of all other things. This twofold expressiveness of the Word in God serves as the ground for understanding the relations that exist between the Word and all created things.

The three-step pedagogy influences Thomas' study of verses three to fourteen, in which he believes John treats the power of the Word. Each step in the pedagogy represents a particular exercise of the Word's power. The Word is Creator and thus has a relation to all creatures, precisely because he is the expression of all created things in God and the conceived Wisdom by which all things are made. God's Word, unlike ours, brings the truth that it expresses (with respect to created reality) into actuality. All created things participate in existence by this Word.

1 Kevin Vaughan has recently provided a close textual study of these first lectures in a joint paper he and I presented at the conference "Reading John with Saint Thomas" held in Detroit, November 2001. I summarize below the findings as they appear in the unpublished paper, Gilles Mongeau and Kevin Vaughan, "The Procession of the Word as Structuring Principle of *Sacra Doctrina*: Reading the *Summa theologiae* in Light of the *Super Ioannem*."

Within this more general participation of all created things in the Word, there is a more particular sharing which John, according to Thomas, makes explicit beginning at verse four: "The Word is the light of all peoples." The Word is light for us in two ways: as the light in which our intellect participates in its knowing and as the light of grace. Both of these created participations in the Word are grounded in the procession of the Second Person as a Word generated from the Father's self-understanding. Our knowing is a participation in the Divine Wisdom conceived by the Father, but we are broken creatures and in need of restoration. The work of restoration by grace is also a function of the Word as our light, because it is by the light of the archetype conceived in the artisan's mind that the artisan repairs what he has previously made.

The final relation of the Word to creatures is the new and surprising one of the Incarnation, which Thomas also proceeds to understand from the psychological analogy. He shows how this new and surprising relation gathers together and moves beyond the previous three. There is thus a pedagogical progression in the prologue which can be summarized as follows: "first, in vv1–2, John establishes the when, where and what of the Word, thereby displaying His distinctive qualities, namely, His immaterial generation from the Father by way of an intelligible procession, and His relation to things outside of His divinity, i.e., creation. Then, in vv3–14a, John begins to differentiate the different ways the power of the Word is related to creation: first, as Creator to creation; then, as the light of knowledge to human beings as having a rational nature; next, as the light of grace to man as in need of salvation; and finally, as the Person of the Word to the flesh of Christ. Each of these elements of the pedagogical order is rooted in the procession of the Word understood according to the psychological analogy. Thus, the procession of the Word becomes the fundamental structuring principle of verses 1–14a."[2]

The Summa theologiae

In order to understand how the contemporary medieval pedagogical techniques concerning the consideration of images that we have seen Thomas present in his commentary on the Gospel of John are also in the *Summa theologiae*, we must first clear away an obvious but unhelpful possibility. Unfortunately, what we have discerned in the commentary on John's Gospel does not correspond to any one section of the *Summa*. In the *Super Ioannem*, Thomas, the disciplined

2 Ibid.

exegete, follows the order of the Gospel's text. In the *Summa*, as he reminds us in its prologue, Thomas pursues the *ordo doctrinae* rather than the order of a book or a disputation. We have seen that the elements of this pedagogy are spread throughout the whole of the *Summa*. Thus, the elements that are united in the first fourteen verses of John's Gospel will not necessarily be found together in the *Summa*, precisely because they will be ordered to the demands of *sacra doctrina* rather than the order of the biblical text. It should, therefore, not surprise us that we will not be able to find confirmation for our theory in a particular section of the text. As we saw earlier concerning his understanding of the nature of God, Thomas often restricts himself to preparatory remarks and postpones his full conception of a given topic until a more appropriate question or article in acccordance with the *ordo doctrinae*.

In the *Lectura super Ioannem*, Aquinas analyzes the pedagogy used by John in the prologue of the Gospel; in the *Summa*, he deploys that same pedagogy to order various doctrines into a dynamic progression of spiritual exercises whereby the theologian, teacher or student, participates in the transforming *sacra doctrina* of God's revelation. This deployment occurs by means of various rhetorical tools, as we have seen. In what follows we will notice these elements and the tasks that they perform as part of the deployment of the pedagogy. We are, in a sense, performing the equivalent of the *divisio textus* exercise with which the medieval theologian began any commentary on Scripture, bringing to light the dynamic structure of the text before exploring its content.[3]

Prima pars: *Questions 1 to 26*

The importance of recognizing the pedagogical role of particular questions becomes clear when we look at the twenty-five questions that precede the treatment of the Trinity. Interestingly, unlike his commentary on John, Thomas does not immediately consider the procession of the Word from the Father because in the *Summa* he follows the pedagogical demands of the *ordo doctrinae*.

3 Thomas Ryan, relying on the research of other scholars and applying it to Aquinas' commentary on the Psalms, has shown that the *divisio textus* is, for the Angelic Doctor, one of the methods by which the very lives of his students will be informed by the Psalms: "the *divisio textus* ... charts the development in the Psalms from penance to praise of heavenly glory and makes that development not just physically accessible in a text but also mnemonically available in a classroom/oral setting so that students can expound on it professionally and enter into it personally." Thomas F. Ryan, *Thomas Aquinas as Reader of the Psalms* (Notre Dame, IN, 2000), 20.

This means that before the psychological analogy can be used, Thomas must treat "knowing" and "willing" as they apply to God in general. This in turn requires that other elements be in place first. The material that comes before the discussion of processions in God not only serves the purpose of defining key notions, but it also establishes what can be said of God's essence. In fact the order of the first thirty-four questions of the *Summa* is the same as the order Thomas discovers in the first verse of chapter one of John's Gospel. In the *Summa* Thomas proceeds from first principles and thus treats of God's existence and nature before the distinction of persons. In this regard, our Christological concerns provide key insights.

Question 1 of the *Prima pars* concerns *sacra doctrina*, and the second article of this question establishes that *sacra doctrina* is a subalternated science, dependent on the science of God and the blessed for its principles. By paying attention to the rhetorical structure of the article, especially to its *sed contra*, an important new piece of theological information appears. Aquinas quotes from Augustine's *De Trinitate* that all things that nourish, beget, protect, and strengthen faith belong to the science of *sacra doctrina*.[4] Because the *sed contra* is usually the starting point of the *respondeo*, it is important to understand why Aquinas invoked this particular passage from chapter one of book fourteen here.[5] In the third chapter of this book Augustine finally proposes the psychological analogy for understanding the Trinity, and in chapter one considers the nature of true human wisdom which is "in fact the true and principal worship of [God]."[6] This wisdom is distinct from the *scientia* that "breeds, feeds, defends and strengthens the saving faith which leads to true happiness."[7] Augustine had discussed this *scientia* more fully in book thirteen, in which he writes that it consists of "all these things that the Word made flesh did and suffered for us in space and time ... ."[8] This knowledge is in us by grace and leads us to contemplate the truth that is the eternal Word and far surpasses that of heathen philosophers: Christ revealed in the flesh is the very knowledge which leads us to the contemplation of the Word which is our wisdom. "Our knowledge therefore is Christ, and our wisdom is the same Christ. It is he who plants faith in us about temporal things, he who presents us with the truth about eternal things.

4 Thomas Aquinas, *Summa Theologiae* 1.1.2.

5 Saint Augustine, *The Trinity* 14.1, trans. Edmund Hill, Works of Saint Augustine: A Translation for the 21st Century (Brooklyn, 1990).

6 Ibid., 370.

7 Ibid., 371.

8 Ibid., 362.

Through him we go straight toward him, through knowledge toward wisdom, without ever turning aside from one and the same Christ … ."[9]

Augustine's identification of *scientia* with the person of Christ sheds a whole new light on Aquinas' use of Augustine as an authority in article two of question one of the *Summa*. It seems a fair assumption that given his familiarity with *De Trinitate* Thomas cannot have been ignorant of this link between *scientia* and Christ. Furthermore, given the pattern we have already observed, i.e., that he uses the *sed contra* as a strategy to appeal to a larger, often scriptural, context wherein the student can understand the *respondeo*, the appeal to just this text of *De Trinitate* is not simple proof-texting. As a pedagogical strategy, the quotation from Augustine introduces the person of Christ as the starting point of reflection on *sacra doctrina*. This links *sacra doctrina* with Christ in his humanity. Thus, when Thomas argues in the response to this question that *sacra doctrina* is a subalternated science, which depends for its principles on the *scientia* of God and the blessed, we can interpret this distinction as equivalent to Augustine's distinction between the Word made flesh as our knowledge and the Word itself as our wisdom and thus between Christ through whom we come and Christ to whom we are directed. The Word as the *Verbum* of God's self-understanding is thus made present by means of a rhetorical strategy. The procession of the Word is the *de facto* principle of the teaching of question one, even if this cannot be made explicit on account of the *ordo doctrinae*.

This distinction between knowledge and wisdom, i.e., between Christ as the way and Christ as the end, occurs again in article six of question one, in which Thomas asks whether *sacra doctrina* is wisdom. In the *respondeo*, he replies in the affirmative and quotes *De Trinitate* book twelve in favor of this solution.[10] In chapter four of that book, Augustine makes the same distinction between knowledge and wisdom. Here the emphasis is on the distinction between knowledge, which is concerned with action in time, and wisdom, which is the contemplation of eternal things. By this fundamental distinction Augustine develops the difference between the Incarnate Word as the way and the Word itself as end. Thus, *sacra doctrina*, insofar as it is wisdom and therefore contemplation of eternal things, is the contemplation of the Word as end. Once again, God's *Verbum* functions rhetorically as the principle of the theological argument.

In question 14 of the *Prima pars* Thomas also deploys the rhetorical use of the Word as principle of *sacra doctrina*. Question 14, which is concerned with

9 Ibid., 363.

10 Thomas Aquinas, *Summa theologiae* 1.1.6.

God's knowledge, begins a series of four questions culminating in the inquiry into God as living. These are the key questions that, in addition to setting the appropriate limits to theological speech about God's knowing, articulate the first set of building blocks for the psychological analogy of the Trinity. In the sixth article of this question, "whether God knows things other than himself by proper knowledge," Thomas quotes Hebrews 4:12–13 in the *sed contra* as the theological basis for his argument.[11] This verse, by which Aquinas argues that because God knows things in particular, he has proper knowledge of them, is a statement about God's "word." Thomas conflates God's knowledge and God's "word" in accordance with his understanding of the passage itself.

In his second lecture on Hebrews,[12] Thomas expounds on verses twelve and thirteen of chapter four in the following way: "… Paul says 'the *sermo* of God is living'. It seems that this phrase comports certain difficulties, so that we ought to consider another translation that is clearer. We have here *sermo*, but in the Greek is found *logos*, which is the same as *verbum*. Thus *sermo* is the same as *verbum* … . The *Verbum* of God is conceived from eternity, in the intellect of the Father is the primordial *Verbum* … . And because it is primordial, from it derive all other words … ."[13] Thomas clearly understands the passage from Hebrews as expressing God's knowledge of things in his Word. Thus, his citation of Hebrews 4:12–13 in the *sed contra* further develops the rhetorical appeal to the Word as his structuring principle.

In question 16 article five, Aquinas considers whether God is truth.[14] The *sed contra* cites John 14:6: "I am the way, the truth, and the life" as the starting point for responding in the affirmative. Interestingly, Aquinas cites the Incarnate Word speaking as God. Rhetorically, the Incarnate Word himself speaks directly to the student in the first person and teaches a truth about God. Thus the Incarnate Word moves from being an implicit rhetorical presence to being the explicit rhetorical actor who fulfills the role of being the way that leads to wisdom. The Word who speaks in his humanity in John's Gospel teaches something about the Word in his divinity. This is a step forward in making the Word the explicit theological principle, as we will see in question 27.

In question 18 article four Thomas moves closer towards the explicit explanation in question 27. In the *sed contra* to this question, Thomas quotes the pro-

11 Ibid., 1.14.6.

12 Thomas Aquinas, *Super Epistolas Sancti Pauli Lectura*, 8th revised edition (Turin, 1953), 373.

13 Ibid., 383.

14 Thomas Aquinas, *Summa theologiae* 1.16.5.

logue to John's Gospel, "what was made, in Him was life," as if John's statement were about God according to God's essence, rather than specifically about God's Word. The Word is rhetorically affirmed in this usage as Creator, as we can easily verify from Thomas' explicit treatment of this passage in his *Lectura super Ioannem.*[15] Aquinas develops this rhetorical affirmation explicitly later in the *Prima pars*.

In question 25 article 5, Thomas continues this movement from question 16 and again makes the Incarnate Word the explicit teacher of truth concerning divinity. The *sed contra* cites Matthew 26:53, "Do you not think I could call on my Father, and he would send twelve legions of angels ... ," as the starting point for showing that God can do what he does not. Unsurprisingly, this usage corresponds with Thomas' treatment of this passage in his commentary on Matthew's Gospel: " ... and this saying destroys the opinion of those who say that God cannot do anything except what he does do: because if Jesus could call out legions that he does not call out, we can see that he could do many things that he does not do. 'How could the Scriptures be fulfilled' ... ."[16] God chooses to act or not to act according to His wisdom, and not because of a lack of power or freedom, and this is revealed by the teaching of the Incarnate Word in his passion.

Prima pars: *Questions 27 to 44*

Beginning with question 27 Thomas explicitly treats the procession of the Word from the Father and consequently, the Word as the structuring principle for *sacra doctrina*. In addition to preparing the way for question 27's use of the psychological analogy, Thomas shapes the first 26 questions of the *Summa* according to the Incarnate Word as revealed through a series of rhetorical devices. The medieval student is either taught by Christ directly or experiences the Incarnate Word as the practical starting point of theological development. He is made to "live" the teaching of Augustine that the Incarnate Word is the way that leads to contemplation of the Word itself as his attention is directed to key scriptural passages. By the time the student confronts this teaching explicitly according to the *ordo doctrinae*, he has been shaped by it through Thomas' pedagogical use of these rhetorical devices.

15 Thomas Aquinas, *Commentary on the Gospel of John*, trans. James A. Weisheipl and Fabian R. Larcher, Aquinas Scripture Series 4 (Albany, NY, 1980), 56–58.

16 Thomas Aquinas, *Lectura super Matthaeum*, ed. J.S.E. Fretté and P. Maré, Doctoris Angelici divi Thomae Aquinatis sacri ordinis F.F. Praedicatorum Opera omnia ... 19 (Paris, 1876), 634.

Aquinas begins his treatment of the Triune God with question 27 of the *Prima pars*. In article 1 he asks whether there is procession in God and responds in the affirmative with a brief statement of the psychological analogy.[17] It is important to notice that the *sed contra* grounds Aquinas' response in a statement made by Christ in John's Gospel. The Incarnate Word reveals the Trinity, and the student begins from the truth He has taught.Concerning the rhetorical development of the response itself, Aquinas explains and refutes the errors that have been made when trying to understand what Christ has revealed. For example, Arius misunderstood procession on the analogy of an effect proceeding from a cause, and for this reason, he taught that the Son came from the Father as the Father's first or primary creature. Others, such as Sabellius, misunderstood procession on the analogy of the cause proceeding to its effect, as moving it or as communicating its character to it. This error leads into the various forms of modalism which confuse the cause and effect. Both misunderstandings stem from the fact that procession is understood "externally," that is, as involving an outward act, but prior to this outward procession, there is an internal procession. From this point, Aquinas introduces the psychological analogy, showing its usefulness in understanding procession in God.

Aquinas here splendidly fulfills the office of the wise teacher. Beginning from what is given, the revelation of the Trinity by the Incarnate Word, he first explains and sets aside the mistaken ways of understanding the revealed data. This examination of famous errors plays an important pedagogical role. The "obvious" way of understanding procession is by analogy to material processions. Indeed, the early Church Fathers used many such analogies for the Trinity. Arius and Sabellius are useful foils here for showing the problem with such limited analogies. By explaining that their mistakes reveal the limitations of using "outward processions" as analogies for procession in God, Aquinas prepares the way for the proper use and understanding of the psychological analogy.

Thomas completes this initial discussion with article 2, which affirms that the procession of the Word is a generation precisely because it is an intelligible emanation.[18] The *sed contra* quotes the second Psalm: "This day I have begotten you."[19] Once again, this is not mere proof-texting, but a careful selection of a text which plays a crucial rhetorical role, as becomes clear from Thomas'

17 Thomas Aquinas, *Summa theologiae* 1.27.1.

18 Ibid., 1.27.2.

19 Ibid.

commentary on the Psalms. Among other things, he interprets this psalm as revealing Christ's sovereignty over the nations,[20] which is founded on his sonship, that is, his eternal generation from the Father,[21] and then discusses the Son's generation as an inner Word from the Father's self-understanding.[22] In the *sed contra* of this article in the *Summa*, Thomas evokes the exact same argument that is set forth in the subsequent *respondeo*: "So in this manner the procession of the Word in God has the *ratio* of generation: for He proceeds by way of intelligible action, which is a vital operation; He proceeds from a conjoined principle, as stated earlier; He proceeds by way of similitude, inasmuch as the likeness of the intellect is a likeness of the object conceived; and He exists in the same nature, because in God the act of understanding and His existence are the same, as shown above. Hence the procession of the Word in God is called generation; and this same proceeding Word is called the Son."[23]

If in question 27 he answers the *an sit* of the Word by means of the psychological analogy, Thomas makes use of the same analogy to discuss the Word's *quid sit* in question 34. Having established in article one that *Verbum* is in God a personal name rather than a name that is common to the divine essence, Thomas proceeds to show that this particular name applies only to the Second Person.[24] His response summarizes and continues the discussion from question 27.

Thomas then determines in the third article of question 34 that the name *Verbum* implies a relation to creatures. The *sed contra* gives Augustine's *Liber de 83 quaestionibus* as the authority, which this is the same text used in Thomas' *Super Ioannem*. From this starting point, Thomas argues that because God knows Himself and all things in Himself by the same act of understanding, the Word that proceeds from this understanding expresses not only the Father but also all created things.[25] Thomas then distinguishes these two expressions. The Word of God is the expression of the Father *simpliciter* and the expression and cause of created things.[26] The procession of the Word thus anchors a relation

20 Thomas Aquinas, *Commentaire sur les Psaumes*, trans. Jean-Éric Stroobant de Saint-Éloy (Paris, 1996), 49.

21 Ibid., 50.

22 Ibid.

23 Thomas Aquinas, *Summa theologiae* 1.27.2.

24 Ibid., 1.34.2.

25 Ibid., 1.34.3.

26 Ibid.

of some kind to created things, a notion which Thomas develops later in the *Summa*.

Before this development, however, Thomas examines another name for the Second Person. In question 35, he treats of the Son as *Imago Dei*. In order for there to be an image in God, there must be similitude in the specific nature as well as an order of origin.[27] Thomas says that the name "Image" properly belongs to the Son because he proceeds from the Father as Word, which implies the "being-of-like-species with that from which it proceeds" that is a requirement of being the Image in God.[28] The Son is the Image because he proceeds as the Word from the Father. This understanding is bolstered by question 39 article 8 of the *Prima pars* concerning the appropriation of the divine attributes by the Son.[29] There are three reasons to do this, which correspond to the three metaphysical conditions for beauty: integrity or perfection, due proportion or harmony, and splendor or clarity. Because the Son has in himself truly and perfectly the nature of the Father, the first condition is met. Because he is the expressed Image of the Father, he has due proportion to the original; an image is said to be beautiful if it perfectly renders even an ugly thing. The Son as Word is, according to the Damascene, the light and splendor of the Father's intellect, thus meeting the third condition. Beauty is appropriated to the Son as a function of the names "Image" and "Word".

Prima pars: *Question 45 to end*

According to the various prologues of the next major sections of the *Summa*, which begins with question 45, the same progression appears that we outlined in chapter two, namely creation, human beings, Christ. At first glance, this seems to be the same general order as in Thomas' *Super Ioannem*, although the two texts have strikingly different *rationes*. In the *Summa* Thomas employs a different kind of language to express the relation of creatures, in general, and human beings, in particular, to the creating God. At the same time, the relation that is explicitly made is not between creatures and the Word but between creatures and the Trinity as a whole.

In question 45 of the *Prima pars* Thomas considers the relation between creation and the Triune God, and in article seven he asks, "Utrum in creaturis sit necesse inveniri vestigium Trinitatis." The term used is "vestige" or "trace,"

27 Ibid., 1.35.1.

28 Ibid., 1.35.2.

29 Ibid., 1.39.8.

and Thomas' explanation of how creatures have a vestige of the Trinity builds upon his response in the previous article, "Utrum creare sit proprium alicuius Personae." The act of creation properly belongs to all three Persons, because it belongs to God essentially. Each Person, however, creates according to an order that is founded on the nature of the processions. Because of this, created things show forth a trace of the whole Trinity. Insofar as they are created and have a principle and cause, they exhibit the Father who is the first principle; insofar as they have form and species, they exhibit the Word, because the work of art comes from the artist's conception; insofar as they are ordered among themselves, they exhibit the Love which is the Holy Spirit.[30] Thomas links the vestiges of the Trinity in created things to the Word by the terms "Image" and "Beauty", which he developed in questions 35 and 39. This is a first rhetorical clue about the link between the Word and creation.

In question 93 of the *Prima pars* Aquinas takes up the question of the particular relation of human beings to God. The term used here is "image." Article 1 seeks to know "Utrum imago Dei sit in homine." Thomas answers that human beings show forth God in a way that non-rational creatures and even angels do not. In article 4 he distinguishes three ways in which there is an image of God in human beings. There is an image first in the natural aptitude to know and love God which resides in the essence of the soul as rational and voluntary. There is also an image when human beings actually know and love God; this is the conformity brought by grace. Finally, there is an image when human beings actually and perfectly know God, which is the conformity of glory, when we will know God by God's knowledge. In article 9 Aquinas specifies that the first and second kinds of image can be distinguished as image and likeness, where image refers to the human being as having reason and will, and likeness refers to the participation in divine virtue that is given to us by grace.

The final rhetorical allusion to Christ in the *Prima pars* occurs in question 104, which begins a series of four questions on the particular effects of the divine governance of creation. This section examines God's power and the ongoing effects of that power. In article 1 Aquinas asks whether creatures need to be conserved in being by God. The *sed contra* anchors his response with a quotation of Hebrews 1:3, " ... upholding all things by the word of his power ... ." In the body of the article, Thomas does not refer explicitly to Christ, focusing instead on an exploration of causality that leads to the clarification of God's causal relation to created being. There is, however, a clear reference to

30 Ibid., 1.45.7.

Christ in the quotation from Hebrews when its full context is examined according to Thomas' commentary on the epistle. He understands Hebrews 1:3 as a statement of Christ's dignity and power in relation to the Father and to creation. In the previous verses, "The apostle showed the excellence of Christ with respect to his own origin, with respect to his majesty as Lord, and with respect to his power of operation."[31] With verse three, the Apostle Paul wants to show "Christ's excellence with respect to His sublime glory and dignity."[32] This is apparent from the two things that make a person fit for any dignity of office, namely, "facility in administering" and "zeal and briskness in seeing things through to the end."[33] Christ is certainly a capable governor because he embodies the three qualities that make for ease in administration. He is, after all, the Wisdom by which governance does not err, he has the nobility of origin which guarantees that his directives will not be despised, and finally he has the strength of power to execute what he decrees: " ... not only is he wise, but he is in fact Wisdom itself ... not only is he noble, but he is in fact Nobility itself ... not only is he powerful, but he is Power itself."[34] Concerning the phrase "by the word of his power," and after he has set the stage with the discussion of Christ's glory and dignity, Aquinas writes, "And here the Apostle is speaking of the creation of all things, that God made all things through the Son ... ."[35] That same Son is the "conserving cause" that keeps all things in being.[36] Thus, in the same way that all things are created in the Word, so are they conserved in the Word.

If we return to the first article of question 104 with this new insight, Thomas' response takes on a whole new light. The language of causality is an expression of the Word's role in God's providence, including all of the Christological material of the previous questions and explaining more clearly the ongoing relationship between the Word and creatures. Thus, although the explicit content of the *Prima pars* links creation to the whole of the Trinity, the theological locus that grounds this link is in fact the Word and its particular relation to created things, grounded in the Word's procession from the Father.

There is therefore a threefold Christological development in the *Summa*. First, Christ is introduced rhetorically as the actual teacher of *sacra doctrina*.

31 Thomas Aquinas, *Super Epistolas Sancti Pauli Lectura*, 341.
32 Ibid.
33 Ibid.
34 Ibid.
35 Ibid., 342–343.
36 Ibid., 343.

Then, the Word is shown to have a particular relationship to all created things and to be the structuring principle of *sacra doctrina* itself by his particular procession from the Father. As Thomas explores the first effect of God's power, i.e., the work of creation and its related work of governance,a third development appears, namely that the Word continues to be the ground of creation's connection to the Triune God.

Prima secundae: *Questions 1 to 108*

The prologue to the *Secunda pars* takes up the notion of "image" and makes it the governing principle of the *Prima secundae*,[37] which culminates in the treatment of grace. Thomas speaks of God as the "exemplar,"[38] thereby recalling the language not only of vestige and image but also of Wisdom. In the questions on the procession of the Word, he considered the Word as the Father's conceived wisdom. Thomas also used the notion of wisdom to link the proceeding Word to all created things as their exemplary cause. He brings all of these ideas forward in this remark at the beginning of the *Prima secundae*, rhetorically kept in awareness so as to be present in the treatment of human beings as God's image.

In questions 1 and 2 of this part, Thomas engages in some necessary ground-clearing (for example, "an sit beatitudo") and definition of terms, so that he asks in question 3 "quid sit beatitudo." The climax of this question occurs in article 8. After identifying the operations whereby beatitude is received in human beings and progressively eliminating possible objects of contemplation, Aquinas considers whether beatitude "consists in the sole contemplation of God seen in His essence."[39] In the *sed contra*, which quotes the First Letter of John, "When He shall appear, we shall be like Him, because we shall see Him as He is," Thomas provides an interesting context for his affirmative response. He believes that seeing God as God is will involve our being transformed into a greater likeness to God. This is precisely the dynamic of the *Prima secundae*, that is, to trace the movement from image to likeness, according to the way in which Thomas defined these two terms in the *Prima pars*.

Aquinas picks up this notion of being conformed to God in question 19 article 9. He quotes Matthew 26:39 in the *sed contra* as the basis for a discussion that shows why the goodness of the will depends on conformity to the divine

37 Thomas Aquinas, *Summa theologiae* 1–2 prologus.

38 Ibid., 1–2 prologus.

39 Ibid., 1–2.3.8.

will.[40] Augustine guides his interpretation of this passage, which points to Christ's behavior in Gethsemane as a teaching of Christ. This same perspective is evident in Thomas' commentary on Matthew.[41] Question 19 comes at the climax of Aquinas' treatment of properly human acts and is part of a series of three questions on the goodness or malice of human acts. Christ the teacher comes to the fore precisely at this climax. Although the content of this section of the *Prima secundae* displays no explicit links to our Christological pedagogy, it does in fact remain under the sign of Christ the teacher. In addition to being a teacher, Christ is also a model to be imitated. The being conformed to God that is characteristic of the progression from image to likeness in the *Prima secundae* is marked by the imitation of Christ.

Questions 22 to 48 are preparatory to the study of the virtues, and the turning point in this consideration of the virtues is question 62 on the theological virtues. The *respondeo* of article 1 of this question has two interesting rhetorical or pedagogical features. First, Thomas refers twice to question 5 of the *Prima secundae*. The first reference establishes the link between beatitude, virtue, and acts of will perfected by virtue, and the second recalls the distinction between natural and supernatural beatitude.[42] This material is subsumed under a text from the Second Letter of Peter: "quod per Christum facti sumus consortes divinae naturae,"[43] by which the gift of the theological virtues is explicitly linked to Christ.

The treatment of the virtues is followed by questions on sin and vice, thus finishing the study of the intrinsic principles of human acts, and the study of the extrinsic principles from God begins with the treatment of law, in which the procession of the Word plays a crucial role. Significantly, the treatise on law reproduces within itself the structure of the *Summa*. It is a microcosm or hologram of the whole.

After he has established the essential characteristics of law in question 90, Aquinas studies in question 91 the various kinds of law. Along the way, he develops an interesting progression. In article 1 he argues that there is an eternal law, which is the *ratio* for the governance of all things, considered in God as Ruler of the universe.[44] This approach corresponds with Aquinas' treatment

40 Ibid., 1–2.19.9.

41 Thomas Aquinas, *Super Matthaeum*, 344.

42 Thomas Aquinas, *Summa theologiae* 1–2.62.1.

43 Ibid., 1–2.62.1.

44 Ibid., 1–2.91.1.

of Christ as the Wisdom of God's art in creation. To confirm this, he makes an explicit appeal to question 22 articles 1 and 2 of the *Prima pars*. These articles treat God's providence in general, and article 2 refers explicitly to God's Wisdom as the art by which all creatures come to be and are ordered to each other. This notion is later explicitly sublated into Christ as God's Word and particularly into the notion of the Word as expressing created things. There is thus a suggestive parallel being drawn between the Word as conceived Wisdom of the Father and the Eternal Law in God.

This parallel is strengthened in article two and made explict in article three. Thomas calls natural law the human creature's participation in the eternal law. All creatures receive the imprint of the eternal law in themselves and thus receive their natural inclinations as participations in the eternal law. Rational creatures receive a more perfect imprint of the eternal law, because their participation is intentional. This participation in the eternal law is properly called natural law in rational creatures.[45] In article 3 Thomas proposes a proportional equation: speculative reason is to Divine Wisdom (which has already been explicitly linked to the Word) as practical reason is to Eternal Law. Thus, Thomas rhetorically links the Eternal Law, which is identified with the Word, and natural law shown to be the creature's participation in this Word, insofar as it is the Word of God's wise government of the universe. In question 91 Aquinas examines human law, which is seen as a participation in the natural law. Article 4 of question 91 looks at the particular case of the Old and New laws revealed by God to Israel and in Christ, respectively. Thomas understands this divine law in exactly the same way as he did *sacra doctrina* in the *Prima pars*. Because the human acts that merit beatitude are beyond the ken of reason to discern, a divine law is necessary to direct human acts beyond what is found in natural and human law.[46] Article 5 sets the Old and New laws in proper relation to each other.[47] Question 91 thus establishes the program of the whole treatise on law, in the sense that the treatise on law functions pedagogically as a summary of what has gone before, as the most concrete point for the study of created realities in preparation for the introduction of grace.

In question 93 article 1, Thomas adduces whole sections of material from the *Prima pars*. In particular, he explicitly restates the relation whereby the Word as God's conceived Wisdom expresses all created things. It is by His Wisdom

45 Ibid., 1–2.91.2.

46 Ibid., 1–2.91.4.

47 Ibid., 1–2.91.5.

that God creates, on the analogy of an artisan in relation to his work. If the technique of God's Wisdom can be understood as God's art, as exemplary cause, or as archetypal Idea, then similarly the principles of God's Wisdom, by which God moves all things in His providence, have the nature of Law. According to this comparison, the eternal law is nothing more than the sum total of the "thoughts" of Divine Wisdom, whereby Wisdom gives direction to all acts and movements in created things.[48] Thomas' reply to the second objection in article 4 of the same question makes the point even more clearly. The Son is the eternal law by a kind of appropriation, as was established by Augustine.[49] According to Augustine's *De vera religione*, chapter thirty-one, to which Thomas refers, the "appropriation" in question is the Father giving judgment over to the Son who is Truth itself and, therefore, the Judge.

In the *sed contra* of article 2 of question 98 ("whether the Old Law was from God"), Aquinas begins with the teaching of Christ in the Gospel of Matthew, that the Old Law was indeed from God. Christ is, once again, the Teacher. Thomas' response is therefore worthy of comment. He writes that, "The Old Law was given by the good God, Who is the Father of our Lord Jesus Christ," thus rhetorically linking Christ and the Old Law. Aquinas exploits this notion by introducing the Pauline notion of the Law as a pedagogue leading to Christ.[50] This link is further developed in question 99, in which Thomas cites the relevant passage from Paul's letter to the Galatians explicitly.[51] In question 100 article 2, Aquinas connects this pedagogical function of the Old Law with the notion of growing into the likeness of God. The moral precepts of the Old Law are about acts of virtue, whereby the human reason is ordered well and becomes more God's image.[52] This is further developed in the study of the ceremonial precepts of the Old Law, which are shown to prefigure Christ.[53]

The treatment of the Old Law's relation to Christ culminates in question 107, in which the New Law in Christ is compared with the Old. In article 2 Thomas shows how Christ fulfills the Old Law in the New. Beginning with the doctrine of type and antitype, Aquinas argues that Christ fulfills the Old Law both in his works and in his doctrine. He accomplishes this in his works, when, for example, he undergoes circumcision and in his doctrine, in three ways,

48 Ibid., 1–2.93.1.
49 Ibid., 1–2.93.4.
50 Ibid., 1–2.98.2.
51 Ibid., 1–2.99.6.
52 Ibid., 1–2.100.2.
53 Ibid., 1–2.101.2.

namely, by explaining the Law, by prescribing the safest way to fulfill the Old Law, and by adding "counsels of perfection."[54] In question 108 Aquinas examines the concrete content of the New Law in itself. Thus, the treatise on law is a microcosm or hologram of the entire *Summa*. It begins with the procession of the Word as Eternal Law and ends with the salvation-historical and very concrete content of the divine law revealed by God. This summary serves as the climax of the treatment of created things, pulling them together and opening them to the next step, the presence and action of grace, which *actually* conforms human beings to the likeness of God. All of this has been shown to be a function of the procession of the Word. In this way, the treatise on law hints at what is to come in the explicit Christology of the *Tertia pars*.

Prima secundae: *Climax – Questions 109 to 114*

There is not much explicit discussion of Christ in the treatise on grace which is the culmination of the *Prima secundae*. The language that is most apparent is that of likeness to God, and this should be expect as the text moves from image to likeness and from the general created participation in the Trinity, which we have as knowing and choosing beings, to the actual concrete participation that is made possible by grace. In the *Prima pars* both of these imitations or participations were grounded in the procession of the Word, who because He is God's *Verbum* is also the Image, the exemplar in whose beauty all created images and likenesses participate. Thus, the lack of explicit reference to Christ or to the Word at this point in the text is not at issue. The focus is rather on how grace is presented as the agent of our growing likeness to God in the Image.

In question 110 article 4, Aquinas argues that the participation in the divine goodness that grace communicates to us forges a kind of likeness between human beings and God. Thomas anchors this understanding in the *sed contra* of the question which quotes the Pauline notion that we have been made "sons of God."[55] In his response, he supports this notion with the example of the theological virtue of faith that conforms our knowing to God's knowing.[56] As Thomas had established earlier, this conformity is the work of God's *Verbum*, and consequently Christ's role in the giving of grace is clear, even if this aspect will not become explicit until the *Tertia pars*. The language of re-generation and re-creation used both in the *sed contra* and in the final lines of the *respondeo*

54 Ibid., 1–2.107.2.

55 Ibid., 1–2.110.4.

56 Ibid., 1–2.110.4.

in question 110, article 4 strengthens this awareness by rhetorically drawing a parallel to the procession of the Word, which was described as a "generation" in the *Prima pars*. Thomas marks the importance of Christ for the proper understanding of the *Prima secundae* in the final question of this part, which examines merit as the fruit of cooperating grace.[57] In article 6 of this question, he asks whether anyone can merit grace on behalf of another and answers that only Christ by the special grace of his office as redeemer can merit for another.[58]

The Secunda secundae

As the most concrete point in the *Summa* for the study of image and likeness in human beings, the *Secunda secundae* explores the specific habits and acts that constitute our concrete likeness to God in Christ under grace. For the majority of this section of the *Summa*, Thomas carefully parses the general principles of this concrete likeness under grace, that is, the theological virtues that actualize the likeness by conforming our knowing and loving to God's knowing and loving. This first part explores our concrete participation in God's knowing and loving, not so much in its historical actualization but in its sources. In this part of the *Secunda secundae*, explicit references to Christ or to the Word are few and far between. The student who Aquinas has brought this far by the Christological pedagogy, however, is aware of the presence of the Word in the language of "being ordered" or "conformed" by this or that virtue.

The theological virtue of faith conforms our knowing to the supernatural truth revealed in the mysteries of our salvation. It is both a new light that is proportioned to the new objects to be known and a reordering and elevating of our knowing. This reordering and elevation is a gift that is already operating in the student, of course, but by conforming our explicit knowing of it to the reality already operative, Aquinas develops our knowing's likeness both to the known object and to its principle, the Word in God. Similarly, the treatment of the theological virtues of hope and charity makes us explicitly aware of the transformation of our willing by God's love, which gives us a more intimate knowledge of the good at work in us, and thus the ability to choose it intentionally and collaborate more consistently with grace.

Aquinas presents charity as the friendship with God by which we are fundamentally reordered in our love for God, creation, and neighbor. Communion with God is the radical horizon within which we act concretely, express-

57 Ibid., 1–2.114.

58 Ibid., 1–2.114.6.

ing love for God and neighbor. The gift of the Holy Spirit that crowns charity is, perhaps not surprisingly, wisdom. Aquinas' treatment of this gift deserves close scrutiny, marking as it does a significant "way-station" in the *ductus* of the *Secunda pars*.

In question 45 of the *Secunda secundae*, Thomas makes explicit many elements that have shaped his understanding of *sacra doctrina* as wisdom. In article 1 he shows that the gift of wisdom is right judgment according to the Eternal Law. Specifically, it belongs to the gift of the Holy Spirit called "wisdom" to judge rightly about divine things because of a certain connaturality with them, a connaturality that is the result of charity; thus the gift of wisdom is borne of love.[59] The merit and reward of this gift is the seventh beatitude: "Blessed are the peacemakers, for they shall be called children of God." Peacemakers make peace in themselves and in others, for peace is the tranquility of order.[60] Such people are rewarded by a more intimate participation in the only-begotten and natural Son of God, who is also the Wisdom by which God foreknew and foreordained all things according to Romans 8. "Hence, by participating in the gift of wisdom, man attains to the sonship of God."[61]

Aquinas presents the cardinal virtues next with prudence considered first. Prudence is practical wisdom that discerns the proper actions to take in order to appropriately express the true and the good that are known and desired by means of the theological virtues. It is a habit that conforms human beings at the natural level (the gift of wisdom having already conformed us at the supernatural level) to the likeness of God's good government of creation, i.e., our created likeness to God as provident lawgiver. The virtue of prudence thus conforms us to the Word in a new way, making us capable of issuing commands that are true images of the Word by which God governs for the common good.[62] Prudence is also the pivot between contemplation and action. In accordance with the pedagogical progression, Thomas now moves to the consideration of the practical virtues by which the concrete forms of Christian life will be lived. Justice, the next virtue in his sequence, includes a consideration of the annexed virtue of religion. In this context Aquinas presents for the first time the categories of sacrifice and satisfaction, which play a significant role in his theology of the Cross. By teaching these values and thereby conforming the student to them at this point in the text, Thomas prepares us to understand

59 Ibid., 2–2.45.2

60 Ibid., 2–2.45.6

61 Ibid.

62 Ibid., 2–2.47.8 and 2–2.47.11.

the mysteries of Christ that we are called to imitate. Aquinas insists that justice is an expression of the charity that is implanted in us by grace. This is particularly true of the external acts of religion, which correspond to a fundamental offering of self to God and which is the chief inner act of religion.[63]

After the study of the general principles or sources of our concrete likeness to God in Christ under grace, Thomas focuses on the actual historical ways in which this likeness is lived. This is, if you will, the "concreteness within the concrete" and the particularity of specific ways of life in the Church and in the world. First, Thomas embarks upon a general study of the active and the contemplative lives, which culminates in a comparison of the two forms of life at question 182. In the first article, Aquinas asserts the superior dignity of the contemplative life. In the *respondeo*, however, he makes use of an interesting argument from *convenientia*. "The contemplative life holds itself in the sphere of the divine, the active life in the human sphere. 'In the beginning was the Word,' writes Augustine, 'This is the one to whom Mary listened. And the Word was made flesh: this is the one whom Martha served.'"[64] The two forms of life are ordered to each other as the procession of the Word is to the Incarnation, both key Christological doctrines. It is interesting that the doctrines have begun to serve as interpretive principles. Although such a use of the doctrines has been implicit in the rhetorical and pedagogical practices of the *Summa* to this point,[65] this is the first explicit use of Christological principles to understand the relations between two theological *loci*. This practice takes on much greater importance in the treatment of Christ in his mysteries in the *Tertia pars*.

From the study of the two forms of life, Thomas proceeds to examine the concrete states of life in the Church. These are the stable historical likenesses which believers encounter in the Church. The diverse offices and states are necessary in the Church precisely because they show the plenitude of grace which flows from Christ as head.[66] In the questions on the religious state, Thomas makes explicit a new relation to Christ, that of the "imitation of Christ." This is, obviously, a classic medieval definition of the spiritual life, but Aquinas orients us specifically to the tasks of preaching, which is the exercise of *sacra doctrina* in the Church that has been implicitly driving the forward movement

63 Ibid., 2–2.82–83.

64 Ibid., 2–2.182.1.

65 It is, after all, an interpretive use of the doctrine of the procession of the Word to make it, even pedagogically, the grounding of the doctrine of creation, as we saw earlier in this chapter.

66 Ibid., 2–2.183.2.

of the *Summa*'s Christological pedagogy, having the Incarnate Word as its structuring principle. Thomas's treatment of the imitation of Christ deserves closer scrutiny.

In the fifth article of question 186 Thomas considers whether obedience belongs to the perfection of the religious state. The *sed contra* reads as follows: "The perfection of the religious state is above all constituted by the imitation of Christ, as we read in Matthew, chapter nineteen: 'If you wish to be perfect, go and sell all you have and give it to the poor, and come and follow me.' But in Christ what is most commended is obedience, according to the letter to the Philippians: 'He was made obedient even unto death.' Thus we see that obedience belongs to the perfection of the religious state."[67] Aquinas considers obedience the chief vow of the religious state, because it is included in the call itself to follow Christ.[68] The imitation of Christ also serves as the justification for the mendicancy of certain vowed religious. The *sed contra* of question 187 article 5 reads, in part, as follows: "It belongs to religious to live the imitation of Christ. But Christ begged, according to this word from Psalm 39: 'As for me, I am a beggar and poor;' about which the Gloss says: 'Here Christ is speaking of himself in the form of a servant;' and a little further 'That one is a beggar, who asks from another and that one is poor who cannot meet his own needs.'"[69]

Secunda pars: *Summary of Pedagogical Progression*

In the *Secunda pars* Thomas thus uses the distinction between image and likeness to order the doctrines of this part into a pedagogical whole which begins from the doctrine of creation in the *Prima pars* and concludes with the doctrine of the imitation of Christ. This doctrine is the key to understanding religious life according to Aquinas and explains why the explicit treatment of Christ comes at this point in the *Summa*. The student must be brought pedagogically to the point where the next natural question is "But who is this Christ I seek to imitate?" Thus the Christological pedagogy has brought the student to the "theological climax" of the progression from vestige through image and likeness to the Image made flesh, but the link to the procession of the Word and the Word's expression of created things remains to be determined. This occurs in the Christology of the *Tertia pars*.

67 Ibid., 2–2.186.5.

68 Ibid., 2–2.186.8.

69 Ibid., 2–2.187.5.

Tertia pars: *Question 3, Article 8*

At first glance, the third question of the *Tertia pars* seems out of place. After examining the *convenientia* of the Incarnation in the first question and determining the nature of the union which the Incarnation is in the second question, Thomas seems to abandon all notions of the particularity and concreteness of what has been revealed to engage in "flights of speculative fancy." Most of the articles of question 3 are devoted to answering hypothetical problems: can nature assume, abstracted from personhood?[70] Can a divine person assume a created nature independently of the other persons?[71] Could a divine person other than the Son have assumed a created nature?[72] Could two divine persons assume one and the same individual nature?[73] Could one divine person assume more than one individual nature?[74] At first, this intrusion seems confusing, and is often used as an example for precisely the problem that plagues scholasticism, namely the multiplication of philosophically determined questions that have little to do with understanding the concrete dimensions of revealed truth. A closer reading, one that is more attentive to the pedagogical dimensions of the text, however, yields some important insights.

The first rhetorical device that is apparent in this question is an extensive use of repetition. The phrase "assumptio duo importat: scilicet, ipsum actum assumentis et terminum assumptionis"[75] and its variants recur frequently throughout the question, sometimes as an interpretive principle or a theological starting point and sometimes as the goal to be reached by understanding. This repetition serves a number of pedagogical purposes. First, each repetition clarifies incrementally what is meant by assumption. Each time it is restated, Thomas limits the principle in a particular way, exploits a new dimension of it, or draws a new consequence from it. Thus, the hypothetical cases in each article become a way of clarifying by contrast or comparison just what is meant by the theological use of the term "assumption". Second, this repetition clarifies reciprocally other key terms as they relate to the mystery of the Incarnation, e.g., person and nature. Again, the speculative "case studies" help the student achieve greater precision in the use of technical theological terms.

70 Ibid., 3.3.3.
71 Ibid., 3.3.4.
72 Ibid., 3.3.5.
73 Ibid., 3.3.6.
74 Ibid., 3.3.7.
75 Ibid., 3.3.5.

This pedagogical use of repetition makes manifest just how free God was in the Incarnation and thus the proper understanding of the radical contingency of the Incarnation itself. It rids one of any false notions of necessity either in God or in creatures that might lead to an understanding of the Incarnation as somehow determined. This usage shows precisely the radical newness of the relation between God and creatures that is inaugurated in the Incarnation. Thus, the use of hypotheticals here is a variation on Aquinas' pedagogical use of historical errors and heresies to clarify the proper understanding of doctrines.

At the same time, the radical newness of the Incarnation, its "never-before-seen" contingency, does not bar the possibility of an analogical understanding of the mystery. In response to the objection of the first article of this question that nothing can be added to God who is already perfect, Thomas proposes an understanding of assumption from the analogy of the grace of adoption, which he had already studied in the *Secunda pars*.[76] Similarly, in the *ad secundum* he replies to the objection that "person" is incommunicable and thus a divine person could not assume a created nature by proposing an analogy based on the co-existence in human beings of several accidental natures to understand how, given God's infinite greatness, a divine person might have several substantial natures.[77] These analogies do not settle the issues but rather suggest ways forward.

It is in the final article of the question that Thomas places the "intelligible newness" of the Incarnation in its proper concrete light. After he has established a space for God's freedom, he directs the student to consider "utrum fuerit magis conveniens Filium Dei incarnari quam Patrem vel Spiritum Sanctum."[78] The fittingness of the Son's assumption of human nature concerns God's sovereign Wisdom and not logical or causal necessity, as the *sed contra* asserts. "[T]he Damascene writes: 'In the mystery of the Incarnation the wisdom and the power of God are made manifest: God's wisdom, in that to the most difficult problem He has provided the best solution; and God's power, because He has made of the vanquished the victor.' But power and wisdom belong to the Son by appropriation, as is written in the first letter to the Corinthians: 'Christ, the power and wisdom of God.' Thus it was fitting that

76 Ibid., 3.3.1.

77 Ibid.

78 Ibid., 3.3.8.

the person of the Son become incarnate."[79] Thomas' invocation of the letter to the Corinthians is not accidental but rhetorically meaningful. His treatment of this passage in his commentary evokes precisely the generation of the Son from the Father as conceived Wisdom.[80] In the *sed contra* Aquinas thus invokes the entire pedagogical procedure that has gone before, which is made explicit and linked to the Incarnation in the *respondeo*. First, he recalls the similitude between the Word and all created things. "The word or conception of the artisan is the exemplary similitude of all he makes from his art. Similarly God's Word, Who is His eternal concept, is the exemplary similitude of all creatures. Thus, since it is by their participation in this similitude that creatures are constituted in their proper species, though they are mutable, it was fitting that by the union of the Word, not by participation but personally, the fallen creature should be restored to its proper order with respect to eternal and immutable perfection. For it is by the ideal form of the artisan's conception, by which he made the thing, that he restores it if it breaks down."[81] This is the same point that Thomas makes in the *Prima pars* in relation to the Word expressing all created things as a function of his procession from the Father precisely as Word but seen now in the additional light of the need for redemption.

This first step of the pedagogical progression is followed by the second and third steps, image and likeness. "In another sense, there is a special harmony between the Word of God and human nature: it comes from the fact that the Word of God is His eternally conceived Wisdom, from which all human wisdom derives. This is why human progress in wisdom, which is the perfecting of human nature as reasonable, is measured by its participation in God's Word: thus the disciple is taught insofar as he receives the word of his master ... . It was fitting, then, for the perfection of human beings, that the Word of God be personally united to human nature."[82] The rhetorical and pedagogical allusions in the *Secunda pars* have now been brought to term and explicitly linked to the procession of the Word in God. Thomas brings the whole pedagogy of the *Summa* to its properly Christological conclusion. In the next chapter we will see how precisely this pedagogical progression allows Aquinas to articulate his systematic understanding of the doctrines pertaining to the person of Jesus the Christ.

79 Ibid.

80 Thomas Aquinas, *Super Epistolas Sancti Pauli Lectura*, 243.

81 Thomas Aquinas, *Summa theologiae* 3.3.8.

82 Ibid.

Conclusion: The Word as Structuring Principle of Sacra doctrina

In the *Lectura super Ioannem*, Aquinas shows how the fourfold pedagogical progression from vestige to Image is rooted in, and structured by, the procession of the Word in God. When he deploys that same pedagogy in the *Summa*, he employs the various rhetorical devices at his disposal in order to relate the pedagogical development of *sacra doctrina* to the Word in various ways. Before the explicit treatment of the procession of the Word in the questions on the Trinity, Thomas evokes the presence of the Incarnate Word as the context within which particular exercises of understanding are to be undertaken. A key example of this is the use of Augustine in a *sed contra* to link the notion of *scientia* to Christ. Aquinas also uses the *sed contra* to present Christ as the teacher of doctrine about God. Once the procession of the Word has been explained, it plays the same role in the development of the pedagogy of the *Summa* that Thomas found it played in the prologue to the Gospel of John. As we come to the end of the *Secunda pars*, we see that the student has been brought to the point where the next question is "Who is this Christ I seek to imitate?" The answer to that question will be the explicit Christology of the *Tertia pars*, the climax of the progression of spiritual exercises in *sacra doctrina*.

CHAPTER SEVEN

Knowing Christ in His Fundamental Principles

In the last chapter I developed a reading of the structure and dynamic of the *Summa theologiae* as a Christological pedagogy with the explicit Christology of the *Tertia pars* as the climax to this pedagogy. This pedagogical dynamic proceeds in four movements, each anchored in the procession of the Word in God. In the *Prima pars*, the movement is that of the vestiges in creation and culminates in the creation of human beings; the *Prima secundae* introduces the movement from the Trinitarian image, the *imago Dei,* in our operations and culminates in the gift of grace; the *Secunda secundae* takes up our likeness, the *imago ad imaginem*, to God in our redeemed living and culminates in the *imitatio Christi*; finally, the *Tertia pars* considers the *Imago Dei*, Christ.

This pedagogical dynamic is only one way that Aquinas' use of rhetorical and other instruments form students into an ever-greater resemblance to God's Wisdom. His Christology itself, at the apex of the spiritual pedagogy of the *Summa theologiae*, conforms the mind and heart of the student to the shape and telos of God's Wisdom. In the next three chapters I present three case studies that show this christoforming pedagogy at work: questions 1 to 6 of the *Tertia pars*, which present the mystery of the Incarnation in its fundamental metaphysical principles; questions 40 to 45, the study of the mysteries of Christ's public life; and questions 46 to 59, Christ's return to the Father through the passion and resurrection. Each case study brings out different rhetorical elements and dimensions of the pedagogy of the *Summa*'s Christology.

Perhaps the most helpful way to begin this task is to state explicitly what it is not. These chapters will not be an in-depth study on Thomas' Christological doctrines. This work has been excellently done by other commentators,[1] who have addressed the more doctrinal questions (qq.1-26). It will also not be a com-

1 See, for example, Inos Biffi, *I misteri di Cristo in San Tommaso d'Aquino*, Di fronte e attraverso 339 (Milan, 1994); Michel Corbin, "La parole devenue chair: Lecture de la première question de la *tertia pars* de la *Somme Théologique*," *Revue des sciences*

mentary on the biblical exegesis that follows because Jean-Pierre Torrell has completed an exhaustive commentary on Aquinas' treatment of "Christ in his mysteries" (qq.27-59).[2] All of these studies have brought out what Torrell calls the objective pole of *sacra doctrina*. The next three chapters move forward from these studies by attending to the subjective pole, the transformations of the person intended by the theologian's collaboration with God's teaching activity in history. I will therefore continue to focus on the rhetorical and pedagogical dimensions of the text that were brought out in the previous chapters. These practices organize the explicit Christology of the *Tertia pars* into a spiritual pedagogy, an ordered and dynamic set of "spiritual exercises" whereby the student is formed as a preacher and pastoral minister capable of interpreting Scripture in a doctrinally sound manner that understands and relies upon the proper concreteness of the Christian message and therefore has no need of fables or non-biblical *exempla*. In this way the preacher or pastoral minister can help others live the Christian life through moral judgments grounded in a wise grasp of the concrete whole as it is expressed in the example of Christ.

The Pedagogical Order of the Dogmatic Christology

A few general remarks about the *ductus* and *skopos* of the first twenty-six questions of the *Tertia pars* are in order. To bring out more clearly the meaning of the path Aquinas sets forth in the *Summa*, it is helpful to compare its dogmatic Christology to his other works, *De articulis*, the *Compendium theologiae*, and the fourth part of the *Summa contra Gentiles*.

Thomas wrote the *De articulis* sometime between 1265 and 1268 for Leonardo, archbishop of Palermo, to expose the creed and the nature of the seven sacraments. In the first part, he follows the order of the articles of the creed. When he comes to the Christological article, he explains the article briefly and then develops the various errors that have arisen historically. The order is simple:

---

philosophiques et théologiques 62 (1978): 5–40; Francis Ruello, *La christologie de Thomas d'Aquin* (Paris, 1987); Édouard-Henri Weber, *Le Christ selon saint Thomas d'Aquin*, Jésus et Jésus-Christ (Paris, 1988); also, finally, Joseph Wawrykow, "Hypostatic Union", in *The Theology of Thomas Aquinas*, ed. Rik van Nieuwenhove and Joseph Wawrykow (Notre Dame, IN, 2005), 222–251.

2 This work has been published in two volumes: Jean-Pierre Torrell, *Le Christ en ses mystères* (Paris, 1999). The first volume covers the material up to and including the transfiguration, the second, the passion and resurrection.

1. Those who say that Christ is only human; those who say that Christ does not have a true body
2. Those who say that he had a celestial body
3. Those who say that Christ did not take flesh from Mary (Apollinaris)
4. Those who say that Christ lacked a human soul (Arius)
5. Those who say that he lacked a human intellect (Apollinaris again)
6. Those who hold that he had a single (mixed) nature after the Incarnation (Monophysites)
7. Those who hold that there is only a divine operation in Christ after the Incarnation (Monothelites)
8. Those who hold that there are two persons after the Incarnation (Nestorius)
9. Those who deny the work of the Holy Spirit and hold that Jesus is born of Mary and Joseph (Carpocrates)
10. Those who hold that Mary had other children from Joseph after Jesus' birth (Helvidius)

There is a similar treatment of errors in the *Compendium*, which is from the same period and was composed for Reginald of Piperno as a digest of Thomas' teaching:

1. Those who say that Christ was merely human
2. Those who hold that there were two persons after the Incarnation (Nestorius)
3. Those who say that Christ had no human soul (Arius)
4. Those who say that he lacked a human mind (Apollinaris)
5. Those who hold that he had a single (mixed) nature after the Incarnation (Monophysites)
6. Those who say that Christ lacked a real body
7. Those who say that he had a celestial body, not taken from Mary
8. Those who hold that there was an accidental union of human and divine in the Incarnation (this was a position contemporary with Aquinas);
9. Those who hold that there are two *supposita* after the Incarnation (also a contemporary position)
10. Those who hold that there is only one will and operation in Christ (Monothelites)

This list has a slightly different order and excludes some errors while adding others. Finally, there is Thomas' treatment of Christology in the fourth part of the *Summa contra Gentiles*:

1. On the Incarnation of the Word according to the Scriptures
2. Those who hold that Christ was merely human (Photinus)
3. Those who hold that he assumed a phantasy, not a real, body (Manicheans)
4. Those who hold that he assumed a celestial body (Valentinus)
5. Those who hold that he did not assume a body from Mary, but somehow a piece of the Word was changed into flesh (Apollinaris)
6. Those who hold that he did not have a human soul (Arius and Apollinaris)
7. Those who hold that he did not have a rational mind (Apollinaris), and those who hold that Christ's soul was preexistent (Origen)
8. Those who hold that there were two persons after the Incarnation (Theodore of Mopsuestia and Nestorius)
9. Those who hold that there was only one nature after the Incarnation (Eutyches)
10. Those who hold that there was only one will after the Incarnation (Macarius of Antioch)
11. Those who hold that there was an accidental union of humanity and divinity (contemporary theological position)
12. Those who hold that there were two *supposita* after the Incarnation (contemporary theological position)
13. What the Catholic faith holds about the Incarnation
14. Objections against faith in the Incarnation
15. How one should understand the Incarnation of the Son of God
16. [A series of explorations of issues flowing from the understanding of the mystery]
17. Solutions to the objections against the Incarnation

It is evident that the treatment of the Incarnation in the *ScG* is more complete than in the other two texts, and that Aquinas' desire to perform the office of the wise man has made a difference to his ordering of materials. This vocation, which is at work throughout the *ScG*, yields the following basic *ductus* and *skopos* to the work:

1. What is found in Scripture
2. Various interpretations that have challenged a full reception of the Scriptures
3. The doctrine of the Church that preserves the meaning of the mystery
4. Understanding this doctrine from first principles
5. Overcoming objections to it by reducing them to basic philosophical mistakes

This movement proceeds from the horizon of Scripture to an exercise of judgment, and to a deepening of one's understanding that includes understanding and overturning errors, which is the true sign of being wise. Interestingly, in the *ScG* Aquinas changes the order of errors that was set forth in *De articulis* and the *Compendium*, even as he includes a fuller treatment and adds the reduction of these errors to basic philosophical positions. The changes can be summarized in the comparative table below, which refers to the three lists above:

De articulis	*Compendium*	*Summa contra Gentiles* IV
Merely human	Merely human	Merely human
No true body	Two persons after Incarnation	No true body
A celestial body	No human soul	A celestial body
Did not take flesh from Mary	No human intellect	Did not take flesh from Mary
No human soul	Monophysitism	No human soul
No human intellect	No true body	No human intellect
Monophysitism	A celestial body	Two persons after incarnation
Monothelitism	Accidental union of body and soul	Monophysitism
Two persons after incarnation	Two *supposita* after the union	Monothelitism
No action of the Holy Spirit	Monothelitism	Accidental union of body and soul
No perpetual virginity of Mary		Two *supposita* after the union

In the first two columns, the errors are grouped according to a logical pattern. In *De articulis*, the groups are those that deny the genuine divinity, those that deny the genuine humanity, and those that deny a genuine union. In the *Compendium*, the order is those that deny the genuine divinity, those that deny a genuine union, and those that deny the genuine humanity. In the *ScG* (third column) this pattern is broken up, and the errors appear in what is essentially historical sequence. Unlike the other two texts, in the *ScG* the analysis of the errors follows upon the explanation of the Catholic position, and the list of errors precedes the definition of Catholic doctrine. The *ductus* in the case of the first two texts already includes an analysis, whereas the order of errors in the *ScG* creates a path to encourage the reader to make the judgment that the Church has made by showing the intelligibility of preserving the whole of the scriptural revelation of the mystery of the Incarnation. Once that judgment is made, the doctrine can be explained and errors overturned.

The Prologue to the Tertia pars

Given that our Saviour the Lord Jesus Christ,
  As the angel attested,
In saving His people from their sins showed forth to us
  the way of truth in Himself
A way along which, rising again,
We can reach the happiness of immortal life,
It is necessary for the completion of the whole theological labour,
After the consideration of the final goal of human life
And of the virtues and vices,
To consider the Saviour of all in Himself
And the benefits he offers the human race.[3]

The first step to understand the order of the Christology of the *Summa* is to examine the prologue of the *Tertia pars*. The prologue begins by invoking "Our Saviour the Lord Jesus Christ," which is the first time that this title is invoked in the *Summa*. This new title signals a new start. The doctrine to be explored is taken as "given." Thomas employs the Latin term *quia*, which according to the Aristotelian logic used at the time, asserts fact as fact, as opposed to a properly scientific understanding (*propter quid*), which requires a knowledge of first principles and causes. The *Tertia pars* then concerns contingent truths that are known to be so (e.g., Socrates is truly sitting if and only if he is sitting in fact) and develops how our Savior, "in saving his people from

3 Thomas Aquinas, *Summa theologiae* 3 prologus.

their sins showed forth to us the way of truth in Himself." This way of truth is a way along which we also travel to reach the happiness promised us. In the Christology of the *Tertia pars*, we are not simply studying the truths of the faith but in so doing travel along the way, which is Christ himself.

There are two interesting points about this section of the prologue. The first concerns the interpretation of the verse from Matthew's Gospel, "in order to save His people from their sins,"[4] which modern scholars have used to make a doctrinal point concerning the reason for the fittingness of the Incarnation.[5] At issue is reading this verse according to a rigorously "Thomistic" interpretation as opposed to one often attributed to the fourteenth-century Franciscan John Duns Scotus and his followers. The so-called "Thomist" position states that the Incarnation happened because of sin and is therefore designated as a post-lapsarian account. By contrast the so-called "Scotist" position is pre-lapsarian, namely that the Incarnation is not dependent on the Fall of Adam and Eve because it effects our union with God. By understanding the Latin as causal, scholars and interpreters have obscured the proper grasp of the pedagogy of this section of the *Summa*. As Michel Corbin has shown, Thomas' approach to the mystery of the Incarnation in fact overcomes the Thomist-Scotist debate.[6] For Thomas, the choice is not between pre-lapsarian or post-lapsarian reasons for the Incarnation. Rather, Thomas holds a delicate balance between the grasp of the Word in God as Wisdom and Truth, and what we can humbly say as the result of what is revealed in the concrete circumstances of the Incarnation. His pedagogy moves us to the deeper communion with Divine Wisdom which is our "pre-lapsarian" destiny, even as his dogmatic content fosters the "post-lapsarian" humility that conforms us to the truth of our historical condition.

4 "Populum suum salvum faciens a peccatis eorum," Thomas Aquinas, *Summa theologiae* 3 prologus. This English translation is that of the older Blackfriars edition.

5 This issue is perhaps most clearly seen in the various translations into modern languages that have been given for the verse. The English Dominican translation rendered the phrase as "in order to save His people from their sins," while the translations from Éditions des Jeunes and more recently Éditions du Cerf give "in saving his people from their sins." The Blackfriars translation has "as he was saving his people from their sins." A more literal translation would be "making saved his people from their sins," which the two French as well as the later Blackfriars translations try to render intelligible with the prepositions "in" or the phrase "as he was."

6 Corbin, "La parole devenue chair," 5–40.

The second point of interest concerns the phrase "showed forth to us the way of truth in himself."[7] From the beginning of the *Summa* Thomas shows that the Word is the way of truth for us. With the treatment of the Incarnation, Thomas can demonstrate this fact for the student explictly, that is, by showing Jesus Christ saving his people from their sins. This is the actual and concrete way in which we attain resurrection and beatitude. The themes previously discussed in the *Summa* are shown here to serve as general principles governed by this specificity and concreteness. Thus, the *Tertia pars* treats the Savior in himself and then the benefits (the Sacraments and the Last Things) that he has brought us. In turn, the consideration of the Savior in himself is in two parts, the mystery of the Incarnation in itself, and then "the things that our Saviour, God made flesh, did and suffered."[8] This last twofold division, between the Incarnation in itself and those things which our Savior did and suffered in the flesh, is unique to Aquinas among his contemporaries.[9] These divisions in the prologue give us the basic structure of the *ductus* of Aquinas' Christology in the *Summa*.

The Ductus *of the Christology of the* Summa theologiae

The order of the Christology proposed by Thomas in the *Summa theologiae* naturally shares some points with that of *De articulis*, the *Compendium theologiae* and the *Summa contra Gentiles* but it also differs from them significantly. At this point, we are well aware of the fundamental pedagogical values Aquinas uses in the *Summa*. He wants to understand the mysteries of faith from first principles. The overall *ductus* of the Christology is as follows:

7 Thomas Aquinas, *Summa theologiae* 3 prologus.

8 Ibid.

9 It is true that other scholastic theologians make theological use of the mysteries of Christ's life, but as Jean-Pierre Torrell points out (*Le Christ en ses mystères*, 26), this use is limited: only those mysteries contained in the creed were discussed, and mainly for their soteriological import and without a concern for their underlying theological unity; or in the case of Peter Lombard, the mysteries are included within his speculative agenda, often at the service of developing an anti-Docetic stance. According to Torrell, Thomas is here retrieving a more patristic mode of theologizing on the mysteries of Christ's *acta* and *passa*, which from our perspective Thomas will apply using rhetorical tools.

- The Savior himself (qq1–59)
  - The mystery of his Incarnation, as this means God becoming human for our salvation (qq1–26)
    - The fittingness in itself of the Incarnation (1)
    - The manner of union of the Word made flesh (2–15)
      - The union itself (2)
      - With respect to the person (3)
      - With respect to the nature assumed (4–6)
      - His perfections (7–13)
      - His disabilities (14–15)
    - Consequent implications of the union (16–26)
  - The things that our Saviour, God made flesh, did and suffered (qq27–59)

Let us begin by noting the *skopos* of the first or dogmatic part of the Christology, which can be found at questions 20 to 26. In these questions Thomas presents Christ, the flesh-and-blood historical agent in his interpersonal relations to his Father (his obedience, his prayer, his priesthood), his interpersonal relations from his Father to him (his adoption, his predestination), and his relationship with us (our adoration of him, and how he is mediator between God and humanity). The first set of relations explores how he will make his offering of love to the Father. It recalls the treatment of charity and religion in the *Secunda secundae* and points to the treatment of the cross and resurrection. The second set shows how Christ is the first principle of our adoption and the cause of our salvation. The third and final set shows how we relate to him and how in this relationship he reconciles us to God by his human self-offering, which brings us benefits.

In question 20 Aquinas introduces a shift in perspective, the second such shift of perspective in the pedagogy that structures the Christology of the *Summa*. His Christology begins with an ontological perspective in questions 2 through 15. Questions 16 and 17 summarize Christ's unity and switch the perspective to the psychology of Christ's willing and operating. This change represents a progression towards the concrete existing Christ, and the psychological considerations, far from being disconnected from the ontological considerations, serve to integrate the ontological developments into a complex whole that more closely approximates the actual existence of Christ understood theologically. Moving from psychological terms and relations, the viewpoint grasps particular persons as terms and tries to understand their complex relations, i.e., the actually existing Incarnate Word's relation to the Father, the

Father's relation to the actually existing Incarnate Word, our relation to the actually existing Incarnate Word, and finally the actually existing Incarnate Word's relation to us. Thus, three terms and four relations constitute the Incarnate Word's social and existential identity. Thomas has analyzed each term in depth at some point in the *Summa* and understood each in the real complexity of its concrete existence: the Father in the *Prima pars*, we ourselves in the entire *Secunda pars*, and Christ the Incarnate Word in the previous nineteen questions of the *Tertia pars*. Each of these four relations are quite complex, integrating even further the matter that has gone before. Christ's relation to the Father is understood according to three elements, whereas, the Father's relation to Christ has two elements. Although our relation to Christ and Christ's relation to us each receive one "name," these names themselves are understood according to various components.

Importantly, in these questions Thomas probes ways of reading Scripture. In questions 20 to 22 he sets out to understand the existential stance of the Incarnate Word before God according to an ordered progression: the stance taken in itself (submission to the Father), the stance in its proper act (prayer, the proper act of religion), and the stance in its salvific effects for us (Christ's priesthood). In questions 23 and 24 Aquinas further examines this last point by considering the two facets of the Father's relation to the Incarnate Word, namely, in what sense filiation and predestination are true of Christ in his human nature.

In question 25, the perspective shifts to Christ's existence with respect to us. This is the question of adoration which is our relation to the Incarnate Word. In the articles that make up this question Thomas displays a masterful combination of practical pastoral problems and theological conclusions about the concrete relation between Christ and ourselves. More precisely, the theological conclusions about this concrete relation are the heuristic structure governing the particular pastoral solutions. Thomas is explicitly directing the student to take a specific stance in relation to the Incarnate Word in final preparation for meeting him in the Scriptural text.

In question 26 the perspective on the relation between Christ and ourselves shifts again from ours to that of Christ, and Aquinas now considers Christ as the mediator between God and human beings.[10] This title of "mediator" corresponds to that of "priest" in question 22 and completes the theological identity of Christ that Aquinas set forth from the beginning of his Christology. Properly speaking, the office of a mediator is to unite those between whom he

10 Ibid., 3.26 prologus.

mediates. This belongs supremely to Christ, who reconciles human beings to God. Others in the Church co-operate in this mediation either dispositively or ministerially.[11] Christ stands between God and human beings in a particular way, only as a man. As a man, he is distant from God by nature, but he is distant from us by dignity of both grace and glory. It is as a man also that he unites us to God, teaching us God's precepts on the one hand and offering satisfaction and prayers to God for us on the other hand.[12] The title of mediator, then, is the title by which Aquinas grasps the ordered whole: the Incarnate Word in himself, his activity *as* revealing God, his activity *of* revealing God, his exemplary causality, and his being the concrete principle of grace. All of these elements are gathered in the title of mediator.

This title of mediator, as we notice in question 26, also serves to order our relation to the Incarnate Word. When we understand Christ in his relation to us, we also understand ourselves in relation to him, so that the title of mediator also unites the matter of the entire *Secunda pars*, which climaxed with the *imitatio Christi*, as we saw in the last chapter. That part of the *Summa* ended with the question "whom do we imitate?" Question 26 closes the pedagogical progression by which Aquinas has been leading us to an answer to that question. Significantly, this title of mediator is the precise role by which Aquinas conceives the mission of the teacher, as we saw in his *principium* or inaugural lecture (chapter four). Here, at the climax of the doctrinal Christology, Aquinas shows that Christ is the principle of all mediation, while others participate "dispositively and ministerially"in his priestly and revealing activity. Here, at last, is precisely what we have been suggesting about the meaning of *sacra doctrina*. It is a complex notion which includes the activity by which the teacher of theology participates in God's revealing activity through Christ, and it also includes the activity of preaching and pastoral care of the priest in the Church.

This, then, is the *skopos*, the destination of the path from questions 1 to 26. We can understand questions 1 through 6, in light of this goal, as setting out the metaphysical conditions under which what actually happens for our salvation in Christ can happen in the way it does. As we shall see, the person of the Word is the primary and most basic explanatory principle of the Incarnation, metaphysically speaking. The natures of the Incarnate Word are secondary, because they explain how things can be truly said of Jesus Christ, especially his actual

11 Ibid., 3.26.1 corp.

12 Ibid., 3.26.2 corp.

human nature. The union itself must be understood, as Aquinas argues, as an order that serves the soteriological purpose of the Incarnation.

The Horizon for Understanding the Mystery: Question 1

In question one of the *Tertia pars* Thomas Aquinas considers the *convenientia* of the Incarnation, which has the following basic structure:

1. whether the Incarnation is appropriate to God (article 1)
2. whether it is an appropriate means to the end (articles 2 to 4)
3. whether it occurred at a time appropriate to its end (articles 5 and 6)

Article 1 considers "whether it was fitting for God to become incarnate."[13] The objections express assumptions about God and the world, and intellectual orientations that prevent giving assent to the mystery of the Incarnation and could also become obstacles to understanding that mystery. They address the horizon for making a proper judgment in faith. In the *sed contra* Aquinas returns to Romans 1:20, which governed the discussion of God in the *Prima pars*: "God's invisible attributes, that is to say God's everlasting power and deity, have been visible, ever since the world began, to the eye of reason, in the things God has made." The repetition of this quotation is not accidental but is a kind of pedagogical chiasmus that proposes a new basis on which to consider the mystery. It promotes a shift of horizon. The shift is from a horizon where ethics and metaphysics are confused, and the Incarnation is considered the model of necessary emanation, to a properly theological and sacramental horizon and a basis in the fundamental character of goodness and God's free agency. Here, the Incarnation is grasped as a totally free communication manifesting divine goodness.

It is most fitting that visible things reveal the invisible God. The entire path of the *Summa* has been governed by this Trinitarian and Christological position. In the *Prima pars*, we apprenticed ourselves to the vestiges of the Trinity in all created things; in the *Prima secundae*, our understanding was shaped according to the image in our operations; in the *Secunda secundae*, it was the graced likeness in our redeemed living. The Incarnation is inscribed within this divine pedagogy as its fulfillment. It makes intelligible God's invisible power through the visible flesh of Jesus Christ, as John Damascene has shown.[14] In the

13 Ibid., 3.1.1.
14 Ibid., 3.1.1 s.c.

response Aquinas offers a simple argument for this, which relies on the self-communicativeness of the good. It belongs to the Supreme Good, which God is, to communicate itself in a supreme way. This supreme communication occurs in the Incarnation, when "Christ so perfectly joins human nature to himself that one person is constituted from these three: Word, soul, flesh."[15] This argument points not to a logical conclusion but to a fitting one. It shows how the event of the Incarnation "fits" concretely into the pattern of God's Wisdom.

This argument of *convenientia* is not merely an idea but is intended to be a new disposition of the student or reader. Aquinas' reply, considered as an idea, is not satisfactory, but as intellectual therapy, which opens possibilities, it promotes a change of perspective in the student. The responses to the objections in this article resolve the issues at the most basic level so that they can be built upon. To the first objection, that the Incarnation would involve a change in God, which is not fitting, Aquinas replies that the change is not in God but in the creature (that is, the human nature taken by the Word). This is a repetition of the solution first developed in the teaching on creation in the *Prima pars*. It becomes in this place a basic pattern for "solving" various questions about the concrete reality of the Incarnation. To the objection that God and humans are infinitely distant because they are so radically different, Aquinas replies that this mystery is indeed beyond the dignity of human nature (a solution repeated many times throughout the *Summa*) but not beyond the goodness of God. Again, this basic pattern serves as a template for understanding various dimensions of the Incarnation, particularly the graces poured out into the humanity of Christ. To the objection that the human condition is evil, Aquinas replies that all created things in their very mutability reveal God and are good. Mutability is not the result of sin. Because the immutable God is revealed in mutable things, nothing stands in the way of the Incarnation. All that remains to be said is that God does not take on sinfulness in taking on flesh. To the last objection, that the finite cannot contain the infinite, Aquinas deploys the sophisticated arguments that he developed in the *Prima pars* to understand the transcendent God's immanent presence in all created things.

In the second article of this question Thomas takes up another aspect of the fittingness of the Incarnation, namely its suitability for redeeming us. The objections propose that the Incarnation is a disproportionate flourish for sav-

15 Ibid., 3.1.1 corp.

ing us, that the agent of our salvation in the Incarnation, being God and not man, is not the proper agent, and that it derogates from the proper reverence due to God. Aquinas roots his response with Jesus' reply to Nicodemus in the third chapter of John's Gospel:

> Is this famous teacher of Israel ignorant of such things? In very truth I tell you, we speak of what we know, and testify to what we have seen, and yet you all reject our testimony. If you disbelieve me when I talk to you about things on earth, how are you to believe if I should talk about the things of heaven? No one ever went up to heaven except the one who came down from heaven, the Son of Man whose home is in heaven. This Son of Man must be lifted up as the serpent was lifted up by Moses in the wilderness, so that everyone who has faith in him may in him possess eternal life. God loved the world so much that he gave his only Son, that everyone who has faith in him may not die but have eternal life. It was not to judge the world that God sent his Son into the world, but that through him the world might be saved.

Aquinas states in the *sed contra* that whatever saves us is *de facto* necessary for our salvation. He goes on to show in his reponse that this necessity is of a particular kind. The Incarnation is not necessary for our restoration in an absolute sense, since God could have chosen any of a myriad ways to save us. It is necessary "quod melius et convenientius pervenitur ad finem."[16] Aquinas then offers ten reasons for this, five from the perspective of our progress in the good and five from the perspective of our withdrawal from evil. Without going into the particulars of these reasons, it emerges that in each case the Incarnation is more suited to our restoration and that it is more appropriate or bears greater fruit. In some cases, Thomas refers to or restates material from earlier in the *Summa*. The series of reasons from the perspective of our progress in the good follows an interesting sequence: certainty of faith, greater hope, deeper love, Christ as model to imitate, and the Incarnation as the greatest participation of humanity in divinity. This is the exact sequence of treatises from the beginning of the *Secunda secundae* to the present treatise on the Incarnation. Each reason for the fittingness of the Incarnation appeals to the fulfillment of material previously considered and gathers it up in the "climax" of the Incarnation, thereby transforming it and bringing it to its fullness of meaning.

16 "[O]ne arrives to the end better and more fittingly." Ibid., 3.1.2 corp.

This pattern continues with the use of *convenientia* in the third article which considers whether, if we had not sinned, God would nevertheless have become incarnate.[17] In the *sed contra* Aquinas appeals to Augustine's commentaries on Luke and Paul. Augustine's comments on 1 Timothy 1:15 state the case most clearly: "There was no cause of Christ's coming into the world, except to save sinners. Take away diseases, take away wounds, and there is no need of medicine."[18] Aquinas begins the *respondeo* with the simple assertion that our assent ought to be given to the opinion that if we had not sinned, the Son of Man would not have come, since this is in line with what God has revealed. We cannot know what God would have chosen to do to effect our union with Him if sin had not intervened. This is beyond our ability to know of our own efforts and could only be revealed to us. Since what has been revealed is that the Incarnation was ordained by God as a remedy for sin, this is where our assent ought to take us. Nevertheless, we must understand that it is a question of revelation in the concrete and not of a negation in principle. God's power is not limited and could have ordained the Incarnation no matter what. In addition, Aquinas' choice of the "self-communicating good" as a starting point for understanding the Incarnation, along with his fundamental option for a pedagogy built on increasing degrees of participation in divinity is not negated by the position taken in this article: "It follows that the event of Jesus Christ, whose contingent nature in the eyes of reason is never denied, seems to be simply a particular case of a general principle concerning what is fitting to God. The argument presents the fittingness of the unique Incarnation within a universal framework which is first with respect to it."[19] By uniting the historical concreteness of the Incarnation with the more universal context of the *Summa*'s pedagogy, Aquinas sees no contradiction between whether Christ became Incarnate on account of sin or not, holding together the elements that will later devolve into the Scotist-Thomist controversy. The further pedagogical importance here is in the option to stay with the concrete and the historically revealed (on both sides of that "issue"). This fits into the thrust of *convenientia* and serves to discipline the spirit of inquiry into a proper humility before the mystery. By contrast, the proponents of an either/or solution are revealed to have eliminated the paradox or tension in the mystery by a kind of intellectual pride.

17 Ibid., 3.1.3.

18 Ibid., 3.1.3 s.c.

19 Corbin, "La parole devenue chair," 33; translation mine.

In light of this point, the reply to the third objection is very helpful. The objection states that, even wounded, human nature is capable of the grace of union (and therefore this grace would be even more appropriate prior to sin). Aquinas replies that human nature was never capable of this grace in itself; union remains always a free and supernatural gift worked by God alone. Indeed, "There is no reason why human nature should not have been raised to something greater after sin. For God allows evils to happen in order to bring a greater good therefrom."[20] This is an appeal to a basic position first taken in the *Prima pars*[21] and repeated a number of times in the *Summa*. Here it finds a properly Christological expression, the fullness of which will become apparent in the treatment of the passion.

In article 4 Thomas establishes that God becomes incarnate first and foremost as a remedy for original rather than actual sin, as a consequence of the position taken in article 3. Articles 5 and 6 examine the fittingness of the timing of the Incarnation in history. Aquinas' position in both articles points to God's pedagogical timing, showing God's wisdom in waiting for the appropriate time. The basis of this position in article 5 is the appeal of Paul in the Letter to the Galatians to the need for a *paidagogos*, i.e., the Law, to prepare us for the coming of God's Son: "... So long as the heir is a minor, he is no better off than a slave, even though the whole estate is his: he is under guardians and trustees until the date fixed by his father. And so it was with us. During our minority we were slaves to the elemental spirits of the universe, but when the term was completed, God sent his own Son, born of a woman, born under the Law, to purchase freedom for the subjects of the Law, that we might attain the status of sons."[22] The initial objections appealed to the difficulty, which is an existential one, of accepting that the Incarnation does not remedy sin by simply removing evil for us without our help. All of the objections are variations on this principle that love should not put off coming to the aid of a friend. Therefore, it would seem that if God had come sooner more people would have been saved, then the principle of saving grace should have been from the beginning.

Aquinas' reply offers reasons of *convenientia* according to his various interpretations of Galatians 4:1–6 as quoted in the *sed contra* and proposes multiple ways of understanding God's pedagogical wisdom. He offers two major rea-

20 Thomas Aquinas, *Summa theologiae* 3.1.3 ad 3.

21 Ibid., 1.22.2 ad 2.

22 Galatians 4:1-6.

sons. First, the Incarnation is medicinal, and medicine can only be safely given when there is illness. He proposes Matthew 9:10–13[23] as an exegesis of the passage from Galatians. Second, the timing of the Incarnation must correspond to the awakening of the human being to the need for a Savior after pride has been defeated. He therefore appeals to Galatians 3:19, the beginning of Paul's treatment of the Law as pedagogue,[24] where Paul points to the Law's role in opening our eyes to our powerlessness against sin. Aquinas adds to this passage Lombard's commentary extending Paul's insight to all people and then provides supplementary arguments that relate to one or other of the major reasons for not sending the Son too soon:

1. He proposes 1 Corinthians 15:46–47 and its teaching on the relationship between the physical body and the spiritual body born from it in the resurrection as a further exegesis of Galatians.[25]
2. He appeals to the cultural experience of his students by pointing out that the greater dignity of the Word is shown forth in his having a greater number of heralds (the prophets) preceding him.
3. The time chosen serves to shorten the time *after* Christ's coming and so ensures that a greater number will still believe at the time of the second coming. This is not a minor point, since it directly opposes the basic assumption of the objections, that a longer delay dooms too many.

Article 6 picks up, in a sense, from this last argument of *convenientia*: if it is best to shorten the time that remains after the Incarnation and before the second coming, then should the first coming not have been postponed altogether? According to Scripture, mercy comes in the last days, perfection in its fullness should come at the end of human history, and finally, it would seem that two comings are wasteful. The *sed contra* appeals to the book of the prophet Habakkuk, in chapter three: "A prayer of the prophet Habakkuk: O Lord, I have heard tell of your deeds; I have seen, O Lord, your work. In the midst of the years you made yourself known, and in your anger you remembered your

23 " ... it is not the healthy who need the doctor, but the sick ... . I did not come to call the virtuous, but sinners."

24 "What then was the purpose of the Law? It was to specifyy crimes, until the posterity came to whom the promise was addressed."

25 " ... first, the one with the soul [Adam] ... and after that the one with the Spirit [Christ]."

mercy." The prayer continues with a plea for deliverance in the midst of oppression and suffering, climaxing in Habakkuk's expression of confidence that God will act now to save: "Yet I will exult in the Lord and rejoice in the God of my deliverance. The Lord God is my strength, who makes my feet nimble as a hind's and sets me to range the heights." Aquinas' *respondeo* is a gem of synthesis. The Incarnation is not merely the perfection of the imperfect in time, but it is also the efficient cause of our fulfillment, and in that sense the perfect comes before the imperfect. The time of the Incarnation corresponds to the need of the human race and to the nature of faith. All these reasons are exegeses of the expression "in the midst of the years" in Habakkuk's prayer. The reply to the first objection offers yet another perspective on this, using Augustine's notion of the ages of man. The reply to the third objection connects to the link made by Habakkuk between judgment and mercy by appealing to John Chrysostom's insight that in God's economy mercy came before judgment.

It is important, at this point, to pause and reflect on the role played by *convenientia* in this first question. Helpfully, Gilbert Narcisse points out that as a strategy, *convenientia*, without prejudice to the exigence of human reason for a full explanation even now of supernatural realities, is able to integrate the excess of intelligibility contained in the mysteries of faith while orienting reason to a humble and respectful stance before them. *Convenientia* invites human reason to a contemplative and silent extension of itself before the mystery.[26] In this way, Thomas makes room for the beautiful, which is the splendor of truth. It profoundly affects discourse and language but cannot be discussed in discourse, because it is born of a communion between the thing known and the intellect which knows it.[27] This communion derives from the intellect's conformity to the thing known, which is why theology, undertaken "normally," tends to order itself to contemplation. It is not a question of substituting one for the other, but of understanding the relation between both.[28] The role of *convenientia* in Thomas' theology is rooted in the importance of the humanity of Christ: " ... through Christ's humanity, ... we are ... adequately (conveniens) purified of all our false affects and conceptions ... By opening us to this meaning of divine wisdom and by demanding a constant dependence on it, argu-

26 Gilbert Narcisse, *Les raisons de Dieu: arguments de convenance et esthétique théologique selon saint Thomas d'Aquin et Hans Urs von Balthasar* (Fribourg, Suisse, 1997), 146.

27 Ibid., 206.

28 Ibid., 287.

ments of fittingness truly purify the intellect."[29] Thus, theological argumentation is a participation in the process of redemption which the Incarnation operates, and arguments from *convenientia* are the privileged pedagogical instrument of this participation.

Question 1 of the *Tertia pars* ensconced us firmly in the perspective of God's love for us as the appropriate horizon for understanding the mystery of the Incarnation. Having oriented the student of theology to a proper participation in the mystery, Aquinas sets out, in questions 2 to 6, to understand the Incarnation according to its fundamental principles.

The Kind of Union the Incarnation Is: Question 2

Question 2 examines the union of the Word Incarnate in itself. The first article considers whether the union took place in a nature. Starting from the teaching of the Council of Chalcedon, "Two natures, without confusion, without change, without division, without separation,"[30] Aquinas shows why the union could not have taken place in a nature. What is of importance here is Aquinas' pedagogical use of errors. We have already seen, in chapter five, that Aquinas uses the errors of the past as a way of teaching theology. As we have seen, by pushing the errors to their limits and overturning them, Aquinas leads students to the appropriate shifts of perspective and horizons that will better allow them to grasp the authentic solution.[31] He usually does this for concerns or questions that lie at the nub or core of issues: get the position right on this point and all sorts of other issues fall into place. The first article of question 2, along with the next article, is a perfect example of this strategy. In these two articles, Aquinas sets the interpretive pattern that will be the key to understanding and solving any issues that arise in the rest of the Christology.

He begins his response by clarifying the meaning of the term "nature". Here it is in the sense of essence or quiddity, that is, in terms of form. One way of understanding union in terms of nature is as one thing made up of two complete things which remain in their perfection, like a heap made up of many stones without order or a house made of stones and beams arranged in order. This sounds like a plausible interpretation of Chalcedon at first glance. Some indeed understood the union of the Incarnation in this way by manner of con-

29 Ibid., 396. Translation mine.

30 Thomas Aquinas, *Summa theologiae* 3.2.1 s.c.

31 See Chapter 5, above, and the articles by Gilles Emery cited at n30.

fusion (without order), or commensuration (with order). In fact, this kind of union remains merely accidental and is only a unity relatively speaking. The result, says Aquinas, is not a nature but a product of art; hence, the approach is self-defeating, because its proponents sought to show that the union took place in a nature.

Another way of understanding union in terms of nature is as one thing made up of several things, perfect in themselves but changed, as a mixture is made up of its elements. In this way, some sought to show that the union was brought about by means of combination. The divine nature cannot be changed, however, because it is incorruptible (cf. question 9 of the *Prima pars*), and neither can anything else be changed into it. Besides, any mingling of human and divine natures would "absorb" the human as a drop of water disappears into a flagon of wine. This analogy depends on the proper understanding of the relation between God and creatures developed in the *Prima pars*. The usually imagined "half-man, half-God" that supposedly results from combination or mixture is metaphysically impossible. This approach is also self-defeating, because it annihilates one nature in the union.

Finally, some have thought of the union as a thing made up of things not mixed or changed but imperfect, as, for example, the soul and body in us. Both the human and divine natures, however, have their specific perfections, as Thomas amply developed in previous parts of the *Summa*. Another possibility would be to understand the union on an analogy from the union of parts of the body to each other, but the human and the divine cannot be "added" to each other as parts, because the divine nature is incorporeal (cf., *Prima pars*). Nor can the two natures be as form and matter, because divine nature is not the form of any creature (*Prima pars* questions 3 and 8). Again, this approach is self-defeating, because it results in a being neither divine nor human. In light of this third kind of error, Aquinas' response to the second objection is important. The objection relies on Athanasius' seemingly unorthodox analogy from the union of soul and matter in us. Aquinas replies to the objection by specifying the particular way in which the analogy is useful, namely that from the union of soul and matter in us there is "an individual subsisting in flesh and soul."[32] This analogy thus serves to point to the unity of one Christ, subsisting in the divine and human natures. This solution introduces the basic pattern clarified in the next article.

32 Ibid., 3.2.1 ad 2.

Article 2 considers whether the union took place in the person. Aquinas again begins from Chalcedon: "[O]ur Lord Jesus Christ is not parted or divided into two persons, but is one and the same Only Begotten Son and Word of God ... ."[33] The *respondeo* begins with the meaning of the term "person," showing its distinction from "nature." The *suppositum*, which in the case of human being is known as "person," is the whole which has the nature as its formal part to perfect it. It is distinct from nature, because it can be the *suppositum* of other realities than the nature, for example, accidents. Whatever adheres to a person is united to it in person, whether it belongs to its nature or not. Having, in the previous article, exhausted the possibilities for a union in nature, what remains is the possibility of union in the person. Inasmuch, then, as the Word has a human nature united to him, which does not belong to his divine nature, it follows that the union took place in the Person of the Word and not in nature. As the first objection points out however, relying on *Prima pars* 39.1, in God nature and person are not really distinct. The reply to the first objection argues that although they may not be ontologically distinct in God, they are meaningfully distinct for us. The reply to the second objection places all this material in the context of the development of the whole *Summa* and points to the fuller development in the eighth article of question 3: the union of the Incarnation is an ennobling fulfillment of the human nature, on an analogy to the sensitive soul, which is more noble through its participation in human reason than it is in brute beasts.

Articles 3 to 6 of question 2 take up various errors to correct them from the perspective of the correct understanding. This serves the pedagogical purpose of further clarifying the meaning of the proper solution by showing how particular consequences flow from it. Hence, Aquinas shows in what proper sense Christ may be called a composite, shows how and why Christ must have a human soul, against both Peter Abelard and Apollinarianism, and corrects the errors of Eutyches, Dioscorus, Nestorius, and Theodore of Mopsuestia as functions of either confusing the natures or separating the persons. Article 7 moves to a more positive set of concerns, using the metaphysical clarifications of the *Prima pars* to show that the union is something created, since it implies a certain relation between the two natures. The term "relation" is important, and Aquinas uses it at key points in the *Summa*. It enters into the definition of persons in the Trinity and into the definition of creation and of grace, as well as qualifies the notion of participation that is so important to the overall peda-

33 Ibid., 3.2.2 s.c.

gogy of the text. "Relation", as Aquinas uses it, is a key theoretical notion, that is, it serves to signal and promote the theoretical differentiation of consciousness that Aquinas is committed to in the *Summa*. In this article, "relation" signals the beginning of a process of theoretical articulation between two terms, the divine and human natures, within the divine person of the Word.

Article 8 clarifies the difference between union and assumption and relates the two terms properly to each other. Article 9 shows how the union of the two natures, precisely as a particular relation, is the greatest of all unions, correcting the excesses, not only of the objections involved, but also of the *sed contra* (from Augustine) upon which the *respondeo* of the article relies.[34] The tenth to twelfth articles clarify in what sense the union may be said to be a grace with respect to the human nature. Here Aquinas relies on the positions developed in the treatise on grace in the *Prima secundae*.

Question 3 returns to the realm of *convenientia*, as it seeks to understand the union on the part of the person assuming. There is a concrete fact to understand, namely, that it is the Second Person that has assumed a human nature and not the First or Third Person. What is the *ratio* of this fact? Article 1 takes a step back to consider whether it is within the proper "competence" of a person to assume a nature. That a divine person can assume a human nature is a strict consequence of question 2, but Aquinas takes the time to further develop the notion of "assumption" by articulating it according to its principle and term (both of which are the divine person of the Word).[35] These two concepts serve as the basis for exploring the fittingness of the Second Person's assumption of a human nature. Article 2 clarifies that, strictly speaking, the divine nature assumes as principle, while the Person of the Word assumes as term. In article 3, we are made to understand that because the divine nature is uniquely the "to-be-subsisting-in-itself," not depending on a distinct act of existence but having strict identity between nature and existing, the divine nature could, in principle, also serve as the "personal" term of the assumption: God as known by the Jewish people is a personal God, even though they do not know persons-in-God, but in fact, says article 4, the assumption of the human nature is by the Second Person as term and accomplished by all three persons as principle.

Article 5 pauses to clarify the obvious issue at this point: if the divine nature could assume as "personal" term in principle, then could not the other two persons assume? We are here in the realm of pure *convenientia*. The article serves

34 Ibid., 3.2.9 s.c and ad 1–3.

35 Ibid., 3.3.1 corp.

three pedagogical purposes. First it sorts out the historical errors in the objections, showing how each depends on a misplaced understanding of necessity; second, it opens our minds to the radical freedom God enjoys by getting us to acknowledge various possibilities; third it prepares us to accept the real and proper concreteness of the mystery, which will be developed in the following three articles. Articles 6 and 7 continue the pedagogical process of shaping our minds into *adequatio*[36] to the divine freedom with respect to the manner of the Incarnation, by further clarifying the distinction between nature and person.

Article 8, however, is the key article and the climax of the process of the question. We have already seen how this article links the Christology to the rest of the *Summa* and is therefore the climax of the overall pedagogy. What we will do here is show how the article in itself is the climax of a growing tension in the understanding of the mystery. If God is not necessitated in any way to work the Incarnation as it in fact occurred, why did it occur in the way it did? What is the wisdom of it? The *sed contra* returns to John Damascene. In the Incarnation God's *power* and *wisdom* are made manifest, but according to Paul in the First Letter to the Corinthians, power and wisdom are appropriated to the Son because of his procession as Word.[37] The *respondeo* begins by showing how this power and wisdom, appropriated to the Son, governs the *ordo doctrinae* developed in the whole *Summa*. Because the Word is the form and principle of *sacra doctrina*, it is entirely fitting that he take on flesh and bring human nature to perfection by union with himself. Aquinas then suggests that there is wisdom in the sending of the Son with respect to the end of the Incarnation, namely our adoptive sonship. It is fitting that the natural heir be the one who communicates to us this grace of becoming God's adoptive heirs. Finally, there is the

36 *Adequatio* here is best understood as it functions in the phrase "adequatio rei et intellectus" where it means "conforming, bringing into greater correspondence with, making more like," and therefore, "conforming the mind to the real."

37 This is also the position found in Aquinas' treatment of the prologue to the Gospel of John with which we began Chapter 6. This position is *not* the one taken by Aquinas in *Summa theologiae* 1.39.8, where he appropriates power to the Father and Wisdom separately to the Son. It is important to remember that appropriations are themselves arguments of *convenientia*, which means that the concrete intelligibility they communicate, precisely because it is concrete, does not exhaust the possible facets of the mystery: there is no contradiction between the two kinds of appropriations, nor is it the case that they are unrelated. In fact, the reply to the second objection neatly clarifies the relation between the two appropriations, carrying forward the solution espoused by Thomas in the *Lectura super Ioannem*.

wisdom revealed in the overcoming of Adam's disordered grasp of knowledge by the Word of true wisdom who orders all authentic knowing. It should be noted that Aquinas takes the tension implicit in the first two reasons and keeps them in perspective by linking them to the third: it *is* true that the Incarnation has a particular link to the order of creation and reveals that link; it *is* true that the human nature is united to God in a particularly fulfilling way in the Incarnation; that this is revealed in the Incarnation is not independent of the redemption. To the first objection, namely, that the Incarnation as it actually occurred led to the misconceptions of Arius with respect to the Son's equality with the Father, Thomas replies that there is nothing that human malice cannot twist or abuse, even God's goodness. Significantly, this reply states explicitly what we have been saying about the pedagogy of the *Summa*. It places responsibility squarely on the human disposition to receive the mystery.[38] To the second objection, that the second creation, like the first, should come from the Father, Thomas replies that the first creation comes from the Father *per Verbum*, which again recalls the careful work of the *Prima pars*. It is fitting that the second creation also comes *per Verbum*. Finally, in the face of the objection that because the Holy Spirit remits sin, it would have been more fitting for it to become incarnate, Thomas shows the even greater fittingness that the Son, who sends the Spirit with the Father, should, by making of the Incarnation a source of the Spirit's sending, reveal his role in the Spirit's sending.

With question 4, Aquinas now turns our attention to the union on the part of the nature assumed and specifically considers the human nature in itself. Some of the material seems at first to be repetitive, but the difference of perspective is paramount. This question is the first of three that consider which things were assumed by the Word of God. Its purpose is to set aside common errors and heresies that arise from an improper understanding of the mode of union viewed from the human side of the event. We are thus being formed to look at the unique relation of the Incarnation from its human term. Article 1 shows the *convenientia* of the human nature to being assumed. We must speak of an "aptness" rather than a natural capability to be assumed, since no creature, of its own natural endowment, is capable of what is a supernatural event, that is, the grace of union. Human nature was apt on two fronts: *secundum dignitatem*, because our operations are ordered to knowing and loving God, which are already forms of union; *secundum necessitatem*, given our need to be rescued

38 Thomas Aquinas, *Summa theologiae* 3.3.8 ad 1.

from the power of sin and death.[39] Irrational creatures lack the aptness of dignity; angels lack the aptness of need. A creature's aptness to be assumed says nothing about God's power, which is not at stake here.[40] The common similitude of vestige is a stamp of the divine in creatures; the similitude of image in human creatures is precisely in the operations of knowing and loving by which we attain some measure of union with God. Vestige does not make the creature *capax Dei*, but image does.[41]

Articles 2 to 5 proceed from this first determination to sort out errors in understanding, in order to clear the way for a return to *convenientia* in article 6, which considers the fittingness of the Son's assumption of a human nature from Adam's lineage. As the *sed contra* makes clear, we are faced with an item of scriptural fact, and therefore with God's wisdom as it has been revealed in *sacra doctrina*. Beginning from the facts of Luke's genealogy,[42] Thomas proceeds to give three reasons that it was fitting for the Son to take humanity from the stock of Adam. It was fitting in justice, which would seem to require that the one who sinned provide restitution; it was fitting in dignity, that the conqueror should spring from the conquered; it was fitting in that God's power is made more manifest, that from weakened and corrupt nature springs up that which God raises to might and glory.[43] The first reason develops the notion of atonement in the direction of God's enabling our restitution of the debt. This was previously hinted at and is now more fully articulated. We are not dealing here with a willful God who seeks to be appeased by the cross, but rather a compassionate God who works the Incarnation within the confines of creation to enable humanity to meet the demands of justice. Thus, once again, the prior developments of the *Summa* are brought forward, transforming key theological notions and also being transformed by them. The third reason is a concrete example of Aquinas' position on metaphor in the *Prima pars*, in article 9 of question 1 on *sacra doctrina*: something low and "far away" from God, namely weakened human nature, gives us a truer sense of what God is.[44] Paradoxically, this reason also recognizes the concrete limits on human nature's ability to be an image. There is a dynamic give-and-take in the pedagogy that refines each notion by testing it against the concrete factuality of our condition.

39 Ibid., 3.4.1 corp.
40 Ibid., 3.4.1 ad 1.
41 Ibid., 3.4.1 ad 2.
42 Ibid., 3.4.6 sc.
43 Ibid., 3.4.6 corp.
44 Ibid., 1.1.9 ad 3.

The fifth question addresses the actually existing humanity of Christ for the first time, by looking at the assumption of the various parts of human nature. The pedagogical task of this question is once again the refutation of errors, in order to clear the way in the mind of the student for the proper understanding. We rediscover here the list of errors from the *De articulis*, but this time ordered from the more fundamental denial of Christian faith to the least fundamental. The errors are also now grouped, and the list is not as exhaustive because Thomas reduces the more extensive lists of the previous texts (*De articulis*, *Compendium theologiae*, *Summa contra Gentiles*) to three fundamental "types" of denial of the mystery. Thomas makes use of a consistent threefold pattern of argumentation: to deny the genuineness of the Incarnate Word's humanity is to (a) go against the witness of Scripture; (b) endanger the authentic understanding of our own redemption, and therefore our ability to collaborate with it; (c) to deny the reality of Incarnation itself, and thus call into question God's power to effect it. Article 1 refutes the error that Christ's was not a real body, an error shared (for different reasons) by Gnostics and Docetists. Article 2 overturns Mani and Valentinus, who maintained in one way or another that Christ's was a heavenly and impassible body. Article 3 refutes the Arians and Apollinarians who denied Christ a human soul, and article 4 refutes the semi-Apollinarians who denied Christ a human mind. The progression is one of gradually excluding all possibilities and focusing the student's attention on what must be the case as a consequence of doctrines already understood.

Question 6 then takes the positive route of considering the "order" of the assumption, the genuine metaphysical constitution of the Word made human. This is not a temporal order with before and after, but rather an order of "mediation" or more precisely of relation and proper proportion. Thomas wants to understand the ordered disposition of the parts.[45] In effect, we are being presented with the proper order of creature to Creator and the proper ordering of humanity in itself. This also further prepares the ordered heuristic that will serve to guide the interpretation of Scripture in questions 27 to 54. This "problem-solving pattern" is applied more explicitly with question 7, which begins the consideration of the perfections co-assumed in the Incarnation, namely grace, knowledge, and power. This is particularly clear in the reply to the first objection in article 1, where the properly understood relation between the two natures helps Thomas clarify that it belongs to the soul of Christ to be divine

45 Ibid., 3.6.1 corp.

by participation, which is by grace.[46] The heuristic is used again in the reply to the second objection, which shows why the human nature enjoyed the grace of glory and habitual grace.[47] The reply to the third objection is important for other reasons. The objection had introduced for the first time the notion that Christ's humanity was an instrumental cause; the reply does not deny this but fine-tunes the notion, which Aquinas will put to important pedagogical use further on. The human nature is "instrumentum animatum anima rationali, quod ita agit quod etiam agitur. Et ideo, ad convenientiam actionis, oportuit eum habere gratiam habitualem."[48]

Conclusion: Redemption through the Incarnate Word

At the end of question 6, the student who has been following Aquinas' pedagogy not only possesses a grasp of the ontological constitution of the Incarnate Word, but also understands why this constitution is the wisest one for the end of our redemption, and has been brought into the personal intellectual and religious horizon within which such an understanding is possible. Precisely because this pedagogical path is one that increases the student's participation in the truth of the Incarnation itself, and because this truth, which is *sacra doctrina*, is at the very same time a participation in the Word itself by which God reveals God's self, the student, by both possessing this truth and being transformed to receive it, imitates Christ more intimately and is thus more capable of being an instrument of this saving teaching in the world, as preacher and formator of Christians in the sacrament of reconciliation. Although this transformation is completely interior and intellectual at this point, it has disposed the student to contemplate the mystery properly and has thus prepared him or her for the next steps, i.e., the consideration of Christ as an agent in Himself, and eventually, in the concrete mysteries by which our salvation is achieved.

46 Ibid., 3.7.1 ad 1.

47 Ibid., 3.7.1 ad 2.

48 "[A]n instrument animated by a rational soul, which is so acted upon as to act. And so for the fittingness of the action, it was necessary that he have habitual grace." Ibid., 3.7.1 ad 3.

CHAPTER EIGHT

Knowing Christ in His Manner of Living

After considering Christ in the fundamental principles of the Incarnation, Thomas Aquinas proceeds to consider the graced psychological constitution of the Incarnate Word (questions 7 to 19) and Christ's concrete existence in history as agent of our salvation (questions 20 to 26). This last section serves as a kind of *skopos* to the first part of the Christology, in which Aquinas has been "re-composing" the mystery of the Incarnation in itself according to the order of teaching. The ontology and psychology of the Incarnate Word sets the foundation for the consideration of Christ in his mysteries, but, as we saw in the last chapter, Aquinas presents this specific ontology because in God's wisdom a particular kind of Savior is given to us, one whose genuine and full humanity is a unique principle of grace.

Aquinas begins the consideration of Christ in his mysteries with question 27,[1] or as he puts it "those things which our Saviour, who is God in our flesh, himself did and suffered." This consideration of Christ proceeds according to a fourfold dynamic: *ingressus*, *progressus*, *exitus*, and *exaltatio*. The unfolding of the life of Christ in this world follows the same order as the unfolding of creation. At the same time, Jesus traces the path we must follow with him to return with him to the heart of the Trinity.

According to Jean-Pierre Torrell, the consideration of Christ in his mysteries is intentionally ordered by an "anti-Docetic" concern: "Ce n'est pas pour rire que le Verbe a pris chair, mais en vérité ... ."[2] This is what we have been calling Aquinas' concern to lead those who will preach and hear confessions to know the Christian message in its appropriate concreteness without recourse to fables and non-biblical *exempla*. Aquinas intends the consideration of Christ in his mysteries to both order and model a theologically fruitful preaching of the Scriptures. The goal is to proceed to a theological investigation of the princi-

1 This felicitous expression is taken from Jean-Pierre Torrell, *Le Christ en ses mystères* (Paris, 1999), 1: 1.

2 Ibid., 89–90.

pal events that marked the existence of the Word made flesh and to uncover their exemplary and efficient causality for our salvation, both of which continue to this day. The two "rules" developed in the first twenty-six questions, i.e., that the humanity of Christ has a unique dignity which makes it the principle of grace and that the humanity of Christ is empowered by grace to fulfill its revealing and reconciling mission, are rigorously applied in the biblical Christology. Nothing in Christ's life is without theological significance.

Aquinas therefore proposes a "re-lecture," a reading again, of the Gospels in light of what has been presented concerning Christ in the first twenty-six questions.[3] This involves a complex practice of both dialectical and rhetorical methods, such that more than in any other part of the *Summa theologiae*, the character of Aquinas' theology as a spiritual exercise ordered to personal transformation is evident. The terrain often seems more exegetical and homiletical than properly systematic. For the most part, Aquinas cites patristic sources in his *respondeo*, providing avenues for further reflection by means of arguments from *convenientia*. If we understand this practice in light of the concern to guide preachers to the proper consideration of Christ's concrete humanity, we discover just how rich this practice is, especially in his choice of authors and in his choice of mysteries to consider. Thomas presents a model of a systematic theology that is shaped by historical particularity to great effect.

Our case study in this chapter considers the unfolding (*progressus*) of Christ's life in the world. As in the last chapter, we are not so much concerned with the content of Aquinas' teaching as with its rhetorical and pedagogical elements.[4] The consideration of Christ in his manner of living proceeds along an itinerary (*ductus*) of six questions:

1. Christ's manner of living among men (question 40)
2. The temptation of Christ (question 41)
3. The teaching of Christ (question 42)
4. Christ's miracles (questions 43 to 45)
    a) In general (question 43)
    b) In particular (question 44)
    c) His transfiguration (question 45)

3 Ibid., 16.

4 The content of Aquinas' teaching has been amply commented upon by Torrell in the two volumes of *Le Christ en ses mystères*; see also his more recent work in *Encyclopédie Jésus le Christ chez saint Thomas d'Aquin* (Paris, 2008).

Each of these questions exhibits the same structure, comprised of exactly four articles. The first article asks "*an sit?*" the question for judgment, and thus establishes that there is a particular mystery to be understood. The following three articles explore the intelligibility of that mystery. Neither before nor after this section do we find this regular structure. Aquinas feels quite free elsewhere to multiply articles as the needs of a question dictate. As we have noted, the repetition of a regular structure is a common memorial practice.

Christ's Manner of Living

In order to understand this section of the consideration of Christ in his mysteries, it is important to recognize that the first article of question 40 proposes a kind of global or "encompassing" reason of fittingness for the whole section. Christ's manner of life must be fitting to the finality of the Incarnation. This encompassing argument from fittingness is signaled metonymically by the *sed contra* from Baruch 3. More than just a convenient proof-text relying on the phrase "God has appeared on the earth and dwelt with men," the passage as a whole is a poetic praise of Wisdom designed to evoke desire for God's Wisdom in the hearts of Israel. Here, the passage identifies Christ with Wisdom and constitutes an appeal to *pathos* (affect) to dispose the student positively to the figure of Christ the teacher of wisdom.

Aquinas supports this "global fittingness" by three rhetorical *exempla*, that is, three inductive appeals without the full induction worked out. Each of these three *exempla* thus invites the student's own creative *inventio* or discovery. The first *exemplum* juxtaposes Christ's own testimony as to the final cause of his coming in John 18 (metonymically represented by John 18:37) with his testimony to his manner of living in Luke 4 (represented by Luke 4:43). John 18 recounts Jesus' trial before Pilate, and the fragment of verse 37 concludes in the biblical text with the words "... whoever seeks truth listens to my voice." Luke's retelling of Jesus' ministry in Capernaum in chapter four climaxes in verse 43, which is immediately followed by the words " ... and he preached in the synagogues of Judea." The juxtaposition of both testimonies invites the student to bring together what Jesus said with what he did and to discover and dwell upon their congruence. It is thus an exhortation to listen to Christ as an authentic preacher.

The second *exemplum* is epideictic, using praise to present Jesus as a model to be imitated, and relies on the testimony of respected authorities on preaching, namely the Apostle Paul and John Chrysostom, the preaching expertise of whom, recognized by everyone, testifies to the truth of their witness. This is, of course, the rhetorical appeal to *ethos*, and Aquinas employs it to call for an imitation of Christ. The third and final *exemplum* is a cause-effect commonplace inviting contemplation of Christ's behavior. Christ's way of welcoming sinners effects their conversion. This *exemplum* also functions as an epideictic appeal.

This global *convenientia* shares elements of the special political topic of the advantageous and disadvantageous and the special epideictic topic of praise and blame. As political, it is hortatory and calls the student to a decision or choice. As epideictic, it appeals to the affect to promote conversion and a shift of horizon. Like his confrères, Thomas sees in Christ's manner of life and preaching the founding of the Dominican order.[5] The manner of Christ's living is directly relevant to learning the way of life of a Friar Preacher, and choosing to enter more deeply into a consideration of the *progressus* of this life moulds the young Dominican more and more into the image of Wisdom Incarnate by which he can participate personally and autonomously in God's *sacra doctrina* as it is mediated in history by the Church (and by the Dominican order). The order of the three inductions is particularly interesting: exhortation to listen to Christ, invitation to imitate him, and presentation of Christ's manner of living for deeper contemplation. In the replies to the objections, in addition to overturning error, Thomas draws out specific conclusions that can be brought forward from the *exempla* of the *respondeo*, although by no means exhausting the inductive power of the *convenientia*. The reply to the second objection is an *analepsis* to the *Secunda secundae* and its discussion of the mixed contemplative and active life as the best form of religious life. The reply to the third objection is particularly interesting, featuring three further *exempla* from Scripture proposing Christ as a model for preachers to imitate.

In article 2 of question 40 Aquinas continues the political and epideictic exploration of Christ's manner of living, by asking whether Christ ought to have led a more austere life. The metonymy of the *sed contra* appeals to Matthew 11, where Christ highlights the "perversity of this generation" who are like

5 See Richard Newhauser, "Jesus as the First Dominican? Reflections on a Sub-Theme in the Exemplary Literature of Some Thirteenth-Century Preachers," and Ulrich Horst, "Christ, *Exemplar Ordinis Fratrum Praedicantium*, According to Saint Thomas Aquinas," in *Christ Among the Medieval Dominicans*, ed. Kent Emery, Jr. and Joseph Wawrykow, Notre Dame Conferences in Medieval Studies 7 (Notre Dame, IN, 1998), 238–255 and 256–270, respectively.

"children playing in the square" convinced neither by John's austerity nor by Jesus' feasting. The climax of this passage, of course, is Christ's statement that "Wisdom is revealed as Wisdom in her children." The *respondeo* proposes a simple enthymeme that begins with a universal commonplace. It is most fitting that the one who wishes to live with others conform himself to their manner of living. This commonplace is confirmed by Paul's behavior among the Corinthians (again an appeal to *ethos*) and Thomas therefore draws the conclusion that it was most fitting that Christ adopt the food and drink of those with whom he dwelt. It is crucial to recognize that this argument is a rhetorical enthymeme moving from general to specific by means of an example as its middle term. Such an argument is a meditative *ductus* with affective as well as aesthetic properties appealing to the whole person. Accordingly, it is not a logical construct.

In his solutions to the objections Thomas once again proposes behaviors to be adopted or attitudes to be emulated as a result of being convinced by the foregoing enthymeme. These are temperance and spiritual detachment and a rhythm of life that combines periods of abstinence with living like those the Friar Preacher wishes to serve. The replies also praise Christ's desire to be with sinners, pointing out that he did not need abstinence to purify his relationship with his own body, and implying that the abstinence of the Friar Preacher is for the sake of a return to help sinners. The solution to the third objection once again invites the student to a more contemplative stance.

The import and meaning of Christ's poverty consumed much theological speculation and polemical writing in the second half of the thirteenth century. It was precisely the charge that the mendicant orders falsified the poverty of Christ and his apostles which the secular masters at Paris brought in the renewed controversy of the late 1260s during Thomas' second regency. The question of the benefit and use of evangelical poverty also consumed the mendicant orders themselves both between Franciscans and Dominicans and within the Franciscan order itself as the controversy between spirituals and conventuals raged, prompted by the famous question: did Christ own property? In article 3 Aquinas finds a solution to this controversial topic. In the *sed contra* he proposes an appeal to *pathos*, that is, an appeal to the student's sympathies and imagination through Jerome's commentary on two Gospel passages: the story of the rich young man ("... the son of man has nowhere to lay his head") and the story of the temple tax ("... go to the sea ..."). The Dominican students addressed by Aquinas have given up everything to follow Christ and were thus disposed to be moved by this appeal.

Aquinas' response builds on this with four different arguments. The first is an appeal to fittingness highlighting the congruence of poverty with itinerant preaching. This first argument is also hortatory, presenting Christ and the apostles as models to be imitated. The second argument is a comparison of degree between the pairs "Christ's bodily death – our eternal (spiritual) life" and "Christ's bodily poverty – our spiritual riches"; this argument also appeals to *pathos* by evoking our gratitude. The third argument is an appeal to authority that also connects with Dominic's insight into the need to imitate the poverty of the Albigensian preachers: if Christ had possessed riches, he might have been accused of preaching for personal gain. The fourth and final argument is an aesthetic appeal to the contrast between Christ's humanity and his divinity: the more deprived Christ's human living, the more his divine identity can shine through.

Question 40 reaches its *skopos* with article 4: did Christ live according to the Law? The *respondeo* is rather short, simply giving four reasons (without supporting arguments) that affirm that Christ wished to live according to the Law. It is the solutions to the objections that do the hard work, overturning objections grounded in particular instances of Christ's seeming to break the Law. Aquinas performs a refutation, that part of a "speech" where the reasons of one's opponents are overturned as part of the process of convincing one's audience to accept one's point as true and good. The whole of question 40 can thus be conceived as a theological address to young Dominicans to convince them to allow themselves to be shaped by Christ's manner of living, using various rhetorical exercises to promote their conversion and assent. If Christ did not follow the Law, this might call into question his status as a model to be imitated, and so he must be shown not to be a Law-breaker, especially since the Law was God's gift to Israel and the Church.[6]

Refutatio can be performed by appeals to *logos* (reason), *pathos* (affect and imagination), *ethos* (character), and wit. The solution to the first objection concerns Christ's healing the paralytic on the Sabbath and appeals to Christ's own *logos* on the occasion: keeping the Sabbath does not forbid doing God's work; the Sabbath does not prohibit works of mercy (i.e., saving works); it does not prohibit those works belonging to the divine *cultus*, in this case the paralytic's

6 We should also note here that in the *Secunda secundae*, Aquinas spends a great deal of time showing how Christ fulfills the Law. For a helpful commentary on this question, see Matthew Levering, *Christ's Fulfillment of Torah and Temple: Salvation According to Thomas Aquinas* (Notre Dame, IN, 2002).

carrying of his bedroll is to God's praise. The solution to the second objection reconciles the seeming opposition between Christ declaring that all foods are clean with the Law's declaration that some foods are unclean. The reconciliation is found in an appeal to *ethos*, namely Augustine's authoritative expertise in the area of symbolism. The Law declares pork to be unclean and lamb to be clean according to a certain symbolism, but in themselves, as proclaimed by Christ, pork and lamb are good by virtue of their creation by God. The solution to the third objection once again appeals to Christ's own argument on the occasion of his disciples' picking corn on the Sabbath: genuine necessity (as in this case, from hunger) does not lead to breaking the Law.

The Temptation of Christ

Christ's manner of living is to be praised, and suggestions that he is a Lawbreaker have been refuted. But why was he tempted? Does this not suggest some weakness in Him and some reason not to follow Him? The whole of question 41 functions, like question 40, as a form of hortatory and epideictic discourse with the events of Christ's temptation in the desert functioning as examples to be imitated. The mysteries involved are presented as exercising exemplary causality in the moral order.

Aquinas appeals throughout to the progress of the Christian in the spiritual life. In the spirit of *tradere aliis contemplata*, he presents a template for interpreting one's own spiritual life and for accompanying others through the sacrament of reconciliation. He places emphasis squarely on conversion or what has been called in classic spiritual theology "the way of purgation."

In article 1 Thomas establishes that Christ wished to be tempted for four complementary reasons: to establish his victory over temptations as the principle of our victory over temptation, just as his death is the saving principle that overcomes our death; to provide a cautionary reminder that the enemy preys most on the holiest; to teach us how to overcome the enemy's temptations; to teach us to trust his mercy. Each one of these reasons is supported by a metonymy from either a scriptural or patristic source, sometimes from both. Aquinas encourages the student to recall the texts and link them together. The solutions to the objections, as in question 40, establish basic hermeneutical principles for interpreting key elements of the narrative of Christ's temptations. After the overall *convenientia* of the mystery has been established, Aquinas asks about the fittingness of the location (the desert) and timing (after a forty-day fast) of the temptations. The reasons for fittingness that he offers point to the pedagogical value of Christ's example, which establishes the importance of times of retreat into solitude and the practices of fasting.

Article 4 is the *skopos* of the question and stands out for a number of reasons. First, Aquinas offers no less than seven objections to the fittingness of the kind and order of the temptations undergone by Christ. His *respondeo* relies on Scripture and on Gregory the Great and Augustine, each an acknowledged master of the spiritual life in the Middle Ages. Aquinas adopts without comment Gregory's sophisticated account of how the enemy proceeds to tempt a soul by progressing from lesser to greater sins. He closes his response with a quote from Leo the Great that alludes to the soteriological purpose of the Incarnation: Satan, who had entrapped human beings by vainglory, is vanquished by the humility of a human being. Finally, each objection receives a significant solution, each one diagnosing a particular kind of sinfulness or addressing a specific spiritual difficulty (the seventh addresses a problem of scriptural interpretation). Each of these becomes a helpful maxim for the student, both for his own spiritual life and for the formation of conscience in the sacrament of reconciliation. There are echoes here of the wider tradition of spiritual theology, such as Gregory of Nyssa's *Life of Moses*, and, closer to Aquinas' own day, the writings of the Victorines.

Questions 40 and 41 establish Christ as an authentic teacher of the spiritual life and as a wise rhetor in the Ciceronian mould. Christ is an authoritative teacher because his own life has been holy and authentically human. At the same time, his manner of life and his victory over temptation are soteriological principles of our own spiritual living, and his choices serve as examples to be followed. The text thus works at three levels: the systematic (the theological account of Christ's causality, and the development of particular hermeneutical principles for reading the Scriptures), the epideictic (here is a life to be praised, listen to him), and the hortatory (follow his example and practices). On the basis of this authority of Christ's authentic human living, Aquinas now turns to Christ's teaching and miracles.

Christ's Teaching

If question 41 suggests elements of the purgative way, questions 42 to 44 suggest a turn to the illuminative. While question 42 continues to make use of scriptural and patristic metonymies, the focus shifts to the mission of the preacher imitating Christ. This includes discerning one's place as a disciple sent by Christ, giving glory to Christ, and testifying to his power by simply being a preacher.[7] But the truly interesting breakthrough comes with article 4, which considers whether Christ ought to have written anything down. Aquinas compares Jesus' practice as a teacher to that of Socrates and Pythagoras. Like them, Jesus chose not to write anything down. As Jean-Pierre Torrell points out, this is a telling point in a culture that is still mainly oral.[8] Our understanding of memorial culture shaped by the practices of rhetoric can develop Torrell's insight much further.

Aquinas received, as part of his general education, a traditional understanding of the place and role of writing in the transmission of culture and learning. Written texts are memory aids, and memory is the place where persons are shaped by experience. The focus of the article on "writing directly on the heart" is not merely biblical. It is an allusion to the rhetorical concern for *punctus*, for "wounding" the heart and mind through the use of powerful symbols. In reply to the first objection that highlights the role of written texts as memory aids, Aquinas does not deny the rhetorical truth of this position but merely the theological error that the objection makes, namely that it forgets the link between Head and members. The writing of the disciples is not independent of Christ, and it is Christ the Head writing down in his members that which must be handed on (*traditio*).

Aquinas' inaugural lecture is key at this point, especially for the significance of teachers as mediators in the process of *sacra doctrina*. Christ's choice to not write anything calls forth mediators in the Church whose vocation is to make the teaching live. This decision fits wisely into God's overall plan of salvation. Thomas gives the young Dominican student a sense of the purpose of his vocation as a preacher and offers Christ as a model to imitate.

Christ's Miracles in General and in Particular

Article 1 of question 43 inquires into the fittingness of Christ's accomplishing miracles. The focus in this question shifts slightly. The concern is still illuminative, but Aquinas' practice is closer to that of other parts of the *Summa*, as a systematic concern comes to the fore. How is the student to think correctly about the miracles and preach correctly about them? In article 2 of this question Aquinas develops the principles of Leo the Great in his *Tome* to Flavian on the two natures in Christ into a rule of exegesis for the miracles in the

7 Thomas Aquinas, *Summa theologiae* 3.42.1 ad 2.
8 Torrell, *Encyclopédie Jésus le Christ*, 679.

Gospels. Although the miracles display Christ's divine power, just as the suffering of Christ displays his genuine humanity, nevertheless both natures act in communion with each other. The human nature acts as instrumental cause in the miracles, and here Aquinas provides an *analepsis* to his earlier discussion of these matters in the *Tertia pars*.[9]

In article 3 Thomas establishes a rule for understanding the purpose of Christ's miracles. "Christ worked miracles in order to confirm His doctrine, and in order to show forth His Divine power." This rule provides a consistent exegetical principle for preaching and is designed to overcome the tendency to equate miracles with magic. This article thus provides a theological and pastoral response to the material religiosity that marked the breakdown of pastoral practice in the rapidly urbanizing Christian West.[10] This argument prefigures the position Aquinas takes on the role and purpose of the sacraments in Christian living. In the reply to the first objection, he also points out that this understanding of miracles provides us with a helpful way to distinguish canonical from non-canonical gospels. The non-canonical gospels offer wonders for the sake of wonder, as opposed to miracles that testify to the teaching and identity of Jesus the Christ while preserving his genuine humanity.

Article 4 is, as we have seen in the previous questions in this case study, the *skopos* of the question. After he has established that the miracles serve a specific purpose, Aquinas shows that they accomplish this purpose fittingly. This fittingness takes the form of three converging reasons, each one presented as a metonymy of one or more Scriptural passages. Once again, the rhetorical structure calls for a meditation on the whole in its concreteness. The miracles bring together divine power and personal authority, as well as witness to the truth of a teaching. This nexus of reasons forms a theological hermeneutic for understanding any miracle, and serves as a memory structure for directing the interpretation of any miracle account in its evangelical context by positing the following questions: How does it show forth divine power? How does it reveal Christ's personal authority? What teaching does it come to confirm?

After he has considered the miracles in general, Aquinas turns in question 44 to their classification. Materially, this question presents some significant structural differences from the other questions in the treatment of Christ's man-

9 This occurs at question 19. This basic position will play a significant role in the next chapter, where we will have an opportunity to explore it further.

10 See Chapter 3, above.

ner of living. First, it does not have a *ductus* like the others. The other questions move from a first article establishing the nature of a miracle through reasons of fittingness and through examination of relevant details to a *skopos* in the fourth article. The four articles that make up question 44 classify the miracles in terms of their fittingness with respect to the whole cosmos: miracles over spiritual creatures, miracles over heavenly bodies, miracles involving human beings, and finally miracles over non-rational creatures.

In addition, question 44 offers the shortest and most succinct responses in this part of the *Summa theologiae*. In each case, a single terse reason of fittingness is offered to serve as a trope or maxim for each class of miracle. The miracles over demons show the purpose of Christ's mission. The reactions of the heavenly bodies recorded particularly by Matthew are proportioned to revealing his identity as creator of all. His miracles involving human beings show him to be the Savior, while the miracles over irrational creatures show the submission of all creation to him. With these four interpretive principles, a student has four simple tropes that serve as interpretive principles for any miracle story. In each case, the trope prevents once again the confusion flowing from the material religiosity that threatens to derail the spirituality of many of those to whom Aquinas' students will preach, and distinguishes miracles from magic. Each article in this question also offers the longest and most detailed replies to objections of the entire treatise. Aquinas reaches the point of highest concreteness and detail and meets specific exegetical difficulties. All of these material differences signal that with this question we have reached a significant *skopos* of the illuminative *ductus* of the whole section.

The Transfiguration

Question 44 represents a significant *skopos* in the itinerary through the consideration of Christ's manner of living and perhaps even a kind of final destination. In order to explain how Thomas' consideration of the Transfiguration adds to the *ductus* of the *Summa*, it is helpful to broaden our perspective and compare the four divisions of Aquinas' consideration of Christ in his mysteries. The consideration of Christ's *ingressus* into the world culminates in the baptism of Jesus at the Jordan, which Aquinas treats as an epiphany revealing Christ's identity. The consideration of Christ's *exitus* from this world in his passion and death culminates in the harrowing of hell, which Aquinas again explains as a revelation of Christ's identity and power. Finally, the consideration of Christ's *exaltatio* culminates with Christ sitting at God's right hand exercising power and judgment. In each case, there is a theological theophany centered on the person of Christ.

The Transfiguration serves the same purpose in the *ductus* of the consideration of Christ's manner of living. The way through these mysteries was first purgative and then solidly illuminative. It culminates here in a mystery of light where, just as at the baptism, the Father and the Spirit testify to the identity of the Son. In this particular case, the miracle of the Transfiguration reveals the final cause of the Son's mission and prepares the apostles for the passion. It teaches in itself (as opposed to testifying to the truth of Christ's teaching like other miracles) and specifically strengthens the theological virtue of hope, i.e., the confidence that although the way be arduous, the goal is achievable by God's grace.

The question on the Transfiguration exhibits the four-article structure and *ductus* common to the consideration of Christ's manner of living. Article 1 considers the fittingness of the Transfiguration itself to establish "an sit?" The *respondeo* is a rhetorical itinerary that links together a number of Scriptural passages. This way of proceeding is akin to that of a classroom *lectio*, which was the kind of commentary on Scripture practiced by Thomas every morning in Paris and Naples. Here, the text being commented upon is Matthew's account of the Transfiguration, which Aquinas cites in the *sed contra*. The method consists of interpreting the Gospel text by means of other Scriptural texts.

This article also makes use of *prolepses* to the consideration of the mystery of the resurrection and to the study of the four qualities of resurrected bodies, which would have occurred at the end of the *Tertia pars* according to Aquinas' plan. There is also a *prolepsis* that links the Transfiguration with Christ's suffering and with our own path, through a metonymic reference to Acts 14. The whole article establishes a kind of creative tension between transfiguration, passion, resurrection, hope for the apostles, and hope for us now. This interpretive framework provides many possibilities for preaching on the mystery, and it also proposes some basic points of pastoral psychology around the theological virtue of hope. The whole article functions at multiple levels. Finally, the article makes links to other mysteries of Christ's manner of living through the exploration of specific qualities of resurrected bodies: when Christ walked on water, he was showing hints of the agility of resurrected bodies; the Virgin Birth testified remotely to their subtility; while the miraculous escape from those who wished to throw Him over the brow of the cliff at Nazareth shows evidence of the impassibility of resurrected bodies. Christ's manner of living revealed the resurrection as final cause of his mission, but the Transfiguration, unlike the other miracles, shows this not in a work but in Christ's very person. It is thus the most complete and fitting witness to the purpose of Christ's mission. Again, Aquinas provides an interpretive grid for explaining the Transfiguration to the faithful and applying the mystery to the pastoral care of urban medieval Christians.

Following upon article 1, article 2 specifies a further interpretive stance that seeks to overturn other opinions. Aquinas, as he inquires into the light of glory that shone from the transfigured Christ, seeks to preserve certain basic principles of his Christology, namely Christ's existence as a genuine *viator* with a genuinely human body. This is in response to the wider context of Docetic or Gnostic presentations of this mystery. This article has a particularly long *respondeo*. In it, Aquinas establishes that the miracle is not that the light of glory shines through Christ's body in this event. As he has pointed out earlier in his Christology of the *Tertia pars*, the light of glory which accompanies the beatific knowing of Christ ought to have been flowing into Christ's body from the beginning of the Incarnation, but was miraculously prevented from doing so in order that the Incarnate Word might fulfill his mission. The Transfiguration is thus not a miracle but the temporary suspension of a miracle for the sake of the same mission and specifically to strengthen the witnesses for what lay ahead.

After he has established the nature of the Transfiguration, Thomas explores the theological significance of the witnesses in article 3. This article is rich in patristic and scriptural resources. It places Jesus squarely at the centre of salvation history: both those who went before Christ (Elijah and Moses) and those who followed him (Peter, James, and John) needed to be reassured and offered hope that the Cross was the more fitting way of bringing about God's Reign.

It is once again article 4 that serves as the *skopos* of the question, which contain a number of interesting rhetorical features. First, Aquinas in this article makes explicit the link between Christ's baptism and his Transfiguration. He uses a simple analogical structure to link the two mysteries at multiple levels. As the gift of grace is to the light of glory, so is the Father's testimony at Christ's baptism to the Father's testimony at the Transfiguration. Our actual adoption at baptism is also related to the fulfillment of this adoptive filiation in the future, which fulfillment is efficiently mediated to us in the mystery of the Transfiguration. In other words, Christ as human before his death in this moment of Transfiguration is an efficient cause of our coming to the light of glory. This does not deny the efficiency of other mysteries, especially that of Christ's resurrection, in our own resurrection and communion with God. It locates the efficient causality of Christ's humanity in a complex web of intelligibility.

It is helpful in this context to notice the significance of the theme of the *Imago Dei* in the Transfiguration. One of the objections in article 1 had raised the question of Christ's body as *figura*, and here in article 4 Thomas' *respondeo* articulates the relation between grace and glory by means of the notion of our resemblance to the *Imago* Incarnate. As we have seen the fourfold *ductus* from vestige, through image, through resemblance by grace to *Imago* made flesh is the narrative of spiritual development that orders the *Summa theologiae* as a Christo-formative pedagogy that brings students into a closer personal conformity to Divine Wisdom, thus enabling them to be autonomous preachers and confessors responding to new pastoral and cultural challenges. At the Transfiguration, Christ's body showed forth the full truth of his identity as *Imago Dei* and Wisdom. At that moment, his body participated fully in *sacra doctrina*, not in an operation but in its very being. The student who considers the mystery along the *ductus* of the *Summa* comes into an even greater personal conformity to the *Imago*, to Wisdom Incarnate. The theological consideration of the mystery thus functions, within the narrative of spiritual development of the *Summa*, in the same way that the historical event of the Transfiguration functioned for Peter, James, and John. The historical event prepared the three apostles for the passion and made them apt teachers of the other apostles and of all the disciples after the resurrection. The theological consideration of the mystery points the young Dominican students to the passion and resurrection and makes of them autonomous preachers and confessors responding to the call of Lateran IV.[11]

Conclusion: Wise Living as Imitatio Christi

The consideration of Christ in his manner of living, if we consider it strictly along the subjective pole of *sacra doctrina* as understood by Jean-Pierre Torrell, articulates a twofold understanding of the mystery. First, it brings to light how Christ's manner of living and teaching, along with his miracles, are efficient and exemplary principles of our own salvation. Second, our case study has

11 We should note, at this point, that this conformity to Christ is also a being conformed to the Trinity, and that it is not insignificant that it is precisely with the Transfiguration, which like the baptism is a revelation of the whole Trinity, that Aquinas makes his point about the relation between grace and glory; see J.P. Torrell's commentaries for a more complete discussion.

shown that Aquinas deploys a large number of rhetorical techniques associated with memory to propose a heuristic structure for interpreting the ministry of Christ in preaching. This heuristic structure also proposes a number of patristic and scriptural resources for interpreting the Gospels. These resources can be ordered in one's memory by the very tropes and maxims proposed in the questions.

We have also shown that these rhetorical techniques call for a personal performance from the student, a performance which has affective, memorial, intellectual, and contemplative dimensions. The student is called to listen, observe, and imitate Christ. The consideration of the mystery is thus a transformative exercise whereby the mind is conformed to the mystery of Christ's manner of living, and in being conformed to the mystery participates more closely in the Divine Wisdom that orders *sacra doctrina*. The student is thus enabled to preach and reconcile as Christ did, and on his own personal authority.

This transformative exercise has a particular *ductus*. Christ's manner of living is shown to be that of a wise teacher in the classical (Ciceronian) mode, and examples that might call this into question are refuted. Christ is established as a model to be imitated through a combination of epideictic and political rhetoric. In a number of places, appeal is made to affect through *pathos*, which disposes the student positively and evokes desire for Christ. The *theoria* of Christ's teaching is then presented for contemplation, and its confirmation by miracles established. The proper relation between teaching and miracles is brought to light. The mind of the student now holds, precisely as a purely spiritual structure of understanding, the truth of Christ's manner of teaching, and can order the meaning of Scripture for himself. He is, in this dimension at least, in the image of Divine Wisdom.

This *ductus* is also a narrative of spiritual progress from conversion (purgation) to growing in likeness (illumination). Elements of the consideration of the mystery invite reflection on one's own spiritual progress, as well as offering an understanding of how particular practices can contribute to that progress. The student thus becomes a more Christ-like confessor who can meet the spiritual and pastoral difficulties of a rapidly urbanizing church with his own wisdom, and can deploy that same wisdom to help others progress in the Christian life.

The explicit use of the language of image and resemblance in the treatment of the Transfiguration and the links established rhetorically in this final question to the other mysteries of Christ's life as well as with key parts of the

Summa as a whole (especially, the overall narrative of spiritual development that orders its whole itinerary) confirms the importance of these questions as spiritual exercises. More than just a presentation of the mystery in itself, and more than an explanation of the Dominican charism of preaching and hearing confessions by reference to Christ and the apostles, these questions aim to further the incorporation of the young Dominican student into that manner of wise living as *imitatio Christi*.

CHAPTER NINE

Knowing the Mystery of Christ's Departure and Exaltation

In chapter eight we followed the itinerary of the consideration of Christ in the mysteries of his public life and highlighted the emergence of a theological grid for reading the Gospels as well as the formative character of the questions. In this chapter we treat questions 46 to 59 of the *Tertia pars*, which explore the saving mysteries of Christ's death and resurrection, or "the manner in which Christ left this world" and "the manner of His exaltation." The seven questions in the consideration of Christ's death divide into two groups: questions 46 to 49 and questions 50 to 52. Question 46 explores the fittingness of the passion from various perspectives and sets the theological context for what follows. Question 47 asks about the efficient cause of the passion, and question 48 explores its efficient causality. Question 49 inquires into the effects of the passion, bringing the consideration of Christ's dying to a climax. Question 50 introduces the mystery of Christ's being dead in itself. Questions 51 and 52 complete the narrative of Christ's departure from this world by presenting his burial and descent into hell. The two groupings are thus related as becoming to term of change.[1]

The seven questions in the consideration of Christ's exaltation also divide into two groups according to the same principle of becoming and term of change: questions 53 to 57 lead through the resurrection and ascension as movement to God, while questions 58 and 59 consider Christ's sitting at God's right hand and his power of judging as a form of resting in God. Question 53 explores the fittingness of the resurrection in relation to the passion in particular. Questions 54 and 55 examine particular aspects of the resurrection in itself, climaxing in question 56, with its interest in Christ's resurrection as cause of our resurrection and justification. Question 57 on the ascension functions as a kind

1 Thomas Aquinas, *Summa theologiae* 3.50.1.

of pivot or transition between the consideration of Christ's resurrection and his sitting at God's right hand.

It is important to remember that for Aquinas each mystery (passion, death, burial, descent into hell, resurrection, ascension, and so on) is connected to our salvation, and that the order of the mysteries among themselves is also theologically meaningful. My purpose in this chapter is to show how Aquinas seeks to "elevate" his student and reader to a "higher position" that can hold together the saving mysteries of Christ's passion and resurrection in one grasp. This "higher position" is a function of ordering the mysteries to each other in the manner of the wise according to a few basic principles. In addition to the basic division between "becoming" and "term of change", Aquinas throughout these questions will deploy the three pairs of related terms "soul-body", "humiliation-exaltation", and "humanity-divinity" to show the intelligibility of these mysteries.

In order to make this strategy clearer, I shall depart in this chapter from my usual pattern of following the itinerary as Aquinas lays it out, and instead begin with questions 47 and 48 and their discussions of causality. I do this to allow for a discussion of satisfaction in the context of the broader *Summa* and to highlight how efficiency is related to a broader web of theological intelligibility that articulates an understanding of Christ's departure from this world. After considering questions 47 and 48, I will go backwards to 46, and finally proceed to a consideration of questions 49 to 59.

The Passion and Efficient Causality

In question 47 Aquinas explores the efficient causes of Christ's death. Those who condemned him and put him to death are the direct efficient cause of his suffering. Christ is indirectly an efficient cause because he gives his life willingly. His obedience can be regarded as a "fitting" efficient cause that achieves a greater confluence of ends. The Father does deliver the Son but not against the Son's will, which would be impious and cruel. Aquinas takes care to exclude this motivation from consideration of the cross. The Father does not want blood but acts out of love for us. It was fitting that Christ suffer at the hands of both Jews and Gentiles, since his salvation flows to both groups. The last two articles explore the question of responsibility for Christ's suffering and degrees of sinfulness that accrue to his persecutors. Significantly, Aquinas apportions responsibility with tremendous nuance.

In question 48 he inquires into the efficient causality of the passion, and builds a nexus of five terms: merit, satisfaction, sacrifice, ransom, and efficiency. These five terms are ordered to each other by a complex intelligibility. Merit is a term that expresses the causality of Christ's soul in the mystery of the passion. Satisfaction, sacrifice, and ransom are terms that explore the causality of his body in its suffering, and thus, merit is related to these three terms as soul to body. Finally, as we shall see, the first four terms are related to efficiency as humanity to divinity.

Merit

In article 1 Thomas explores the notion of merit. The just and loving man who suffers for justice merits his salvation. The notion of merit has already appeared within its own proper nexus of intelligibility in the theology of grace in the *Prima secundae*. In question 114 article one of the *Prima secundae*, Aquinas discusses merit as a part of justice. It is an act of justice to make a return for the labor of another on one's behalf. In ordinary cases, there is an absolute equality between the laborer and the one who rewards her labor, but in the case of the just order between God and human beings, God is the source through grace of any meritorious good that human beings do. Nevertheless, the good that is done is properly the operation of the human being, and God, who is the source of this order, wishes to preserve it and so grants these operations their just reward. God derives no profit from our labors, which are simply ordered to the manifestation of God's goodness. What God gives as a reward for faithful labor is eternal life, and so the category of merit expresses the elevation of the human soul by grace to communion with God. In this way, the proper context for understanding meritorious acts in this life is the theological virtue of charity, by which we bring our friendship with God to act. Thus, the passion of Christ understood as meritorious expresses the gift of communion with God which it brings to us. Since we are united as Christ's body to Christ our Head, this moral effect of his suffering for justice comes to us as to one man. The passion and the cross are presented as the climax of the whole life of Jesus from his conception. The cross is the most intense expression of this life of friendship with God.

Satisfaction and Sacrifice

In question 48 article two, Thomas places satisfaction squarely in the context of a relationship rooted in love, and satisfaction breaks free of considerations of mere justice. In article three of this question he shows that the satisfaction offered by Christ takes the form of a sacrifice, i.e., an offering of self. Ransom is then understood in article 4 as a metaphor for the satisfaction that frees one from the consequences of a broken relationship. We pass from servitude to the devil to that of our proper Lord, and we are released from the suffering that was a consequence of sin. This is not a literal ransoming because no price is paid to the devil.

Thus, we witness in these three articles a complex intelligibility that holds together charity, satisfaction, and sacrifice. Bernard Lonergan argues that we must understand satisfaction by analogy to the sacrament of reconciliation, an insight which has been confirmed in more recent studies.[2] That analogy, however, has itself a complex intelligibility that needs to be explored. Question 48 provides only a partial clue to this intelligible nexus among charity, satisfaction, and sacrifice. Charity governs satisfaction, and the satisfaction which Christ offers takes the form of sacrifice. This is not all there is, however, because Aquinas' exploration of the passion occurs within a memory structure, which he created rhetorically by the journey through the *ductus* of the *Secunda secundae* of the *Summa theologiae*. A student performing the intellectual tasks proposed by question 48 would insert the familiar terms charity, satisfaction, and sacrifice into this existing structure, which would provide a set of intelligible terms and relations ready-made to serve as an explanatory framework for the passion and the cross. It is to that memory structure that we must now turn.

In order to take a first approximation of the memory structure generated by the *Secunda secundae*, we begin with the fittingness of the Incarnation as presented in question one article two of the *Tertia pars*. Aquinas proposes five reasons for this fittingness based on our furtherance in the good. A close examination reveals that these five reasons represent the path from faith to hope to charity to *imitatio Christi* to communion of natures in one person, which is the development of the *Secunda secundae* that climaxes in the *Tertia*'s Christology. Significantly, there is no consideration of the cardinal virtues at this point. If we look at the five reasons for our greater avoidance of evil which Aquinas

2 See, for example, Jean-Pierre Torrell, *Encyclopédie Jésus le Christ chez saint Thomas d'Aquin* (Paris, 2008); Albert Patfoort, "Le vrai visage de la satisfaction du Christ selon saint Thomas" in *Ordo Sapientiae et Amoris: Hommage au Professeur Jean-Pierre Torrell*, ed. Carlos-Josaphat Pinto de Oliveira (Fribourg, Suisse, 1993), 247–265; Gustaf E.H. Aulen, *Le triomphe du Christ*, Foi vivante 124 (Paris, 1970); Louis Bouyer, *Le fils éternel* (Paris, 1974); Bernard Sesboüé, *Jésus Christ, l'unique médiateur* (Paris, 1988); Matthew Levering, "Juridical Language in Soteriology: Aquinas' Approach," *Angelicum* 80 (2003): 309–326.

offers in the second part of his reply, however, we note that each of these reasons is a promotion from disorder to a cardinal virtue. The first reason highlights a return to justice, and particularly to genuine religion. The second reason also highlights justice, this time doing justice to oneself as possessing a certain dignity. Presumption is overturned by magnanimity, which is related to fortitude. Pride is overturned by humility, a virtue related to temperance. The fifth and final reason is that of a satisfaction that is fitting and proportionate to human existence. Thus, the cardinal virtues are indeed present, but in the ways in which they exist in light of the Incarnation as correctives to and medicine for sin. The cardinal virtues are instruments that serve to specify and express the freedom from sin and the growth in Christ that lead to the *imitatio Christi*. With this in mind, let us look at the intelligible relation between charity and justice in the *Secunda secundae*.

Aquinas uses Aristotle's analysis of the love of friendship to understand the theological virtue of charity. The love of friendship includes three elements: the disposition to desire and work for the good of the other; the mutual reciprocation of this goodwill between the two friends; an actual *communicatio* and *conversatio*, an exchange of concrete goods that express the love of friendship. Aquinas' analysis of charity surpasses his Aristotelian source in two ways. First, charity involves a love of friendship between two unequals (God and the human person). Second, on the basis of this primary friendship we can have genuine love of those who are not equal in virtue (sinners) and those who are our enemies.

In questions 25 and 26 Aquinas examines the object of charity, that is, both what it is to be loved and in what intelligible order it is to be loved. We love God as friend, and the neighbor in herself by charity, but the "in herself" of the neighbor is understood as "what she is in her best self," that is, the friend of God (3.25.1). Sinners are loved by charity as still capable of beatitude, although they are "hated" qua sinners (25.6). Thomas clarifies this "hatred" of the sinner in his reply to the first objection in article 6. To hate their evil and desire their good have the same motivation, namely that they should flourish in beatitude, so that to hate their evil is, in fact, to love them with the love of charity and to work for their conversion.

Aquinas' analysis in question 25 article 8 on the love of enemies is particularly relevant to our inquiry and deserves careful exegesis. We do not love enemies in their "enemy-nature," that is, we do not love them because of, or by reason of, their enmity. This would be perverse, because it would constitute loving the evil of others or valuing an objective disvalue. We do love them on the basis of their humanity and dignity as loved by God. Our enemies are contrary to us as enemies, but not as human and not as capable of communion with God. It is on this basis that we love them. This love of the enemy takes particular forms when it moves to the concrete. On the one hand, charity does not oblige us to love-in-act each and every person in existence, which is impossible. This means that we are under no necessity to actually love each and every enemy. On the other hand, it is a necessary dimension of the disposition which charity is that we be prepared to love a particular enemy, if this is necessary for his well-being. To ensure a person's human survival, for example, is a duty of charity. Beyond necessity in this basic sense, to actually love the particular enemy before me is a function and expression of the perfection or depth of charity in us. Aquinas explores this question further in article nine of question 25,which asks the question: what marks of charity are to be shown to the enemy? Two things are required, namely, to offer those general concrete goods and marks of love which we must offer to every neighbor, i.e., to pray for their well-being and preserve and defend their common good. To refuse to do this constitutes vengeance. We must also offer specific help in case of necessity (famine, medical crises, and so on). Additional marks of friendship are not required but express the perfection of the virtue in us. This is to act so as to get the enemy to love us by doing them good. Love of one's enemy is in this sense more perfect than love of a friend and is a more perfect act of *dilectio*, because the movement of the will demands greater self-transcendence. One loves the enemy as a potential friend, which manifests a deeper and wider-ranging charity.

In question 26 Thomas explores the proper ordering of our loving. He does not establish a rigid logical grid, but rather an ordered series of questions for discernment to help navigate a particular situation, which is a kind of heuristic anticipation of what a well-ordered response looks like in the concrete. In effect, because the goal of the *Summa* is the formation of confessors, this heuristic structure guides the questioning and discernment of such a confessor who is faced with a particular penitent. In article four of question 26 Thomas makes an interesting point in connection with the notion of atonement. The second objection in this article suggests that we ought to love the other more than ourselves, because the book of Proverbs enjoins us to suffer for love of a friend. In the reply to the objection, Aquinas agrees but specifies that this is a form of higher and more spiritual self-love through a perfection of charity.

The notion of friendship is quite broad. Aquinas deploys the terms *amor*, *caritas*, *dilectio*, and *amicitia* with great precision and dexterity. *Caritas* and *dilectio* both translate *agape*. While *caritas* highlights the "dear-ness" and the "to-be-dear-to" dimension of *agape*, *dilectio* brings to light the voluntary character of this love and the movement of the will as spiritual (rather than sensitive) appetite. *Caritas* thus suggests the use of friendship as an explanatory category. This friendship, following Aristotle, exists wherever there is community, that is, a grouping of persons around a common good. There is familial friendship, friendship of citizenship, and so on. The character of friendship then, is not merely intersubjective (me and God) but social. What is opposed to friendship is not the enemy, not the unloved or not chosen, but the stranger, the one outside the common good which binds us together. Every friendship comes into existence and develops around and through a common working for an authentic good. One realizes here the depth which Aquinas' analysis gives to Paul's statement in the Letter to the Ephesians that we are no longer strangers but fellow citizens and members of God's household.

Aquinas defines the moral virtue of justice as follows: it is the "habit whereby a person with a lasting and constant will renders to each his due." The object of the moral virtue of justice is the right or the just, understood in the basic and objective sense as what is objectively due according to a relationship of balance or *aequalitas*, which can be determined by right reason. There is also a subjective meaning, derived from this more basic meaning, according to which to be just is to have the ability to adjust or adapt oneself to the universe and to society by making claims and discharging duties to others. This is a question of discerning and choosing what is proportionately due to the other, a question of being disposed to valuing the other over my own particular pleasure. In this sense, the virtue of justice helps Aquinas articulate the shift from self to other in human moral and spiritual development. In other words, the virtue of justice captures the human reality which Bernard Lonergan expresses by the term moral conversion, and the relation between charity and justice could be analogously construed as the relation between religious and moral conversion.

Within the horizon of justice, the virtue of religion is that habit by which we pay a debt of honor to God and thus establish the proper relationship or order between ourselves and God, as a matter of natural justice. Religion reverences God only under the aspect of being the first principle of creation and of the government of all things. The fitting worship of religion does not attain God strictly speaking. Worship is a natural act, and acts such as offering sacrifice reach God only in the sense that they express due reverence for God. The balance in religion is not absolute, because we cannot give God his due, even if we exclude the complication of original sin. The balance is based on our limited ability and on God's acceptance of our offering.

The essential and principal acts of religion are both interior acts, namely devotion and prayer. Devotion is the willingness to give oneself promptly to those things that pertain to God's service. Prayer expresses our subjection to God as the source of all of our good. The external acts of justice are various ways of expressing our internal devotion. Sacrifice in particular is a fitting mode of expression of tendering honor and submission, because it uses sensible signs proportionate to us: "the exterior sacrifice signifies an interior sacrifice by which the soul offers itself to God." (2–2.85.2) Sacrifice is a matter of natural justice, offered "insofar as God is the principle of its creation and the goal of its happiness." The worth of the sacrifice is not determined by the value of the thing offered, but by the meaning of the more or less total gift of self (85.2 ad 2). The acts of the other virtues can be directed to divine reverence (as, for example, temperance coming to act in fasting): "the act of any virtue assumes the character of sacrifice if it is performed in order to cling to God in spiritual union" (85.3 ad1).

It is within this whole network of intelligible relations that we must understand the meaning of satisfaction. The most basic category for understanding satisfaction is that of reparation, the act whereby the equality of persons is restored. Whatever else Aquinas may be doing in his treatment of justice, in this area he shares the concerns of what contemporary scholars call restorative justice. Reparation is the act that seeks to restore, repair, and renew the social relations between persons. If reparation for injustices involves things, the particular name given to reparation is restitution. If reparation concerns actions and passions, that is, what has been suffered and done (for example, attacking the worth or dignity of a person), then the particular name given to reparation is satisfaction.[3] Satisfaction is a form of making amends, an act of restorative justice that seeks to restore the balance between persons.

How then are we to relate these two virtues intelligibly? In question 23 of the *Secunda secundae* Aquinas outlines two elements of particular interest. First, charity is a governing virtue because it has *imperium* over the moral virtues of prudence, justice, temperance, and fortitude. This means that like the architect who governs the work of stonemasons, sculptors, and carpenters or like God in his provident government of the cosmos, charity sets a new and wider horizon within which the cardinal virtues are deployed, and orders them to each other and to their tasks within that horizon.

3 Thomas Aquinas, *Super Sententiarum* 4.15.1.5 questiuncula 1, corpus.

Charity is also understood in question 23 as the form of the moral virtues, and it is important that we understand the significance of this term. For Aquinas, charity makes faith and hope, the other theological virtues, to be living virtues. Without charity, faith is present but dead. In addition, charity has a vastly different relationship with the moral virtues. Charity and the moral virtues are related as act to potency, e.g., as form to matter. This means that not only are the acts of the moral virtues ordered to a higher final cause in a wider horizon as governed by charity, but they are also the matter which gives concrete specificity to the acts of charity. We can only discern the love intended by the lover in acts that are shaped by prudence, justice, temperance, and fortitude. Thus, if you will, the complex human act shaped by the moral virtues mediates the supernatural love that is its higher intelligibility and its central form. It is like an outer, "sacramental-because-material," expression of an inner word of love.

Justice, in the wider horizon set by charity, takes on a twofold character. Acts of justice are concrete ways of expressing love for God, that is, they are offerings of myself to God out of love. Acts of justice are also specific ways of expressing love of the other. If the other is a friend, then it is as part of the goodwill I have for this friend. If the other is an enemy, then it is as an act of goodwill that seeks to bring a friendship-in-potency to act.

We see then that a complex set of relations emerges from the path we have traveled. Charity and justice (of which both satisfaction and sacrifice are a part) are related as form and matter. Charity elevates justice to a horizon of higher intelligibility, coordinating justice and the other moral virtues and making of them instruments of a higher reality, namely supernatural love for God and neighbor. In turn, justice is the matter that individuates love. In the case of the love of enemy that seeks to make the enemy into a friend, the corresponding act of justice is satisfaction, which restores the balance between persons in the realm of action and passion. When this satisfaction concerns the relation between God and human beings, it takes the form of sacrifice, an offering of self to God that expresses due reverence for God. This offering of self need not take the form of a ritual giving, but can take the form of the act of any virtue performed in order to cling to God. For example, as Aquinas points out in 1–2.113.4 ad 1, the act of mercy shown to a neighbor satisfies for sin, since being merciful to a brother or sister restores honor to God who created and loves the other.

Christ's passion, then, is a genuinely human offering of self to God in an act of genuine religion. This act of religion expresses sorrow for human sin on our behalf and restores us to God's friendship in an act of satisfaction. This satisfaction is the concrete mediation of a supernatural love of friendship for God, and so reaches beyond the mere overturning of sin to reestablish communion between God and us.

Ransom or Deliverance

In articles 4 and 5 of question 48 in the *Tertia pars* Thomas explores the notion of *redemptio*, because it forms a significant part of the Pauline account of the passion. *Redemptio* can be translated variously as "ransom, buying back, deliverance from." Aquinas certainly knows the tradition whereby the passion and the cross are understood as a ransom paid to the devil, but following Augustine and Anselm he firmly rejects this understanding of the term. After noting that the language of *redemptio* is highly metaphorical, he restricts its meaning to deliverance. *Redemptio* brings to light our passage from bondage to the enemy back to service of our rightful Lord, as well as deliverance from our bondage to suffering. Aquinas then connects this passage and this deliverance to satisfaction as effect to cause.

The Efficiency of Christ's Passion

The climax of question 48 is reached with article 6, which explicitly raises the question of the efficiency of the passion. If we recall the treatment of the causality of Christ's humanity in the passion, we may summarize the itinerary of the question as the reconstruction of a complex moral causality of that humanity in itself. Article 6 asks whether this moral causality is also efficient. The answer Aquinas gives harkens back to the beginning of the *Tertia pars*. The principal efficient cause of our salvation is God, but because Christ's humanity is the instrument of his divinity, it follows that "all that Christ does and suffers operates our salvation by mode of instrumentality" (48.6 corp.). The importance of this final article cannot be underestimated. It reaffirms that God is the one who saves us, effecting both our communion with him and our deliverance from bondage. Merit and satisfaction are instruments of this divine power. In this sense, the passion and the cross are connected with all the other saving mysteries of the Incarnation.

The Larger Network of Intelligibility for Understanding the Cross

Efficient causality only answers one kind of question regarding the theological meaning of the passion. In question 46 article 1, Aquinas explores the necessity for the passion and develops the distinctions between different kinds of necessity much more carefully, especially when compared to the treatment of the necessity of the Incarnation in question 1 of the *Tertia pars*.

In the first question of this part Aquinas distinguishes between absolute necessity and necessity of fittingness (the means are more suitable to achieving the end). In question 46, he multiplies the distinctions by a factor of three, from two kinds of necessity to six. There is, first, the absolute necessity that flows from the very structure of reality, where Christ's suffering follows logically and deterministically from the ontological situation. Aquinas states clearly that Christ's suffering is not necessary in this way; there is nothing in the order of the universe that mechanistically determines the event of Christ's passion. He then considers the necessity that follows upon the action of an exterior cause. An efficient cause would result in a necessity of constraint. Christ's suffering does not fall under this kind of necessity either. The Father's will in sending the Son is not constrained by created causes but is a free choice of love. The Son chooses freely to suffer, and he is therefore not constrained because the definition of constraint is precisely the action of a cause that goes against the will of the one suffering, even though his persecutors arrest him, flog him, force him to appear before Roman justice, and condemn him to death.

The exterior cause, however, can be a final cause, creating a necessity from the end. If the end cannot be achieved at all except by this means, then we have recovered a kind of absolute necessity. Again, Aquinas points out that Christ's suffering is not of this kind, because God remains free to save us in any way God wants. This leaves the necessity of fittingness, where the end is achieved better by the means under consideration. Aquinas argues that the necessity of Christ's suffering is of this kind, and proposes three kinds of fittingness, each one flagged by a metonymic citation from Scripture: with respect to us, with respect to Christ, and with respect to God.

With respect to us, there is the necessity adduced by John 3:14–15, "The Son of man must be lifted up, that whoever believes in Him may not perish, but may have life everlasting." If we remember, since this is a metonymy, that the whole passage represented is the nighttime conversation between Jesus and Nicodemus, we notice two things. First, the language of lifting up is part of John's pattern of vertical descent and ascent, which is a language of conversation and communion between God and his human creatures. Second, the speech by Jesus positively excludes condemnation as part of God's desires or motives. Those who are condemned are condemned by their own refusal to believe. Our contemplation is directed away from the passion as involving God's desire to condemn and towards God's desire for communion and friendship.

The second reason of fittingness is with respect to Christ himself, "who merited the glory of being exalted, through the lowliness of His Passion." Aquinas cites Luke 24:26: "Ought not Christ to have suffered these things, and so to enter into His glory?" This represents the story of the disciples on the way to Emmaus, and the citation introduces Jesus' explanation of the cross in light of the entire Hebrew Scriptures. Christ's death and resurrection express a pattern that is reproduced again and again in the Hebrew Scriptures, a pattern of humiliation and exaltation by which Israel turns to God and recovers the covenant relationship with God.

Finally, Aquinas offers a reason of fittingness with respect to God, who has arranged the history of salvation so that it might come to this point. This appeal to fittingness is an appeal to God's wisdom and providence which has achieved our salvation in a way that yields much fruit. Accordingly, Aquinas cites two scriptural sources, Luke 22:22 and Luke 24:44 and 46. Luke 22 is from the Last Supper, and shows that Judas' betrayal is not outside of God's purview; Luke 24:44–46 is part of Jesus' last instructions to the Twelve and highlights the surplus that flows from the death and rising of Jesus. Repentance is preached to all the nations, and the power from on high (the Holy Spirit) will soon come to the community to empower them to go out.

Aquinas' treatment in this article achieves three key ends. First, he brings us to the contemplation of the passion as showing forth in a better and more fruitful way God's and Christ's love for us. Second, he maps out the points he will explore in the questions on the passion, which we will examine below. Third, perhaps most interestingly, he introduces a series of negations and exclusions which will be repeated throughout the treatment of the passion. These exclusions imprint upon us what the passion and cross are not, namely a reality rooted in God's desire for revenge or punishment.

Beginning with article 2, Aquinas explores key aspects of the fittingness elucidated in the first article. Aquinas recalls what he already proposed at the beginning of the *Tertia pars*, that speaking purely and simply in the absolute, the passion (like the Incarnation) is not necessary for our salvation, since God can free us by other means. The reply to objection three is significant. The objection raises the question of God's requiring satisfaction, and in his reply, Aquinas states that it is true that objectively speaking, God's honor has been wounded, and this, again objectively speaking, requires objective restoration to remedy the disorder introduced into reality. A third-party judge, faced with this situation, would rule that some kind of satisfaction was required. An earthly prince who was harmed, however, could forgive the offence against him without requiring satisfaction. In point of fact, God is in the same situation: he can forgive without receiving satisfaction, and as the supreme governor of the cosmos, his forgiveness would make the relationship whole, simply by his creative word. There must be some reason of fittingness, then, for the passion and cross.

In article 3 of question 46 Thomas addresses this issue with the principle that a means is all the more fitting when a greater number of advantages accrue from it. The passion of Christ, in addition to freeing us from sin, reveals God's love, shows us an example of the human virtues necessary for salvation, merits right relationship with God and communion in beatitude (our authentic end), elicits or evokes greater participation and effort from us in our own salvation, and redounds to our greater dignity (here Aquinas repeats the last reason for our being removed from evil from 3.1.2). The passion as removing sin is placed within a larger nexus of intelligibility.

The crucifixion itself, suggests Aquinas in article 4, has a fittingness of its own. It gives us an example of virtue in the face of death, because Christ dies a most ignominious death while trusting God (an act of the theological virtue of faith). There is also an aesthetic proportion captured in the wood of the cross, which corresponds to the wood of the tree of our condemnation. The two trees serve as an image of the two Adams. Aquinas lists several other reasons of fittingness. I want to highlight these two to draw attention to a shift that has occurred. Aquinas now treats only the level of Christ's human nature, proposing reasons of human virtue and material metaphors that promote our own self-consideration in relation to Christ.

In question 46, then, Aquinas inserts the passion and the cross into the context of the saving power of the mysteries of the whole life of Christ from conception to resurrection. The surplus of effects beyond mere liberation from sin serves to render complex the intelligibility of the passion. In addition, the path traveled through these articles includes repeated spiritual exercises to eliminate and exclude mistaken notions that distort the intelligibility of the passion and cross as saving. We cannot, then, reduce the theological intelligibility of the passion to just one factor. Aquinas builds a complex network of terms and relations that holds together humanity and divinity, charity and justice, and the gift of eternal life and deliverance from sin. By the use of arguments of fittingness, Aquinas is inviting students to perform meditations, both scriptural and patristic, that shift their affective disposition and aesthetic sensibility so that it will be easier for them to hold together the surplus of meaning that Aquinas discovers in the mystery of the passion and death of Jesus the Christ.

The Effects of Christ's Passion

In question 49 Aquinas explores in greater detail the two principal effects of merit and satisfaction, namely the gift of eternal life and deliverance from sin. The six articles in this question form two groups: articles 1 to 4 examine aspects of deliverance from sin, while 5 and 6 look at communion with God in eternal life. Each of these articles is occasioned by the need to understand a biblical passage, and so the whole of question 49 forms an interpretive grid linking the work of questions 46 to 48 to the task of scriptural exegesis in preaching.

In article 1 Thomas summarizes the results of question 48 under three headings: provocation to charity, redemption, and instrumental efficiency. Articles 2 and 3 explore the theme of deliverance from sin at greater length by inquiring into the way in which we are freed from the devil's power and from bondage to suffering. Article 4 is a kind of climax in this first part of question 49, showing how deliverance from sin effects reconciliation with God. This article also serves as a kind of pivot into considerations of communion with God. Article 5 then asks whether the passion opened for us the gates of heaven: Aquinas answers in the affirmative, linking the opening of the gates of heaven to the removal of the obstacles of original and actual sin.

At the climax of the *ductus* of question 49 in article 6, Aquinas links the effects of the passion to the resurrection, the ascension, the manifestation of Christ's divinity at God's right hand, and his role as judge. Each of these is a saving mystery of Christ in its own right. Nevertheless, here the student is invited by a series of scriptural references to meditate on the relation between the passion of Christ and each of these mysteries. The basic theological position is this: Christ renounced what was due him in justice and thus merited a greater reward, namely, that of his exaltation. This exaltation is fourfold, and each mode is expressed by an aesthetic or moral fittingness. With respect to his resurrection, the passion is linked to Psalm 139, the cry of the just person confronted by evil. The Gloss interprets the sitting and rising of the second verse as humiliation and resurrection, and Aquinas offers this interpretation here. With respect to Christ's ascension, Aquinas offers an aesthetic fittingness rooted in Ephesians 4: just as Christ is the one to descend into the depths of hell, so he is the one who fittingly ascends to the highest heavens. With respect to his sitting at God's right hand and revealing his divinity, there is an aesthetic fittingness rooted in the contrast between the disfigurement of the Suffering Servant in Isaiah 52 and the Servant's exaltation; this is taken up by the Philippians hymn. Finally, there is a moral fittingness of contrast between the unjust judgment Jesus receives and the office of the judge he now exercises. Aquinas thus disposes the student to keep the considerations of Christ's passion and death open to the mysteries that will follow and proposes some meditations that can "punctuate" the memory. The goal is not to offer causal explanations, but merely to prepare the way through the ordering of memory and affect. The more explanatory considerations of these mysteries appear in their proper place in the itinerary.

Death, Burial, and Descent into Hell

Questions 50 to 52 function as a group that explores the saving power of Christ's being dead.[4] Question 50 asks about the death in itself, question 51 about the saving power of the burial, and question 52 about the descent into hell. The theological work of question 50 proceeds in three steps: article 1 explores the fittingness of Christ's being truly dead; articles 2 to 5 determine the *quid sit* of Christ's death; article 6, the climax of the question, shows the efficiency of Christ's being dead for our salvation.

Aquinas offers five reasons of fittingness for Christ's being dead. The first recalls the satisfaction offered by Christ in the passion and points out the "homeopathic" nature of Christ's being actually dead. Because death was the consequence of sin, Christ's satisfaction is fittingly offered by a death like ours. Christ's death, states the second reason of fittingness, also bears witness to the genuineness of Christ's human existence: God, in God's wisdom, has provided a witness that contradicts Docetism. Christ's being dead also frees us from the fear of death and is the exemplar of the being dead to sin which marks the life of every Christian. Finally, the genuine being dead of Christ points to the truth of the resurrection, giving us hope in our own resurrection through God's grace. Thus, satisfaction is once again included in a complex nexus of intelligibility that links the passion and death with the life, the ministry, and the resurrection of Christ.

4 These questions merit a deeper examination which space requirements prevent me from developing. One of the key rhetorical strategies such a development would show, however, is the use of metonymic citations of Scripture to invite further meditation, a strategy we have seen many times now in our study of Aquinas' use of rhetorical tools.

The death of Christ in itself is determined to be specifically the dissolution of the union of soul and flesh, but death does not alienate the separated soul and flesh from the person of the Word. Each remains hypostatically united to the divinity of the Word and so each can be the instrument of the divinity's saving power. Thus the being dead of Christ is an efficient cause of our salvation as instrument in its own right. Specifically, the being dead removes the obstacles that prevent our salvation, namely the death of the soul and the death of the flesh. Each remains united to the principle of life, namely the divine power. Question 51, on the burial, is concerned with developing the consequences of this continuing union with respect to the flesh; question 52, on the descent into hell, develops the same concern with respect to the soul.

The burial of Christ was fitting for three reasons, each one linking the burial to other parts of Aquinas' Christology. A genuine burial bears witness against Docetism and to the truth of the resurrection. It serves as an example, as we saw in question 50, for our own dying to sin, which resides in the flesh. Even the mode of Christ's burial is fitting because it confirms the reality of the resurrection. It offers praise for the *pietas* of those who buried him, and thus is a form of epideictic rhetoric encouraging us to do likewise. Finally, it teaches those "who are buried with Christ in his death." By the repetition of key reasons of fittingness throughout these articles and questions, Aquinas is developing a set of tropes that can be used in preaching. Throughout this section, references to Scripture abound, inviting more profound meditation. This is especially true of the replies to the objections in this second article. Aquinas notes that while the body was genuinely corruptible and was truly corrupted in the sense of being apart from the soul, it was preserved by its union with the person of the Word from complete dissolution. This is precisely the participation of Christ's flesh in the victory over death which bears fruit in the resurrection on the third day.

The descent into hell saves us from our own going to hell, delivers those held captive there, and is the occasion for Christ's revealing his power in hell itself, so that all creatures and all parts of creation will have known that power. The soul, united to the divinity, is the instrument through which the universal cause of the passion is applied to the particular case of those already dead. Christ is present in all of hell, even the hell of the damned, but by different modes and for different purposes. The whole person of the Word is personally present in the tomb and in hell, and Christ is present in hell for the same length of time as the body is in the tomb. Christ frees the patriarchs and those ready for salvation, shows his power to the damned to their condemnation, and sets those in need of purgation on the way to heaven.[5]

Resurrection, Ascension, Sitting at God's Right Hand in Judgment

The first article of question 53 makes explicit what has already been adumbrated in the treatment of the passion and death of Christ. The saving mysteries of the passion and resurrection are related to each other as humiliation to exaltation. Aquinas expands this by pointing out that the passion achieves our deliverance from evil while the resurrection achieves our furtherance in the good. This second pair evokes, of course, the fundamental structure of fittingness at the beginning of the treatment of the Incarnation, which is itself to be understood within the complex relation of charity to justice, as we have already seen. Article 1 expands this connection further by offering five reasons of fittingness for the resurrection. God's justice is made evident when he exalts the one who humbled himself for the sake of that justice. The resurrection also strengthens our faith in Christ's divinity. Here, Aquinas offers two metonymies from Scripture, which are 2 Corinthians 13:4 (part of Paul's challenge to the Corinthians to find proof of his authority in their own experience of faith in Christ) and 1 Corinthians 15:14, which represents Paul's use of argumentation to show the resurrection from the dead from the "premise" of Christ's own resurrection. The resurrection of Christ also confirms our hope, and Aquinas invites his students to meditate on Job's hope in the face of adversity: "I know that my redeemer lives." The resurrection is a new "form" for our own life, as Paul says to the Romans, we are dead to sin and alive for God. Finally, while the passion delivers us from evil, the resurrection moves us to the good.

Article 2 introduces the pair humanity-divinity, so important already in the treatment of the passion, to connect the passion with the resurrection. The resurrection is a promotion to a higher kind of living beyond death. Christ as God raises himself by his own power (shared with the Father and the Spirit), but

5 Aquinas also points out that Christ cannot save those children who died in original sin before being able to exercise the charity and faith that would have connected them to Christ in the same manner as the patriarchs. While this is difficult for us today to accept, it is consistent with what Aquinas has offered to this point and relies on the notion of an objective order of justice.

as human he receives from the Father the gift of being raised, because the body and soul do not have the power to reunite of themselves. This distinction and relation between humanity and divinity is further developed in question 54, where Aquinas shows how Christ's being raised (as human) is both the exemplary and instrumental cause of our own resurrection.

The study of the resurrection finds its *skopos* and climax in question 56, which asks whether Christ's resurrection is the cause of our own resurrection and justification. Resurrection and justification are distinguished here as body to soul. Resurrection is of our bodies, and justification is the resurrection of our souls. The resurrection of Christ, as first in its genus, is an exemplary cause of our own resurrection; it is also an instrumental (and therefore efficient) cause serving God's justice. The efficiency of Christ's resurrection extends to the raising of both the good and the bad, but its exemplary causality extends only to the good. It is also the cause of our justification as resurrection of our souls, and here both efficient and exemplary causality apply (since justification is what makes us good).

In question 57 Thomas considers the ascension. The ascension is fitting because it achieves "right order": Christ ascends to the proper place, the place that corresponds to his incorruptible glory. It was not necessary but achieves a kind of *bene esse*. We can think of the ascension as a rhetorical adornment on God's part, a way of showing forth more beautifully the full meaning of the goods that await us. Article 6 develops this exemplary causality at length by showing how the ascension causes our salvation in two ways, with respect to us and with respect to Christ. With respect to us, Aquinas offers four reasons of fittingness that show how the ascension turns our spirits more completely to Christ: by increasing our faith, our hope, and our love, and by deepening our reverence for the person of Christ. With respect to Christ, the ascension is cause of our salvation in terms of the work he accomplishes in ascending to the Father: he prepares a way for us (and here Aquinas points to John); he enters the heavenly sanctuary as our great high priest (Hebrews); he sits at God's right hand of power to send us divine goods (Ephesians). The ascension also shares in the same instrumental efficiency as the resurrection.

Many of the reasons of fittingness offered in these questions are expressions of aesthetic *convenientia*: Aquinas wants his students to dwell upon the beauty of God's wise dispositions whereby we are saved. It is very important to notice this orientation in the text. Theologically, it implies that Aquinas considers that these mysteries are effective in their concrete particularity, that the student grows in grace and wisdom by contemplating them as expressions of God's art.

Questions 58 and 59, as we have already suggested, stand to questions 53 to 57 as rest to motion. We will only point out here that Aquinas shows that Christ's sitting at God's right hand is proper to him not only in his divinity but also in his humanity, insofar as he possesses in a unique fashion all the perfections of graced and glorified humanity and is thus the first principle of our own glorification. The power to judge flows from this perfection, by which Christ is constituted the head of all humanity, the first instrumental principle of our own resurrection and the visible (in his humanity) judge even of the wicked who cannot see God's glory.

Conclusion: Dying, Living, and Ministry in Christ

This chapter has articulated the complex theological intelligibility that Aquinas develops as he seeks to understand Christ's departure from this world and his exaltation to God's right hand. Christ's departure is related to his return to the Father as humiliation to exaltation. Within the mystery of Christ's death there are two basic mysteries, that of Christ's dying and that of Christ's being dead, and these are related as motion to rest. Similarly, Christ's return to the Father can be divided according to motion and rest. Resurrection and ascension are "becoming," while sitting at God's right hand in judgment is "term of change."

The mystery of Christ's dying is related to the whole of Christ's living and ministry as the fullest expression of Christ's relationship to us and to the Father, and cannot be understood outside of this context. At the same time, the dying cannot be understood apart from the resurrection. If we do consider the dying in itself, it exhibits a complex intelligibility that holds together, as we have seen, the healing and elevating character of our salvation, under the headings of satisfaction and merit, respectively. Satisfaction is itself a complex reality that unites charity and justice together as form to matter. The satisfaction which Christ offers takes the form of sacrifice, and this act of justice is taken up in the higher intelligibility of love as its concrete expression in this case. This complex nexus of intelligibility at the level of human moral causality is an instrumental cause whose efficiency is that of the divinity of Christ. The mystery of Christ's being dead is effective by the same divine power. Christ's being dead is genuine and consists of the separation of soul from body. Soul and flesh remain each united to the person of the Word, and each separately is an instrumental cause of our salvation, the flesh by being buried and the soul by the descent into hell.

At the beginning of the *Summa contra Gentiles*, Aquinas presents the office of the wise, which is to show forth the intelligible order of the whole while overturning the errors that prevent people from grasping and delighting in that whole. For Aquinas, God is the one who is supremely wise. God is able to take evil and not just overturn it but order it to a greater good. At the centre of this wise action is the cross, understood as a satisfaction that takes the form of an offering of self out of love. This basic intelligibility, however, must be understood within a network of intelligibly ordered surplus meaning that makes of the passion and death of Jesus God's supremely persuasive appeal to humankind, his artistic rendering, in the concrete human life that is the life of the Word made flesh, of the divine love that reaches out to us. The whole life of Christ, which reaches its climax in the offering of himself on the cross, is, for Aquinas, the particular shape that divine love takes in a world of sin.

The exaltation of Christ is articulated as the *skopos* of Christ's whole life and is shown to be a fitting principle of our own salvation. The passion frees us from evil, but the exaltation attracts us to the good. Each mystery of the exaltation – resurrection, ascension, sitting at God's right hand and exercising judgment – is an exemplary and efficient cause of our own salvation. Exemplary causality expresses God's wisdom and art, as well as the beauty that attracts us to the good.

All of these mysteries invite further theological meditation, which Aquinas signals by copious use of metonymic citations from Scripture. In the end, the student has developed a complex but single viewpoint that grasps together the mysteries of Christ's death and resurrection so as not only to read Scripture in his own authority but also be wise with respect to key theological debates (for example, the theology of Christ's satisfaction or the relation between Christ's death and resurrection as principles of our salvation). We can say with some conviction, then, that Aquinas' treatment of the cross and the resurrection brings to light the genuine beauty of this complex whole, showing forth the splendor of the wisdom of divine love.

CHAPTER TEN

Adequatio mentis ad rem: Retrieving the Unity of the Spiritual and the Intellectual Life

The castle of Roccasecca, where Thomas Aquinas was born, sits high on a mountainous plateau and overlooks the valley in which the present-day village of Roccasecca sits. When visitors have climbed as far as the ruins of even the first set of defensive walls, they are rewarded with a tremendous panoramic view of the valley. On three sides of the mountain, everything is visible. It is easy to discern patterns of land use and patterns of movement below. On certain days, falcons soar below but not above the viewer. It is quite possible that only someone born to and raised in such surroundings could conceive of the kind of breathtaking vision of the whole of theology to which the *Summa theologiae* aspires to lead the student of *sacra doctrina*.

From our study of the *ductus* of *Summa*'s text, it has emerged that a key mechanism of its pedagogy is an *adequatio mentis ad rem*, making the mind or spirit of the student equal to the real and conforming the student to the mysteries of faith by means of spiritual exercises. These exercises are the result of Aquinas' use of classical and mediaeval rhetoric, the science of aesthetic-dramatic meaning which allows him to promote certain kinds of dispositions and judgments in his students. Rhetoric works at two levels in the *Summa*. At the macro level, rhetoric determines an overall aesthetic that orients the student to a more intellectualist and theoretical grasp of the mysteries, and shapes a *ductus* that moves the student towards an ever-greater likeness to the Word Incarnate for the purpose of forming him as a preacher and confessor who can discover the right consoling word on his own authority and out of a truly personal wisdom. At the micro level, rhetoric proposes a set of practical intellectual and experiential practices which actively shape the student's memory, understanding, and judgment in particular questions and articles.

In the first part of this book, I attempted to promote in the reader a particular *adequatio mentis ad rem* of my own. By gathering and organizing research into the cultural and pastoral context of Aquinas' theological ministry, I offered a horizon within which the text of the *Summa* ought to be properly interpreted. As Bernard Lonergan wrote in a number of places, the scholar is the one who has learned to live comfortably in the common sense of another culture, that is, someone who has entered into another cultural horizon and has become capable of grasping meaning and value within it. It remains my contention that unless one enters as fully as one can into the cultural and pastoral crisis of the thirteenth century, and into the creative solutions developed by Lateran Council IV and the Dominican Order as they coalesce in the person of Friar Thomas Aquinas, one will not in fact be able to understand and bring forward the full treasure of his theological achievement. His truly universal achievements can only be appreciated and received for the present, paradoxically, in their unique particularity.

In the second part of the book, I retrieved the *ductus* that leads students of the *Summa theologiae* to the *skopos* of a truly Christoform wisdom by means of which they become pastoral agents of *sacra doctrina* in preaching and the hearing of confessions. As they grow in likeness to the Incarnate Word, they are also conformed more and more to the image of the triune God, whose compassionate governance of creation out of love sent the fitting consoling Word, Jesus of Nazareth, to take flesh in time and become the means of our salvation. In the same way, the young student of the *Summa* would have been enabled to give flesh to the right consoling word to meet the cultural and pastoral exigencies of the day.

It is important to note here that we have often explored only some general elements of this *ductus*, descending into details when it seemed important to make a particular point about the importance of this or that "stop along the way." The overall *ductus* of spiritual progress according to growing resemblance to the Word is itself composed of multiple *ducti* that govern the journey through particular questions and treatises. Each question has a *ductus* and *skopos* arranged to promote a particular development of memory, understanding, judgment, and sometimes choice or command.

When I present this material to my students, they are often perplexed at first and find it difficult to put awareness of the rhetorical dimensions of the text into practice in their reading. But as they become better able to discern rhetorical devices and act on them, I see spiritual transformation and the practice of the theological craft coming together in their written work and in their classroom intervention. Their understanding of the text improves as a function of their rediscovery of fundamental scriptural or religious starting points, all in connection with awareness of the rhetorical dynamics of the text. Recovery of this dimension of Aquinas' theological method alongside dialectic and grammar promotes also its fruits in contemporary researchers and readers.

Aquinas was not only aware of the aesthetic-dramatic dimension and constitutive power of meaning, he was able to make use of it in the craft of theology to promote the kind of pastoral transformation of culture that he, following Lateran IV and his own Dominican spirit, saw as important and necessary. By studying his work in this area, we have been able to observe, as in a kind of controlled environment, a particular instance of the mediation of Gospel and culture in the creation of a particular kind of pastoral agent for the urbanized thirteenth century. Many of the principles we have uncovered, while they will need proper transposition, remain valid for theology today. It is only fitting, then, to give Thomas the last word:

> Dear brothers, what delight, what charm, what sweetness in the words of heavenly wisdom! This is just as true for the Philosopher, who writes about the *scientia* of created things: "All delights follow upon operations. Now, the greatest pleasure is that which comes from the bringing into play of wisdom; the most delightful work is that which is done according to the operation of wisdom." What is more, the theologian-philosopher [Aquinas is referring to Solomon] writes in the Book of Wisdom that he preferred it to the splendour of gold, that is, the heavenly wisdom of which we speak. For this reason, as we begin, we will ask our Lord Jesus the Christ, the source of all wisdom, that very one who, according to the blessed Denys, is the first master of all heavenly spirits and of all devout souls, to enlighten our intelligence, to inflame our hearts, to make our mouths fruitful for the honour of his name or else for the teaching of the Gospel and the edification of our souls.[1]

1 *Praefatio* to the sermon *Caelum et terra transibunt* on Matthew 24:35, for the second Sunday of Advent according to the Dominican usage (my translation).

Bibliography

Primary Sources

Aristotle. *On Rhetoric: A Theory of Civic Discourse*. Trans. George A. Kennedy. Oxford: Oxford University Press, 2007.

Augustine, Saint. *The Trinity*. Trans. Edmund Hill. Works of Saint Augustine: A Translation for the 21st Century. Brooklyn: New City Press, 1990.

Cicero, Marcus Tullius. *De oratore*. Trans. H. Rackham. Cambridge, MA: Harvard University Press, 2004.

Dante Alighieri. *The Divine Comedy: Paradiso*. A Verse Translation by Robert and Jean Hollander; Introduction and Notes by Robert Hollander. New York: Random House, 2007.

John of Salisbury. *Metalogicon*. Trans. Daniel D. McGarry. Gloucester, MA: Peter Smith, 1971.

—. *Policraticus*. Trans. Cary J. Nederman. New York: Cambridge University Press, 1990.

Thomas Aquinas. *Albert and Thomas: Selected Writings*. Trans. Simon Tugwell. The Classics of Western Spirituality. New York: Paulist Press, 1988.

—. *Commentaire sur les Psaumes*. Trans. Jean-Éric Stroobant de Saint-Éloy. Paris: Éditions du Cerf, 1996.

—. *Commentary on the Gospel of John*. Trans. James A. Weisheipl and Fabian R. Larcher. Aquinas Scripture Series 4. Albany, NY: Magi Books, 1980.

—. *Contra impugnantes Dei cultum et religionem*. Ed. H.-F. Dondaine. Opera omnia iussu Leonis XIII P.M. edita 41A. Rome: Santa Sabina, 1969.

—. *De articulis et Ecclesiae sacramentis [ad Archiepiscopum Panormitanum]*. Ed. H.-F. Dondaine, 207–257. Opera omnia iussu Leonis XIII P.M. edita 42. Rome: Editori di San Tommaso, 1979.

—. *De perfectione vitae spiritualis contra pestiferam doctrinam retrahentium homines a religionis ingressu*. Ed. H.-F. Dondaine. Opera omnia iussu Leonis XIII P.M. edita 41B–C. Rome: Santa Sabina, 1969.

—. *Expositio libri Posteriorum*. Ed. R.-A. Gauthier. Opera omnia iussu Leonis XIII P.M. edita 1*/2. Roma–Paris: Commissio Leonina–J. Vrin, 1989.

—. *Expositio super Isaiam ad litteram*. Ed. H.-F. Dondaine and L. Reid. Opera omnia iussu Leonis XIII P.M. edita 28. Rome: Editori di san Tommaso, 1975.

—. *How to Study: Being the Letter of St. Thomas to Brother John (De modo studendi)*. Trans. Victor White. 7th edition. London: Aquin Press, 1960.

—. *Lectura super Matthaeum*. Ed. J.S.E. Fretté and P. Maré. Doctoris Angelici divi Thomae Aquinatis sacri ordinis F.F. Praedicatorum Opera omnia ... 19. Paris: Vives, 1876.

—. *Light of Faith: The Compendium of Theology*. Trans. Cyril Vollert. Manchester, NH: Sophia Institute Press, 1993.

—. *Opuscules*. Ed. M. Védrine, M. Bandel, and M. Fournet. Paris: Librairie de Louis Vivès, Éditeur, 1857.

—. "Prologue." In *Commentary on the Sentences*, trans. Joseph Kenny <http://dhspriory.org/ thomas/Sentences.htm#01>.

—. *Quaestiones quodlibetales*. Ed. R Spiazzi. 8th edition. Turin: Marietti, 1949.

—. *Scriptum super libros Sententiarum magistri Petri Lombardi*. Ed. Pierre Mandonnet and Maria Fabianus Moos. 4 vols. Paris: P. Lethielleux, 1929–1947.

—. *Sentencia libri De sensu et sensato cuius secundus tractatus est De memoria et reminiscencia*, [ed. R.-A. Gauthier]. Opera omnia iussu Leonis XIII P.M. edita 45.2. Rome–Paris: Commissio Leonina–J. Vrin, 1985.

—. *The Sermon-Conferences of St. Thomas Aquinas on the Apostles' Creed*. Trans. Nicholas Ayo. Notre Dame, IN: University of Notre Dame Press, 1988.

—. *Somme théologique*. Ed. Albert Raulin. 4 vols. 1984–1986. Repr. Paris: Éditions du Cerf, 1999–2004.

—. *Summa contra Gentiles 1: God*. Trans. Anton C. Pegis. Notre Dame, IN: University of Notre Dame Press, 1975.

—. *Summa contra Gentiles 2: Creation*. Trans. James F. Anderson. Notre Dame, IN: University of Notre Dame Press, 1975.

—. *Summa theologiae*. Opera omnia iussu Leonis XIII P.M. edita 4–12. Rome: Santa Sabina, 1888–1906.

—. *Super Decretalem [Expositio super primam et secundam Decretalem ad Archidiaconum Tudertinum]*. Ed. H.F. Dondaine, 1–53. Opera omnia iussu Leonis XIII P.M. edita 40E. Rome: Santa Sabina, 1968.

—. *Super Epistolas Sancti Pauli Lectura*. 8th revised edition. Turin: Marietti, 1953.

—. *The Teacher, the Mind: Truth, Questions X and XI*. Trans. James V. McGlynn. Chicago: Henry Regnery, 1962.

William of Saint Thierry. *Le miroir de la foi, Speculum fidei*. Ed. and trans. Jean M. Déchanet. Sources chrétiennes 301. Paris: Éditions du Cerf, 1982.

Secondary Sources

Allard, Guy-H. "Le *Contra Gentiles* et le modèle rhétorique." *Laval théologique et philosophique* 30 (1974): 237–250.

Aulen, Gustaf E.H. *Le triomphe du Christ*. Foi vivante 124, Paris: Aubier-Montaigne, 1970.

Baldwin, John. *Masters, Princes, and Merchants: The Social Views of Peter the Chanter and His Circle*. Princeton: Princeton University Press, 1970.

Balthasar, Hans Urs von. *Word and Redemption*. Trans. A.V. Littledale. Montreal: Palm Publishers, 1965.

Biffi, Inos. *I misteri di Cristo in San Tommaso d'Aquino*. Di fronte e attraverso 339. Milan: Jaca Book, 1994.

Blanche, F. "Le vocabulaire de l'argumentation et la structure de l'article dans les ouvrages de saint Thomas." *Revue de Sciences Philosophiques et Théologiques* 14 (1925): 167–187.

Bouyer, Louis. *Le fils éternel*. Paris: Éditions du Cerf, 1974.

Boyle, Leonard, E. *Pastoral Care, Clerical Education and Canon Law, 1200–1400*. London: Variorum Reprints, 1981.

—. *The Setting of the* Summa Theologiae *of Saint Thomas*. Etienne Gilson Series. Toronto: Pontifical Institute of Medieval Studies, 1982.

Burrell, David. *Exercises in Religious Understanding*. Notre Dame, IN: University of Notre Dame Press, 1974.

Candler, Peter M. *Theology, Rhetoric, Manuduction, or Reading Scripture Together on the Path to God*. Grand Rapids: Eerdmans, 2006.

Cannon, Joanna. "Dominic *Alter Christus*? Representations of the Founder in and After the *Arca Di San Domenico*." In *Christ Among the Medieval Dominicans*, ed. Kent Emery, Jr. and Joseph Wawrykow, 26–48. Notre Dame Conferences in Medieval Studies 7. Notre Dame, IN: University of Notre Dame Press, 1998.

Carruthers, Mary. *The Book of Memory: A Study of Memory in Medieval Culture*. Cambridge Studies in Medieval Literature. 2nd ed. Cambridge: Cambridge University Press, 2008.

—. *The Craft of Thought: Meditation, Rhetoric, and the Making of Images, 400–1200*. Cambridge: Cambridge University Press, 2000.

Chenu, Marie-Dominique. *Nature, Man, and Society in the Twelfth Century*. Ed. and Trans. Jerome Taylor and Lester K. Little. Toronto: University of Toronto Press, 1997.

—. *Toward Understanding Saint Thomas.* Trans. A.M. Landry and D. Hughes. Chicago: Henry Regnery Company, 1964.

Cherubini, Giovanni. "The Peasant and Agriculture." In *Medieval Callings*, ed. Jacques Le Goff and trans. Lydia G. Cochrane, 113–138. Chicago: University of Chicago Press, 1990.

Collins, John J. *Introduction to the Hebrew Bible.* Minneapolis: Fortress, 2004.

Corbin, Michel. "La parole devenue chair: lecture de la première question de la *tertia pars* de la *Somme théologique.*" *Revue des Sciences Philosophiques et Théologiques* 62 (1978): 5–40.

Cousens, Ewert. "The Humanity and the Passion of Christ." In *Christian Spirituality: High Middle Ages and Reformation*, ed. Jill Raitt, Bernard McGinn, and John Meyendorff, 375–391. New York: Crossroad, 1987.

Dauphinais, Michael, and Matthew Levering. *Knowing the Love of Christ: An Introduction to the Theology of Thomas Aquinas.* Notre Dame, IN: University of Notre Dame Press, 2002.

Deferrari, Roy. *A Latin-English Dictionary of St. Thomas Aquinas.* Boston: Daughters of St. Paul, 1986.

Donneaud, Henri. "Insaisissable *Sacra Doctrina*?" *Revue Thomiste* 98 (1998): 179–224.

Doran, Robert M. *Theology and the Dialectics of History*. Toronto: University of Toronto Press, 1990.

Emery, Gilles. "Le photinisme et ses précurseurs chez saint Thomas." *Revue Thomiste* 95 (1995): 371–398.

—. "Le traité de saint Thomas sur la Trinité dans la *Somme contre les Gentils.*" *Revue Thomiste* 95 (1995): 5–40.

—. "Saint Thomas d'Aquin et l'Orient Chrétien." *Nova et Vetera* 4 (1999): 19–36.

Ernst, Cornelius. "Metaphor and Ontology in *Sacra Doctrina.*" In *Multiple Echo: Explorations in Theology*, ed. Fergus Kerr, 57–75. London: Darton, Longman, and Todd, 1979.

Ferruolo, Stephen C. *The Origins of the University*. Stanford, CA: Stanford University Press, 1985.

Finnis, John. "Historical Consciousness and Theological Foundations." In his *Religion and Public Reasons: Collected Essays* 5, 139–162. Oxford: Oxford University Press, 2011.

Foreville, Raymonde. *Latran I, II, III et Latran IV*. Histoire des conciles oecuméniques. Paris: Editions de l'Orante, 1965.

Gauthier, René-Antoine. *Thomas d'Aquin, Somme contre les Gentils: Introduction*. Paris: Éditions Universitaires, 1993.

George, Marie I. "Mind-Forming and *Manuductio* in Aquinas." *The Thomist* 57 (1993): 201–213.

Glorieux, Palémon. "L'enseignement au Moyen Âge." *Archives d'histoire doctrinale et littéraire du Moyen Âge* 35 (1968): 65–186.

Gottwald, Norman K. *The Hebrew Bible: A Socio-Literary Interpretation*. Philadelphia: Fortress, 1987.

Gurevich, Aron. *Medieval Popular Culture*. Trans. Jano M. Bak and Paul A. Hollingsworth. Cambridge: Cambridge University Press, 1988.

—. "The Merchant." In *Medieval Callings*, ed. Jacques Le Goff and trans. Lydia G. Cochrane, 243–283. Chicago: University of Chicago Press, 1990.

Hadot, Pierre. *Philosophy as a Way of Life*. Trans. Martin Chase. Oxford: Blackwell Publishers, 1995.

Hibbs, Thomas S. *Dialectic and Narrative in Aquinas: An Interpretation of the "Summa Contra Gentiles."* Notre Dame, IN: University of Notre Dame Press, 1995.

Hinnebusch, William. *The History of the Dominican Order*. 2 vols. New York: Alba House, 1965.

Horst, Ulrich. "Christ, *Exemplar Ordinis Fratrum Praedicantium*, According to Saint Thomas Aquinas." In *Christ Among the Medieval Dominicans*, ed. Kent Emery, Jr. and Joseph Wawrykow, 256–270. Notre Dame Conferences in Medieval Studies 7. Notre Dame, IN: University of Notre Dame Press, 1998.

Johnson, Mark. "God's Knowledge in our Frail Minds: The Thomistic Model of Theology." *Angelicum* 76 (1999): 25–45.

Jordan, Mark D. *Ordering Wisdom: The Hierarchy of Philosophical Discourses in Aquinas*. Notre Dame, IN: University of Notre Dame Press, 1986.

Lamarche, Paul. "Image et Ressemblance" (1971). In *Dictionnaire de* spiritualité, 7: 1402–1472. 17 vols. Paris: Beauchesne, 1932–1995.

Laporte, Jean-Marc. *Aquinas' Summa Theologiae: Christ at the Center?* Unpublished manuscript, 2001.

—. "Christ in Aquinas' *Summa Theologiae*: Peripheral or Pervasive?" *The Thomist* 67 (2003): 221–248.

Le Goff, Jacques, ed. *Medieval Callings*. Trans. Lydia G. Cochrane. Chicago: University of Chicago Press, 1990.

—. *Time, Work, and Culture in the Middle Ages*. Trans. Arthur Goldhammer. Chicago: University of Chicago Press, 1980.

—. *Your Money or Your Life: Economy and Religion in the Middle Ages*. Trans. Patricia Ranum. New York: Zone Books, 1990.

Levering, Matthew. *Christ's Fulfillment of Torah and Temple: Salvation According to Thomas Aquinas*. Notre Dame, IN: University of Notre Dame Press, 2002.

—. "Juridical Language in Soteriology: Aquinas' Approach." *Angelicum* 80 (2003): 309–326.

—. *Scripture and Metaphysics: Aquinas and the Renewal of Trinitarian Theology*. Malden, MA: Blackwells Publishing, 2004.

Lonergan, Bernard. *De verbo incarnato*. 5 vols. Rome: Pontificia Universitatis Gregoriana, 1961.

—. *Early Latin Theology*. Collected Works of Bernard Lonergan 19. Toronto: University of Toronto Press, 2011.

—. *Method in Theology*. Toronto: University of Toronto Press, 1990.

Marshall, Bruce D. "*Quod scit una vetula*: Aquinas on the Nature of Theology." In *The Theology of Thomas Aquinas*, ed. Rik van Nieuwenhove and Joseph Wawrykow, 1–10. Notre Dame, IN: University of Notre Dame Press, 2005.

Matera, Frank. *Galatians*. Ed. Daniel J. Harrington. Sacra Pagina 9. Collegeville, MN: Liturgical Press, 1992

McGinn, Bernard. *The Flowering of Mysticism: Men and Women in the New Mysticism (1200–1350)*. The Presence of God: A History of Western Christian Mysticism 3. New York: Crossroad Publishing Company, 1998.

McLuhan, Marshall. *The Classical Trivium: The Place of Thomas Nashe in the Learning of his Time*. Ed. Terrence Gordon. Toronto: Ginkho Press, 2006.

McPartland, Thomas. *Lonergan and Historiography: The Epistemelogical Philosophy of History*. Columbia, MO: University of Missouri Press, 2010.

Miccoli, Giovanni. "Monks." In *Medieval Callings*, ed. Jacques Le Goff and trans. Lydia G. Cochrane, 36–74. Chicago: University of Chicago Press, 1990.

Michel, Alain. *In hymnis et canticis: culture et beauté dans l'hymnique chrétienne latine*. Paris: Presses Universitaires de France, 1976.

—. *La parole et la beauté: Rhétorique et esthétique dans la tradition occidentale*. Paris: Belles Lettres, 1982.

—. *Les rapports de la rhetorique et de la philosophie dans l'œuvre de Ciceron: Recherches sur les fondements philosophiques de l'art de persuader*. Leuven-Dudley, MA: Peeters, 2003.

—. *Rhétorique et philosophie chez Cicéron*. Paris: Presses Universitaires de France, 1960.

—. *Théologiens et mystiques au Moyen Age*. Paris: Gallimard, 1997.

Mongeau, Gilles. "Classical Rhetoric and the Control of Elemental Meaning." In *Meaning and History in Systematic Theology: Essays in Honor of Robert M. Doran, SJ*, ed. John D. Dadosky, 353–373. Milwaukee: Marquette University Press, 2009.

Mongeau, Gilles, and Kevin Vaughan. "The Procession of the Word as Structuring Principle of *Sacra Doctrina*: Reading the *Summa Theologiae* in Light of the *Super Ioannem*." Unpublished paper presented at the conference "Reading John with Saint Thomas," Detroit, November 2001.

Mulchahey, M. Michèle. *"First the Bow is Bent in Study ...": Dominican Education Before*

1350. Studies and Texts 132. Toronto: Pontifical Institute of Medieval Studies, 1998.

Narcisse, Gilbert. *Les raisons de Dieu: Arguments de convenance et esthétique théologique selon saint Thomas d'Aquin et Hans Urs von Balthasar*. Fribourg, Suisse: Presses Universitaires de Fribourg, 1997.

Newhauser, Richard. "Jesus as the First Dominican? Reflections on a Sub-Theme in the Exemplary Literature of Some Thirteenth-Century Preachers." In *Christ Among the Medieval Dominicans*, ed. Kent Emery, Jr. and Joseph Wawrykow, 238–255. Notre Dame Conferences in Medieval Studies 7. Notre Dame, IN: University of Notre Dame Press, 1998.

Nicholas, David. *The Evolution of the Medieval World*. New York: Longman, 1992.

Ofilada, Mina M. "The Role of the Teacher as a Condescending Mediator as Viewed from Aquinas's Notion of *Sacra Doctrina* and Its Bearing on the Nature of the Theological Enterprise." *Angelicum* 77 (2000): 373–396.

Panofsky, Erwin. *Gothic Architecture and Scholasticism*. New York: Meridian Books, 1957.

Patfoort, Albert. "Théorie de la théologie ou réflexion sur le corpus des écritures?" *Angelicum* 54 (1977): 459–488.

—. *La Somme de saint Thomas et la logique du dessein de Dieu*. Saint-Maur: Parole et Silence, 1998.

—. "Le vrai visage de la satisfaction du Christ selon saint Thomas." In *Ordo Sapientiae et Amoris: Hommage au Professeur Jean-Pierre Torrell*, ed. Carlos-Josaphat Pinto de Oliveira, 247–265. Fribourg, Suisse: Éditions Universitaires Fribourg Suisse, 1993.

Pesch, Otto Hermann. *Thomas d'Aquin: Grandeur et limites de la théologie médiévale*. Trans. Joseph Hoffmann. Paris: Les Éditions du Cerf, 1994.

Pinckaers, Servais. "Recherche de la signification véritable du terme 'spéculatif'." *Nouvelle Revue Théologique* 81 (1959): 673–695.

Pinto de Oliveira, Carlos-Josaphat, ed. *Ordo Sapientiae et Amoris: Hommage au Professeur Jean-Pierre Torrell*. Fribourg, Suisse: Éditions Universitaires Fribourg Suisse, 1993.

Rabbow, Paul. *Seelenführung: Methodik der Exercitien in der Antike*. Munich: Kösel-Verlag, 1954.

Rhonheimer, Martin. *Natural Law and Practical Reason: A Thomist View of Moral Autonomy*. Trans. Gerald Malsbary. Moral Philosophy and Moral Theology 1. New York: Fordham University Press, 2000.

Rogers, Eugene. *Thomas Aquinas and Karl Barth: Sacred Doctrine and the Natural Knowledge of God*. Notre Dame, IN: University of Notre Dame Press, 1995.

Rossiaud, Jacques. "The City-Dweller and Life in Cities and Towns." In *Medieval Callings*, ed. Jacques Le Goff and trans. Lydia G. Cochrane, 139–179. Chicago: University of Chicago Press, 1990.

Ruello, Francis. *La Christologie de Thomas d'Aquin*. Paris: Beauchesne, 1987.

Ryan, Fáinche. *Formation in Holiness: Thomas Aquinas on Sacra Doctrina*. Leuven–Dudley, MA: Peeters, 2007.

Ryan, Thomas F. *Thomas Aquinas as Reader of the Psalms*. Notre Dame, IN: University of Notre Dame Press, 2000.

Schoot, Henk J.M. *Christ the 'Name' of God: Thomas Aquinas on Naming Christ*. Publications of the Thomas Instituut te Utrecht n.s. 1. Leuven: Peeters, 1993.

Sesboüé, Bernard. *Jésus-Christ, l'unique médiateur*. Paris: Desclée, 1988.

Tanner, Kathryn. *Theories of Culture: A New Agenda for Theology*. Guides to Theological Inquiry. Minneapolis: Fortress, 1997.

Tanner, Norman P., ed. *Decrees of the Ecumenical Councils* 1: *Nicaea I - Lateran V*. Washington, DC: Georgetown University Press, 1990.

Taylor, Greer M. "Function of *Pistis Christou* in Galatians." *Journal of Biblical Literature* 85 (1966): 58–76.

Tillman, Helena. *Pope Innocent III*. Europe in the Middle Ages: Selected Studies. New York: North-Holland, 1980.

Torrell, Jean-Pierre. *Encyclopédie Jésus le Christ chez saint Thomas d'Aquin*. Paris: Éditions du Cerf, 2008.

—. *Initiation à saint Thomas d'Aquin, sa personne et son œuvre*. Fribourg, Suisse: Éditions Universitaires de Fribourg, 1993.

—. *Le Christ en ses mystères*. 2 vols. Paris: Desclée, 1999.

—. "Le savoir théologique chez saint Thomas." *Revue Thomiste* 96 (1996): 355–396.

—. *Saint Thomas Aquinas: Spiritual Master*, trans. Robert Royal. Washington, DC: Catholic University of America Press, 2005.

—. *Saint Thomas d'Aquin, maître spirituel*. Fribourg, Suisse: Éditions Universitaire de Fribourg, 1996.

—. "Saint Thomas d'Aquin et la science du Christ: Une relecture des Questions 9–12 de la *Tertia Pars*." In *Recherches Thomasiennes: Études revues et augmentées*, 198–213. Bibliothèque thomiste. Paris: J. Vrin, 2000.

Tugwell, Simon. "The Spirituality of the Dominicans." In *Christian Spirituality: High Middle Ages and Reformation*, ed. Jill Raitt, Bernard McGinn, and John Meyendorff, 15–31. New York: Crossroad Publishing Company, 1997.

van Engen, John. "Dominic and the Brothers: *Vitae* as Life-Forming *Exampla* in the Order of Preachers." In *Christ Among the Medieval Dominicans*, ed. Kent Emery, Jr. and Joseph Wawrykow, 7–25. Notre Dame Conferences in Medieval Studies 7. Notre Dame, IN: University of Notre Dame Press, 1998.

Venard, Olivier-Thomas. *Thomas d'Aquin, poète théologien I: Litterature et théologie – Une saison en enfer*. Geneva: Ad Solem, 2002.

Vernet, F. "Le catharisme" (1910). In *Dictionnaire de théologie catholique*, 2: 1997–1999. 15 vols. in 18. Paris: Letouzey et Ane, 1910.

Walsh, Liam G. "The Divine and the Human in St. Thomas' Theology of the Sacraments." In *Ordo Sapientiae et Amoris: Hommage au professeur Jean-Pierre Torrell*, ed. Carlos-Josaphat Pinto de Oliveira, 321–352. Fribourg, Suisse: Éditions Universitaires Fribourg Suisse, 1993

Wawrykow, Joseph. "Hypostatic Union." In *The Theology of Thomas Aquinas*, ed. Rik van Nieuwenhove and Joseph Wawrykow, 222–251. Notre Dame, IN: University of Notre Dame Press, 2005.

Weber, Édouard-Henri. *Le Christ selon saint Thomas d'Aquin*. Jésus et Jésus-Christ. Paris: Desclée, 1988.

Weisheipl, James A. "The Meaning of *Sacra Doctrina* in *Summa Theologiae* I, q.1." *The Thomist* 38 (1974): 49–80.

Index of Names